AF624177

ANCIENT INDIAN TRADITION AND MYTHOLOGY SERIES

[PURĀṆAS IN TRANSLATION]

Volumes Released

ŚIVA 1-4
LIṄGA 5-6
BHĀGAVATA 7-11
GARUḌA 12-14
NĀRADA 15-19
KŪRMA 20-21
BRAHMĀṆḌA 22-26
AGNI 27-30
VARĀHA 33-36
VĀYU 37-38
PADMA 39-48
SKANDA, PARTS I-XXI, 49-69
VĀMANA 72-73

Volumes Under Preparation

SKANDA, PARTS XXII-XXIII, 70-71
BHAVIṢYA
BRAHMAVAIVARTA
DEVĪBHĀGAVATA
KĀLIKĀ
MĀRKAṆḌEYA
MATSYA
VIṢṆU
VIṢṆUDHARMOTTARA

ANCIENT INDIAN TRADITION & MYTHOLOGY

Translated by
A BOARD OF SCHOLARS

Edited by
Prof. J. L. SHASTRI

VOLUME **6**

THE
LIṄGA-PURĀṆA

Translated and Annotated by

A BOARD OF SCHOLARS

PART II

MOTILAL BANARSIDASS PUBLISHERS
PRIVATE LIMITED • DELHI

Reprint: Delhi, 1982, 1990, 1998, 2009
First Edition: Delhi, 1973

© MOTILAL BANARSIDASS PUBLISHERS PVT. LTD.
All Rights Reserved

ISBN: 978-81-208-0341-1

MOTILAL BANARSIDASS
41 U.A. Bungalow Road, Jawahar Nagar, Delhi 110 007
8 Mahalaxmi Chamber, 22 Bhulabhai Desai Road, Mumbai 400 026
203 Royapettah High Road, Mylapore, Chennai 600 004
236, 9th Main III Block, Jayanagar, Bangalore 560 011
Sanas Plaza, 1302 Baji Rao Road, Pune 411 002
8 Camac Street, Kolkata 700 017
Ashok Rajpath, Patna 800 004
Chowk, Varanasi 221 001

UNESCO COLLECTION OF REPRESENTATIVE WORKS—*Indian Series*
This book has been accepted in the Indian Translation Series
of the UNESCO Collection of Representative Works,
jointly sponsored by the United Nations Educational,
Scientific and Cultural Organization
(UNESCO) and the Government of India

PRINTED IN INDIA

By Jainendra Prakash Jain at Shri Jainendra Press,
A-45 Naraina, Phase-I, New Delhi 110 028
and Published by Narendra Prakash Jain for
Motilal Banarsidass Publishers Private Limited,
Bungalow Road, Delhi 110 007

PUBLISHER'S NOTE

The purest gems lie hidden in the bottom of the ocean or in the depth of rocks. One has to dive into the ocean or delve into the rocks to find them out. Similarly, truth lies concealed in the language that with the passage of time has become obsolete. Man has to learn that language before he discovers that truth.

But he has neither the means nor the leisure to embark on that course. We have, therefore, planned to help him acquire knowledge by an easier course. We have started the series of *Ancient Indian Tradition and Mythology* in English Translation. Our goal is to universalize knowledge through the most popular international medium of expression. The publication of the Purāṇas in English Translation is a step towards that goal.

Acknowledgement

It is our pleasant duty to put on record our sincrere thanks to Dr. R.N. Dandekar and the UNESCO authorities for their kind encouragement and valuable help in the publication of the volumes in this series.

PREFACE

The present volume contains *Liṅgapurāṇa* Part II in English translation. It is the sixth in the series of fifty Volumes on *Ancient Indian Tradition and Mythology*.

The project of the Series was envisaged and financed in 1970 A.D. by Shri Sundarlal Jain, the veteran interprizer in the field of Oriental Publication and the leading proprietor Messers Motilal Banarsidass. In this project six volumes of the series (that is, four vols. of the Śivapurāṇa and two vols. of the Liṅgapurāṇa completing both the Purāṇas) have been published and made accessible to the reader.

The present English translation is based on the Sanskrit text of the Liṅgapurāṇa published in India by Messers Kṣemarāja Śrīkṛṣṇadāsa. This text, constructed on the collation of Mss. is fairly reliable, although here and there it suffers from certain lapses and defies our efforts for accurate translation. But these lapses are few and far between and they do not vitiate the quality of translation as a whole.

In this translation we have followed the text as closely as possible but at places we have been a little freer with a desire to maintain the spirit of the language in which the original is so rendered. At the same time we have excluded all far-fetched, forced or fancied interpretations including those that are suggested by the author of the Śivatoṣiṇī, though we have often quoted him in the footnotes.

The reader will find that the Purāṇa deals with a variety of subjects—geographical, historical, philosophical, religious and the like which need elucidation. This task could not be accomplished by a mere translation. We have therefore provided footnotes on these topics. The footnotes are very brief but illuminative. They supply the background without which the exegesis of the text would not be possible.

A critical introduction has been prefixed to Part I of this Purāṇa. The reader will find therein some interesting information on the nomenclature, authorship, authenticity, date and general characteristics of this work. We have suffixed to the present Part II a general index which lists among other words the names of persons, tribes, places, rivers, lakes, mountains etc. of which the identity already discussed in the footnotes is marked here by introducing a letter of abbreviation put within the bracket against the name. But we have eschewed all unnecessary repetitions and therefore have included the constantly recurring names, as those of the deities, kings and sages, only when there is some special reason for specifying them.

It is our pleasant duty to put on record our sincere gratitude to Dr. S.K. Chatterjee, Dr. V. Raghavan, Dr. R.N. Dandekar, Shri K.R. Kripalani and the authorities of the UNESCO for their kind encouragement and valuable help which render this work more valuable to scholars than it would otherwise have been. We must also thank Shri T.V. Parameswar Iyer for his valuable spade-work which lightened our labours especially in their initial stage.

In fine, we avail of this opportunity to state that any critical suggestions and advice for improvement are welcome and will receive proper consideration from us.

Translators and Editor

ABBREVIATIONS

AB	Aitareya-Brāhmaṇa
AG	Ancient Geography of India : Cunningham
Agni	Agnipurāṇa
AIHT	Ancient Indian Historical Tradition : Pargiter
Amara	Amarakośa
AU	Atharva-Upaniṣad
BD	Bṛhaddevatā
BG	Bhagavadgītā
Bhāga	Bhāgavatapurāṇa
Bhaviṣya	Bhaviṣyapurāṇa
Brahmāṇḍa	Brahmāṇḍapurāṇa
Devī Bhāga	Devībhāgavatapurāṇa
Droṇa p.	Droṇa Parva of the Mahābhārata
GAMI	Studies in the Geography of Ancient and Medieval India : D.C. Sarkar
Garuḍa	Garuḍapurāṇa
GD	Geographical Dictionary of Ancient and Medieval India : N.L. Dey
G. Dh. S.	Gautama-Dharmasūtra
GEAMI	Geographical Encyclopaedia of Ancient and Medieval India
GP	Geography of the Purāṇas : S. M. Ali
H. Dh. S.	History of Dharmaśāstra : Kane
HG	Hiraṇyakeśi-Gṛhyasūtra
HM	Hindu Mythology : Dawson
Harivaṁśa	Harivaṁśapurāṇa
Hyp	Haṭhayogapradīpikā
JIH	Journal of Indian History
JRAS	Journal of the Royal Asiatic Society (Great Britain)
KP	Kālikāpurāṇa
KRS	Koṭirudrasaṁhitā of Śivapurāṇa
KU	Kaṭha Upaniṣad
KŪ	Kūrmapurāṇa

Liṅga	Liṅgapurāṇa
Mārk	Mārkaṇḍeyapurāṇa
Mbh	Mahābhārata
Mbh. Ādi. P.	Mahābhārata Ādiparva
Mahān. U.	Mahānārāyaṇa Upaniṣad
Manu (MS)	Manusmṛti
MP	Matsyapurāṇa
MP. —A Study	Matsyapurāṇa—A Study: V.S. Agrawal
Mark.	Mārkaṇḍeyapurāṇa
Matsya	Matsyapurāṇa
N.	Nirukta
PE	Purāṇic Encyclopaedia
PGS	Pāraskara Gṛhyasūtra
Rāmą	Rāmāyaṇa
RV.	Ṛgveda
SG	Śivagītā
Sk	Skandapurāṇa
SK	Sāṅkhya Kārikā of Īśvarakṛṣṇa
ŚP	Śiva-Purāṇa
ŚRS	Śatarudrīyasaṁhitā of Śiva-Purāṇa
ST	Śivatoṣiṇī, a commentary on the Liṅgapurāṇa
SV	Sāmaveda
Śvet	Śvetāśvatara Upaniṣad
TA	Taittirīya Āraṇyaka
TB	Tattirīya Brāhmaṇa
TS	Tattirīya Saṁhitā
TU	Taittirīya Upaniṣad
Vā, Vāmana	Vāmana purāṇa
Varāha	Varāhapurāṇa
Vāyavīya (VS)	Vāyavīya saṁhitā of Śivapurāṇa
Vāyu	Vāyupurāṇa
Viśva	Viśvakośa
Viṣṇu	Viṣṇupurāṇa
VS	Vājasaneyisaṁhitā of Śuklayajurveda

ABBREVIATIONS (Index)

c—city, f—forest, k—king, l—lake, m—moun tain, r—river, t—tribe.

CONTENTS

CHAPTER NINETYSIX

Prayer to Śiva

The sages said :

1-3 "How did lord Mahādeva the cause of the annihilation of the universe, assume the hideous and very terrible form called Śarabha ? What all daring acts were performed by him ? Tell us everything."

Sūta said :—

Thus requested by Devas, Parameśvara the abode of mercy resolved to curb the powerful lord called Nṛsiṁha. For that purpose he remembered Vīrabhadra of great strength.

4-5. Vīrabhadra was the terrible form of himself and the cause of the great Dissolution. Immediately he came smiling in front of[883] the lord at the head of the Gaṇas. He was surrounded by extremely terrible leaders of the Gaṇas who were in their crores, who laughed boisterously, who had the forms of lionlike men and who were jumping about.

6-11. He was encircled by others also who were of the same number, who had not been seen before, who were joyful and who were playing with Brahmā and others of great courage as though with balls. He was saluted by heroes. He had the flames of the fire that occur at the end of the kalpas. He had three shining eyes and he wielded arms. He was embellished by the crescent moon that shone amidst his matted hairs. He had two curved fangs that resembled sprouts and had the shapes of two crescent moons. He possessed eyebrows which resembled parts of the bow of Indra (rainbow). By means of his fierce Huṁkāra (the gruff sound of "Hum") he deafened all quarters. He had the features of the blue cloud and collyrium. His moustaches were terrible. He had a wonderful form. With his invincible arms he frequently whirled his all-conquering trident. Lord Vīrabhadra was fluttering in his heroic power. He submitted this to the lord :— "O lord of the universe, command us, What caused you to remember me ? May favour be granted unto me."

883. purā—pūrvabhāge *ST*: but probably for puraḥ—in front of.

The lord said :—

12-16. A great terrible fear has cropped up untimely unto Devas. The fire of Nṛsiṁha is blazing. He cannot be approached. Subdue him. At the outset console him and make him understand. If he does not become calm thereby, show him my extremely terrible features. Destroy the subtle things by the subtle and the gross things by the gross splendour. At my behest make him realize his duty [884] (or bring him in front of me.)

Thus commanded, the presiding deity of the Gaṇas assumed a calm physical form and hastened to the place the Man-lion was present. Thereafter, Vīrabhadra identical with Śiva enlightened Viṣṇu Nṛsiṁha. Like a father unto his bosom-born son Vīrabhadra spoke these words :—

Vīrabhadra said :—

17-22. O lord Viṣṇu, you have incarnated for the happiness of the world. You have been engaged by the great Parameṣṭhin for the purpose of sustenance. Multitudes of creatures have been saved by you in the form of a fish. You moved about in the vast ocean-like sheet of water formerly, after tying up the boat to your tail. You held aloft the Mandara mountain in the form of a tortoise; the earth was lifted up by the Boar. With this leonine form Hiraṇyakaśipu was killed. Again Bali was bound by you in the form of Vāmana taking up three steps. You alone are the unchanging lord of all living beings. This is your prowess : whenever any misery befalls the world, you take incarnations and make your devotees free from ailments. O lord, devoutly attached to Śiva, no one excels you; there is none equal to you.

23-24. Dharmas and the Vedas were established along auspicious lines by you. O lord, the Asura for whom this incarnation was taken has been killed. O lord, your physical form of

884. vaktram ānaya kṛttiñ ca—vaktraṁ mukhaṁ kṛttiṁ tvacañ ca ānaya *ST*. you bring his head as well as his skin. There is a variant kṛtyam for kṛttim which the translators have adopted here. But this does not suit the context. The translation may be emended according to the NS. reading 'kṛttim' for 'kṛtyam.'—Editor.

Manlion is extremely terrible. O soul of the universe, kindly withdraw this form yourself in my presence.

Sūta said :—

25. Thus addressed in mild words by Vīrabhadra, lord Nṛsiṁha (Man-lion) blazed more than before with extremely terrible wrath.

Lord Nṛsiṁha said :—

26-32. O dear, go back to that place wherefrom you have come. Do not be presumptuous enough to advise me what is beneficial to me. I shall now annihilate this universe of the mobile and immobile beings. There can't be the annihilation of the annihilator at his own hands or from others. My sway extends everywhere. There is none to boss over me. Thanks to my favour that everything functions within limits. I alone am the instigator and restrainer of all Śaktis. O Gaṇādhyakṣa (presiding deity over the Gaṇas), know that everything that is glorious, rich, powerful and energetic in the world is a display of my splendour.[885] Those who are conversant with the reality of deities know that I alone am the greatest deity. Brahmā, Indra and other Devas who are equipped with power are my parts. The four-faced deity Brahmā was born out of my umbilical lotus formerly. The bull-bannered lord originated out of his forehead. The creator is well-endowed with Rajo-Guṇa; Rudra is called Tāmasa (abounding in Tamo-Guṇa). I am the restrainer and controller of everything. There is no deity greater than myself.

33-35. I am superior to the universe. I am independent lord of all. I am the maker and unmaker (annihilator). This is my greatest splendour. Who then wishes to hear your suggestion ? Hence, seek refuge in me, be rid of ailments and go back. O great lord of the Bhūtas, understand this great feature of mine. O Vīrabhadra, I am Kāla (Time, Death). I am the cause of the destruction of Kāla. I am engaged in the activity of annihilation. Know me as Death unto the god of Death. It is due to my favour that these Devas are alive.

885. With minor variations, the verse occurs in the Bhagavad Gītā, X. 41.

Sūta said:—

36. On hearing these haughty words of Nṛsiṁha, Vīrabhadra of unmeasured exploits laughed in derision. With throbbing lips he said thus.

Vīrabhadra said:—

37. Don't you know the Pināka-bearing lord of the universe who is the annihilator? Wrong assertions and disputes will bring in only destruction unto you.

38. Out of your different incarnations what are they that remain now? Whatever may be the purpose for which they have been taken, it is only the story thereof that remains.[886]

39. See this defect that you have attained such a plight. Within a trice, you will court destruction through Śiva who is an adept in annihilation.

40. You are Prakṛti and Rudra is Puruṣa. Power has been induced in you, it is not natural. The five-faced Brahmā was born of your umbilical lotus.

41. Brahmā who was engaged in a severe penance thought of Śaṅkara within his forehead. It was for effecting creation that he thought of Nīlalohita the ancestor of the universe.

42. For the purpose of creation Śiva originated from his forehead. That is not disparaging to the lord Śiva. I am a part of the lord of Devas. I have assumed the form of Bhairava.

43-44. I have been employed to subdue you with humility at the outset, and if that fails, with force afterwards. You are endowed with the digit of his Śakti. Thus, you have torn asunder the Asura. Merely on account of this you are crying hoarse with haughtiness again and again. A help rendered to the wicked is conducive only to a malicious misbehaviour.

45. O lion, if you consider Maheśāna (lord Śiva) to be one born after you, you are mistaken. You are neither the creator nor the annihilator and never independent.

46-50. Like the potter's wheel you have been activised by the Śakti of the Pināka-bearing lord. O immature one, even now, your skull is strung in the necklace of Śiva when you had

886. As your past incarnations in the form of fish, boar, tortoise, etc. have remained as mere tales, so you too in this (man-lion's) form will become a thing of the past, to be remembered merely in tales.

assumed the form of a tortoise. Why don't you understand it? Have you forgotten that your physical form of the Boar was tormented by Skanda, the enemy of Tāraka, with an imprecation and curved fang was partially uprooted? O Viṣvaksena (i.e. Viṣṇu), due to your deception, you have been burned at the tip of his trident. At the sacrifice of Dakṣa your head was cut off by me even as you had assumed the form of sacrifice. Even today the fifth head of Brahmā[887] your son has been cut off by me. He is born of your umbilical lotus. His strength is so only partial (?). You have been defeated by Dadhīca[888] along with the Maruts in the course of a battle, even as he was scratching his head. How is it forgotten by you?

51-54. O Cakrapāṇi the discus is your favourite weapon, thanks to its exploits. Whence has it been acquired by you? By whom was it made? Even that has been forgotten by you. All your worlds have been seized from you. Overwhelmed by slumber you lie down in the ocean. How then can you be a Sāttvika? Everything beginning with you and ending with blade of grass is the display of Rudra's Śakti. The fire-god and you, though powerful all round, were deluded. Both of you were incompetent to realize the greatness of his splendour.

55-58. Only to the gross intellect appear the great forms of Viṣṇu, Indra, Agni, Yama, Varuṇa, of heaven and earth. You are born in the belly of the moon.[889] You are Kāla. Parameśvara is Mahākāla. Maheśvara is Kālakāla. Hence, you will become the victim of Death through the burning digit of Ugra (Śiva). The lord with a steady bow is imperishable, heroic and superior to the universe. He destroys fear of fever.[890] He is the lord of all animals and birds and gold (?). Neither you nor the four-faced deity can be the overlord and ruler of the entire universe.

887. See p. 60. note. 78.

888. Cf. *Liṅga*, part I. chs. 35, 36.

889. Vīrabhadra refers tauntingly to the various forms of Viṣṇu, such as Vāmana from Aditi, Jayanta from Indra, Kārttikeya from Agni, Nārāyaṇa from Yama, Bhṛgu from Varuṇa and Budha from Soma, implying thereby the subordinate position of Viṣṇu.

890. upahastā jvaram—jvaraṁ tatsaṁjñaka-rogam upahastā upahāsakaraḥ *ST.*—said of Śiva who scoffs even at the dreadful disease called *jvara.*

59-62. Thus viewing everything, restrain and withdraw the Ātman through the Ātman. Otherwise, death will befall you like the thunderbolt on a stump. You will be the victim of a severe wrath that has the form of great Bhairava.

Sūta said :

Nṛsiṁha who was thus addressed became agitated through anger. He roared and roared and then seized Vīrabhadra with the force and velocity of his body.

In the meantime, the extremely terrible form of Vīrabhadra born of the brilliant splendour of Śiva manifested itself as invincible, spreading through the firmament and causing terror among his enemies.

63. It was not a golden splendour. It was not one pertaining to the moon or the sun nor was it fiery in origin. It was not similar to lightning or the moonlight. It belonged to Maheśvara and it was incomparable.

64. Then all fiery splendours merged into the splendour of Śaṅkara. The highly brilliant and immanent (i.e. Vīrabhadra) became manifest.

65. He assumed a hideous form characteristic of Rudra. Then Parameśvara became visible in the form of the annihilator.

66. Raising auspicious shouts of victory Devas stood observing. Vīrabhadra adopted thousand arms. His hairs were matted. The crescent moon adorned his head.

67. Half of his body was an animal's.[891] With wings and a beak he was a bird. His great curved fangs were very sharp. Adamantine claws were his weapons.

68. He was blue-necked and long-armed. The beak and the feet were born of fire as it were. His majestie roaring sound resembled the terrible thunder of the cloud rising up at the close of a yuga.

69. His three eyes became round and furious like fiery balls. His lower lips and curved fangs became prominent. He thundered a Huṁkāra.

70-75. At his very sight Nṛsiṁha lost his strength and exploit. He had the same uneasiness and flutter as that of a glow-worm

891. This refers to the Śarabha incarnation of Śiva. Śarabha is an animal with eight legs, stronger than a lion.

beneath the thousand-rayed sun. Then Vīrabhadra seized him tying up his legs with his tail and inclosing the region of his arms within his arms. He whirled him [or shook him] with his wings clutching at his umbilicus and feet and hit in his chest. Just as the bird of pray lifts up a serpent and flies high up into the sky so also Vīrabhadra lifted up Nṛsiṁha. He was followed by Devas and sages out of fright. Sometimes he lifted up Man-lion and sometimes he let him fall down. Soaring high up into the air he struck him with his wings and rendered him unconscious. Devas followed that excellent Vīrabhadra, lord of the universe, who was carrying off Nṛsiṁha. They eulogised him with obeisance. Even as he was being carried away, Nṛsiṁha in his helpless state eulogised Parameśāna (Śiva) with palms joined in reverence. His pitiable plight was evident in his face. He eulogised the lord in elegant and graceful words.

Lord Nṛsiṁha said:

76-80. Obeisance to Rudra,[892] to Śarva, to one who is all-consuming, all-pervading. Obeisance to Ugra,[893] to Bhīma[894] (the terrible), to Krodha (anger), to Manyu[895] (wrath), to Bhava, to Śarva. Obeisance to you, to Śaṅkara, to Śiva,[896] to Kālākāla, to Kāla, to Mahākāla, to Mṛtyu, to the heroic Vīrabhadra; to the trident-bearing lord, to Kṣayadvīra[897] (he who destroys powerful persons), to the great Mahādeva, to the

892. rudrāya—For the derivation of the name rudra, see ŚP. Vāyavīya 12.25-30—rodanād dravaṇāccaiva te rudrā nāmataḥ smṛtāḥ. On the authority of Ahobala-*rudrabhāṣya ST.* gives another derivation: one who brings about the union of the individual soul with the supreme soul by means of 'Om'.

अथवा परमात्मानं रुत्या प्रणवरूपया।
प्रतिपादयतीत्येवं रुद्रशब्दं प्रचक्ष्महे ॥

893. ugrāya—ucyati(krudhā)sambadhyate iti ugraḥ *ST*. Cf. Ahobala-*Rudrabhāṣya*—cited in *ST*.

894. bhīmāya—cf. bhīṣā'smāt pavate vātaḥ.

895. manyave—manyur avabodharūpaḥ, kraturūpo vā *ST*. of the form of knowledge or sacrifice.

896. śivāya—kalyāṇarūpāya *ST*. Cf. Ahobala:

शिवो निष्कल्मषो यद्वा सच्चिदानन्दलक्षणः।
यद्वा निर्धर्मिको यद्वा कल्याणात्मेति मन्महे॥

897. kṣayadvīrāya—kṣayad vīram pāpaṁ yasmād asau *ST*. For vīra=pāpa, see Sy. on Rudra-bhāṣya, as cited by *ST*.

lord of Paśus, to the sole,[898] to Nīlakaṇṭha, to the Pinākabearer, to Śrīkaṇṭha, to the infinite, to the subtle, to death,[899] to wrath, to the greatest and noblest Īśa, to the greater than the greatest.[900]

81-87. Obeisance to the lord greater than the greatest.[901] Obeisance to Viśva, to Viśvamūrti (cosmic-formed), to Viṣṇukalatra (one with Viṣṇu as bride[902] (since Viṣṇu represents Prakṛti), to Viṣṇukṣetra (having Viṣṇu as wife), to Bhānu (the blazing one), to Kaivarta (fisherman), to Kirāta (hunter), to the great hunter, to the permanent being, to Bhairava worthy of being sought refuge in, to one of the form of Mahābhairava, to the annihilator of Man-lion, to the slayer of Kāma, Kāla and the Tripuras, to the destroyer of great tangles of Pāśa (bondage), to one who causes the end of Viṣṇu's Māyā, to Tryambaka (three-eyed), to Tryakṣara (three-syllabled one), to Śipiviṣṭa[903] (bold man in the midst of rays of light), to the bountiful one, to the conqueror of Mṛtyu (death), to Śarva, to Sarvajña (the omniscient), to the enemy of sacrifice. Obeisance to the lord of Makha (sacrifice), to the most excellent one, to you of the form of fire, to Mahāghrāṇa (one of huge nose), to Mahājihva (one of long tongue), to the deity that sets Prāṇa and Apāna in motion, to one of three Guṇas, to the the lord who identifies himself with the continuous flow of mundane existence, to the deity who makes the great Yantra function, to one having the moon, fire and sun (as his eyes), to the cause of the mysterious liberation, to the bestower of boons, to the incarnation, to the cause of all reasons.

898. ekāya—advitīyāya *ST*. non-dual. Cf. "ekaṁ sad viprā bahudhā vadanti"—cited in *ST*.

899. mṛtyu-manyave. Cf. "namaste rudra manyave", *VS*. 16.1; *TS*. 4.5.1.1.

900. parāt paratarāya. para is jīva (the individual soul) : paratara is Śiva (the supreme soul).

901. parāt parāya—uttama-puruṣa-rupāya *ST*. Cf.

उत्तमः पुरुषस्त्वन्यः परमात्मेत्युदाहृतः ।
यो लोकत्रयमाविश्य बिभर्त्यव्यय ईश्वरः ।। cited in *ST*.

902. Viṣṇu-kṣetrāya—Viṣṇuḥ kṣetram strī yasya. Cf. Kūrma. योऽनन्तः पुरुषो योनिर्लोकानामव्ययो हरिः। स्त्रीवेषं विष्णुरास्थाय सोऽनुगच्छति शूलिनम् ।। or Viṣṇuḥ Kṣetraṁ Bījanirvāpaṇaṁ yasya, Cf. Liṅga : prakṛtis tvam pumān rudras tvayi vīryam samāhitam / tvannābhīpaṅkajāj jātaḥ pañcavaktraḥ pitāmahaḥ// Compare also the preceding name: Viṣṇukalatra.

903. śipiviṣṭāya—śipiṣu pāśuṣu Viśatīti. Cf. Ahobala: yajñarūpaḥ śipir Viṣṇuḥ paśavaḥ śipayaḥ smṛtāḥ—cited in *ST*.

88-91. Obeisance to Kapālin [one having the skull (in the hand)], to the terrible one, to the lord of meritorious renown, to the Amogha (one who is never futile), to the fiery-eyed one, to Nakulīśa, to Śambhu, to the greatest physician, to one having shaven head, to one holding a staff, to one of yogic form, to the lord having the cloud for vehicle. Obeisance to the lord of Pārvatī, to the unmanifest, to one devoid of grief, to the steady one, to one with steady bow, to Sthāṇu, to one having tigerskin as garment, to the cause of the five substances, to the bestower of boons, to one of a simple foot, to one who has the crescent moon on his head, to the king of Adhvaras[904] (sacrifices), obeisance to the lord of yogins.

92-94. Obeisance to the lord of yogins, to the permanent Being, to the truthful Being, to Parameṣṭhin, to the Ātman of all, to the lord of all, to you once, twice, thrice, four times, five times, ten times, a thousand times, unlimited number of times infinite number of times. Obeisance, obeisance, obeisance, again and again to you.

Sūta said :

95. After eulogising Śarabheśvara (Śiva) with these hundred and eight names identical with nectar, Nṛsiṁha prayed again to the lord (in the form of a Śarabha).

96. O Parameśvara, whenever I am defiled by ignorance and great haughtiness I must be saved by you.

97-98. The delighted Man-lion thus submitted to Śaṅkara. Then Vīrabhadra, said: "O Viṣṇu, you are indeed a weakling. You have been defeated till the end of your life". Then Vīrabhadra skinned off his body which was now left only with bone and then reduced him to a mere face.[905]

Devas said:

99-101. "O Vīrabhadra, all of us including Brahmā have been enlivened by you by your mere sight like the trees by the cloud. You are that deity fearing whom the fire burns, the sun

904. adhvara-rājāya—the lord of sacrifice: Cf. ā vo rājānam adhvarasya rudram—*RV*. 4.3.1; *TS*. 1.3.13.1.

905. tadvaktra—Vīrabhadra reduced Man-lion to a mere skeleton of bones, devoid of skin, but having a face.

rises, the wind blows. You are that Mṛtyu who destroys the five elements. O lord, the expounders of Brahman say that you are Sadāśiva, beyond the digits, unmanifest, the greatest firmament and Bhava (the source of all).

102. O Parameśvara, who are we to understand you the support of the universe?[906] Know that we are unable to describe your beauty of form.

103. O Overlord of the Gaṇas, protect us in the course of all calamities. O lord with eleven souls, you are the embodiment of Śiva.

104-105. O Śiva, on seeing these incarnations of yours let not doubt about you enter us. Let no worry trouble us. You have unmeasured forms as black berries on the ridges of mountains.[907] Please withdraw this form. Let it not frighten the world.

106. The brahmins conversant with the Vedas know that Rudra has two bodies: one Ghora (the terrible) and the other Śiva (calm and pleasing). Each one of them is manifold.

107. O lord, whose great strength is never obstructed, protect us here. Indeed, the entire universe is pervaded by you with your own splendour.

108. O Maheśvara, we, the chief of Devas, Brahmā, Viṣṇu. Indra, Soma and all other Devas and Asuras are born of you.

109-110. O lord, you support the universe after dividing your body as Brahmā, Indra, Viṣṇu, Yama, etc. in eight ways.[908] Protect us, Devas, by granting us our desired gifts.

111-112. The lord Vīrabhadra spoke to Devas and the ancient great sages. Just as water mixed with water, milk with milk, and ghee with ghee, all merge into one, in the same manner Viṣṇu has merged into Śiva. This deity in the form of Nṛsiṁha has great strength and is haughty.

113. This man-lion has been made to function by him who causes the annihilation of the universe. He should be

906. dhātukye—jagaddhārakāya *ST*. the support of the universe.

907. *ST*. interprets 104-105 as follows: 'O lord, on looking at these incarnations of yours, let not a doubt enter our mind. May we not give up thinking on you. Withdraw your dreadful form, shining as the black berries on a mount. Do not destroy this world which you pervade by your soul.

908. aṣṭadhā tanum, see p. 208 note 326.

worshipped and made obeisance to by those who desire to achieve my pleasure.

114. After saying this, lord Vīrabhadra of great strength vanished there itself, even as all the Bhūtas were watching.

115. Ever since that day, Śaṅkara is said to wear the skin of Nṛsiṁha (as his garment). The lion's face is also set as the leading bead in the garland of skulls.

116. Thereafter, Devas became free from agony. They began to repeat and glorify this story. Their eyes became beaming with wonder. They went back to their respective abodes.

117. If any one reads or listens to this great and holy narrative pertaining to Devas he becomes free from miseries.

118. It is conducive to the attainment of wealth, renown, longevity and good health. It increases nourishment, subdues all obstacles and dispels all ailments.

119. It prevents premature death. It causes great peace. It is auspicious. It subdues multitudes of enemies and destroys all mental agonies.

120. It removes evil dreams; it prevents evil spirits; it reduces the ill effects of poison and evil planets; it causes the increase of sons and grandsons.

121. It bestows yogic Siddhis; it illuminates the knowledge of Śiva; it is the staircase leading to the world of Śeṣa; it is the sole means of attaining all desired objects.

122. It dispels the Māyā of Viṣṇu; it gives the real knowledge of the deities; it bestows the Siddhi of all ambitions; it is the means of achievement of prosperity and wisdom.

123. This great form of the Pināka-bearing lord having the shape of the Śarabha should be revealed among devotees and also when great endeavours are undertaken.

124. In the course of all festivals of Śiva on Caturdaśī (fourteenth) and on Aṣṭamī (eighth) days, this should be read and listened to by devotees whose minds dwell in Śiva.

125-128. If one reads this at the installation of Śiva's image, it establishes the presence of Śiva. It shall be read when there is fear from kings and from thieves, tigers, serpents and lions. It shall be read on the following occasions too, viz:—when there are evil portents, earthquakes, forest fires, dust storms, falling of comets and meteors, stormy gusts of winds without rain and heavy downpour. The learned devotee of Śiva, firm in the observance of holy rites shall read this always.

He who reads or listens to this excellent hymn fully will attain Rudra-hood and then become a follower of Rudra.

CHAPTER NINETYSEVEN

Death of Jalandhara

The sages said:

1-5. O Romaharṣaṇa of good holy rites, it behoves you to tell us how lord Hara the destroyer of the eyes of Bhaga, having matted hairs, killed Jalandhara whose exploit was like that of Indra.

Sūta said:

There was once an Asura born of the vast sheet of water (ocean). He was known by the name Jalandhara. He resembled the god of death. It was by penance that he acquired his exploits. All Devas including Gandharvas, Yakṣas, Nāgas and Rākṣasas, and even the unborn lord Brahmā were defeated by him in battle. After conquering Devas and Brahmā, Jalandhara went to the lord of the chiefs of Devas, Viṣṇu, the destroyer of the universe (?), and the preceptor. A battle ensued between them without respite for a whole night and day.

6-10. Lord Viṣṇu was defeated by him. After defeating Viṣṇu the lord of Devas, Jalandhara said to the sons of Diti, "To conquer Śiva is only a justifiable thought. All the rest have been conquered by me in the battle. Only Śiva has not been conquered by me. O leading Dānavas, after conquering him within a short while along with Nandin and the leaders of the Gaṇas, I shall distribute among you the position of Śiva, Brahmā, Viṣṇu and Indra."

On hearing the words of Jalandhara all those base Dānavas roared aloud. Those sinners were eager to face death. Accompanied by these Daityas the powerful Asura set out against Śiva, fully equipped with chariots, elephants and horses.

11-13. Śiva saw the leader of the Daityas stationed on the peak of the Meru. He had already heard about his indestructibility through others. The destroyer of the eyes of Bhaga, the lord and protector of the worlds wanted to keep his promise to Brahmā. He was accompanied by Ambā and Nandin and his Gaṇas. He said laughingly:—"O lord of Asuras, what purpose shall be served now with a fight?

14-16. You have joyously attempted to die with your limbs pierced and split by my arrows."

On hearing these words that rent his ears, Jalandhara the lord of the army of Asuras spoke thus to the lord of Devas.

"O bull-bannered lord of Devas, having mighty arms, enough of words. O Śiva, I have come here to fight with you with weapons as bright and piercing as the rays of the moon."

On hearing his words the trident-bearing lord evolved a discus, the terrible weapon, by drawing sportingly on the surface of the vast sheet of water with the toe of his leg.

17. After making the sharp features of the discus on the water-surface of the ocean the lord thought that the three worlds and Devas had been killed by him. The destroyer of Dakṣa, Andhaka, Antaka, Tripuras, the sacrifice and the annihilator of the three worlds said laughingly.

18-19. "O Jalandhara, O Asura, if you are strong enough to lift up the weapon evolved by me by my leg, stand face to face for fighting, and not otherwise"

On hearing his words the Asura became angry with blazing eyes. He looked over the three worlds as though he would burn them with the pair of his eyes.

Jalandhara said:

20-21. O Śaṅkara, I will lift up my iron club and kill Nandin as well as you. Even as Garuḍa kills the water snakes I will destroy the worlds along with Devas. I am competent to annihilate all mobile and immobile beings, including Indra. O Maheśvara, who is there in the three worlds who cannot be pierced by my arrows?

22. Even during my childhood, the lord was defeated by

my penance. The powerful Brahmā, and the sages along with the leading Devas were defeated during my youth.

23. Within a short while, the three worlds consisting of the mobile and immobile beings were burnt by me. O Rudra, was any lord defeated by you by means of penance?

24. Just as the serpents cannot bear even the odour of Garuḍa, the lord of the birds, so also Indra, Agni, Yama, Kubera, Vāyu, Varuṇa and others cannot bear me.

25. O Śaṅkara, neither in the heaven nor on the earth could my arms get rival. O lord of the Gaṇas, I have gone to all the mountains and attacked them.

26. Mandara[909] the lord of the mountains, the glorious Nila[910] and the splendid Meru[911] have been attacked by me with my staff-like arms. The mountain Meru fell when I scratched it with arms for removing their itching sensation.

27. Just for a sport, the Gaṅgā was restrained with my arms on the mountain Himavān. A group of celestial women was caught and imprisoned by my servants.

28. The mouth of the submarine fire was held by me and choked with the hand. Instantaneously all this was tnrned into a vast sheet of water.

29. Airāvata and other elephants were cast off by me into the water of the ocean. Lord Indra was hurled a hundred yojanas along with his chariot.

30. Garuḍa too was bound by me along with Viṣṇu by means of Nāgapāśa. Urvaśī and other women were imprisoned by me.

31. With very great difficulty Indra got back Śacī alone after bowing down to me. O lord of Umā, you do not know me, Jalandhara the leader of the Daityas.

Sūta said:

32. Mahādeva who was addressed thus, burned his chariot then with the fire of his eye.[912]

33. Since the lord of the Daityas was surrounded by the

909. Mandara—a mythical mountain.

910. Nila—a mountain sacred to the manes. Cf. *Matsya*. 22. 70; 121.

911. Meru, p. 98 note 127.

912. netrāgni—by the one-fourth (ardhārdha) of the digit of his ocular fire *ST*.

invincible army of the Daityas, consisting of the horses, elephants and Nāgas, he did not undergo destruction by the fiery glance of the Tripuras. The silly and weak-minded Asura spoke to the lord of Devas thus.

34-35. What purpose of mine can be served in the battle by the mutual clash of Devas and Asuras? I alone am competent to destroy all these in an instant. I have no fear of fighting. O Īśa, this is my earnest desire. Hence, O enemy of Kāma, Dakṣa, Yajña and Tripuras, if you have strength to fight with my heroes with the help of your leading Bhūtas and the monkey-faced Nandin, then you stand here to fight with me.

36. After saying thus to Mahādeva, the great demon did not move nor did he think of his kins killed in battle.

37. Urged by evil haughtiness that demon of impolite nature clapped his hands together and then seized the discus called Sudarśana. He attempted to kill Śiva with that discus.

38. O excellent brahmins, he placed the heavy discus on his shoulders with an effort. With that he was pierced into pieces.

39. O brahmins, just as the excellent mountain fell down when it was pierced by the thunderbolt of Indra so also the powerful Daitya fell down dead like a mountain of collyrium.

40-43. Instantaneously, the place was covered with his terrible blood. At the behest of Rudra his blood and flesh reached Mahāraurava hell and lo, it became a deep pit of blood. On seeing Jalandhara killed, Devas, Gandharvas and Pārṣadas made leonine shouts and cried : "O lord well done." He who reads or listens to this story of the suppression of Jalandhara or he who narrates it duly will attain the leadership of the Gaṇas.

CHAPTER NINETYEIGHT

Thousand names of Śiva

The sages said:

1. O Sūta, how was the discus Sudarśana acquired from Maheśvara, the lord of Devas, by lord Viṣṇu ? It behoves you to recount it.

Sūta said:

2-3. A terrible fight ensued between Devas and the leading Asuras causing destruction to all living beings. On being pierced and hit by lances, iron clubs, javelins and arrows of bent knots Devas became extremely terrified and fled.

4. The vanquished Devas with minds agitated due to grief bowed down to the lord of Devas, to Viṣṇu the lord of the chiefs of Devas.

5. On seeing them standing aside after bowing down to him, lord Viṣṇu, the lord of the chiefs of Devas, spoke to them these words:—

6. "O Devas, O dear ones of good holy rites, wherefore have ye come here with so much of distress and forgetful of your former exploits ? It behoves you to speak out".

7. On hearing his words, the excellent Devas who were in a miserable plight bowed down to Viṣṇu, the lord of Devas, and recounted everything in the manner it had happened.

8. O lord Viṣṇu, O lord of the chiefs of Devas, O victorious Viṣṇu, all of us are afflicted by Dānavas. We have sought refuge in you.

9. O Puruṣottama, the lord of the chiefs of Devas, you are our goal. Indeed, you alone are the greatest Ātman; you are the father of the worlds.

10. O Janārdana, you alone are the sustainer, annihilator, enjoyer and donor. Hence, O suppressor of Dānavas, it behoves you to kill them.

11-15. Since they have acquired boons, they cannot be killed with any of these arrows and miraculous weapons:— such as those belonging to Viṣṇu, Brahmā, Rudra, Yama, Kubera, Soma, Nirṛti, Varuṇa, Vāyu, Agni, Varṣa, Sun, Īśāna, and other terrible missiles which make others tremble and powerless. O lotus-eyed one, all of them defy death due to their boons. O preceptor of the universe, the blazing Cakra (discus) that belongs to you, and that has originated from the solar disc has been rendered blunt by Dadhīca, son of Cyavana. Your staff and bow, your miraculous weapons have been acquired by Daityas through your grace. Formerly, a terrible and sharp-pointed discus was evolved by lord Śiva, the enemy of the Tripuras in order to kill Jalandhara. It behoves you to kill them with that weapon.

16-19. They can be killed with that weapon and not by any of the hundreds of other weapons.

On hearing their words the discus-bearing lotus-eyed Viṣṇu spoke to those Devas—Brahmā and others.

Lord Viṣṇu said:

O Devas, I shall approach lord Śiva now along with all the eternal Devas and shall carry out your task in full. O Devas, after acquiring the discus, formerly made by the slayer of the Tripuras in order to kill Jalandhara, I shall kill all the six thousand eight hundred great Asuras and Daityas beginning with Dhundhu. Thus, instantaneously I will redeem all of you, along with your kinsmen.

Sūta said:

20-26. After saying this to the excellent Devas, Viṣṇu, the excellent one among Devas, remembered lord Śiva and worshipped him. On the splendid summit of the Himavān he duly installed the Liṅga that resembled the mountain Meru. It had been made by Viśvakarman. Repeating the hymn called Tvarita-Rudra and the Rudrasūkta he bathed the Liṅga and worshipped it with scents. It was charming in its flame-like form. He eulogised Rudra; worshipped him in the fire and bowed down to him. Repeating the thousand names in order he worshipped lord Śiva. Each name was begun with Praṇava and ended with Namaḥ (obeisance). The first name among the thousand was Bhava. With every name he worshipped Śaṅkara, Maheśvara, with a lotus once. With sacrificial twigs he performed ten thousand Homas for every name beginning with Bhava. He duly performed the Homa, repeating the word

Svāhā after every name [i. e. Om Bhavāya Svāhā, etc]. He then, again eulogised Śambhu, Bhava, Īśvara with the names beginning with Bhava.

Lord Viṣṇu said:—

27-40. (1) Bhava (2) Śiva[913] (3) Hara, (4) Rudra (5) Puruṣa[914] (6) Padmalocana (lotus-eyed) (7) Arthitavya (one who should be requested) (8) Sadācāra (one having good conduct) (9) Sarvaśambhu (benefactor of all) (10) Maheśvara (11) Īśvara (12) Sthāṇu[915] (13) Īśāna (14) Sahasrākṣa (thousand-eyed) (15) Sahasrapād (thousand-footed) (16) Varīyān (the excellent one) (17) Varada (the bestower of boons) (18) Vandya (worthy of being saluted) (19) Śaṅkara (20) Parameśvara (21) Gaṅgādhara (one who holds Gaṅgā) (22) Śūladhara (Trident-bearing one) (23) Parārthika-prayojana (one whose sole purpose is to work for other's benefit), (24) Sarvajña (omniscient) (25) Sarvadevādi (the cause of all Devas) (26) Giridhanvā[916] (one who used the mountain as his bow) (27) Jaṭādhara (wearing matted hairs) (28) Candrāpīḍa (29) Candramauli (having the moon on the head as an ornament) (30) Vidvān (scholar) (31) Viśveśvara (lord of the universe) (32) Amareśvara (lord of the immortal) (33) Vedāntasārasandoha (one who is the cumulative essence of the Vedāntas) (34) Kapālin (having the skull in the hand)

913. In fact, the names exceed the required number. In order to arrive at one thousand number *ST* treats some substantives as adjectives and excludes them from the list of names. For example, in 'bhavāya śivāya namaḥ' 'bhavāya' is used as an adjective qualifying 'Śivāya' and not included in the list of one thousand names. Our translation does not follow *ST* in this respect.

Śivaḥ—Śiva is the fourth (turīya) state of the soul in which the other three states merge, losing their identity. Cf. Śivam advaitam turīyaṁ manyante—cited in *ST*. Cf. also Ahobala :

वस्तुत: शिवशब्दार्थो ब्रह्माद्यैरपि तत्त्वत: ।
नैव ज्ञातस्तदर्थोऽत: शिव: सर्वोत्तमोत्तम: ।
जानाति तत्त्वतो यस्मात्स स्वतस्तत्त्ववित्तम: ।। —cited in *ST*.

914. Puruṣaḥ—Viṣṇurūpaḥ *ST*. Cf. sahasraśīrṣā puruṣaḥ. RV. X. 90.1. —cited in *ST*.

915. Sthāṇuḥ—gamanāgamanaśūnyaḥ *ST*. static. Cf. Vṛkṣa iva stabdho divi tiṣṭhatyekaḥ. —cited in *ST*.

916. Giridhanvā—giriḥ Meruḥ dhanur yasya *ST*. one who has a bow in the form of the mountain Meru. Cf. Bhag. Gītā "Meruḥ śikhariṇām aham."

(35) Nīlalohita (blue-blooded) (36) Dhyānādhāra (basis for meditation) (37) Aparicchedya (one who cannot be accurately defined) (38) Gaurībhartṛ (husband of Gaurī) (39) Gaṇeśvara (lord of the Gaṇas) (40) Aṣṭamūrti (one having eight cosmic bodies) (41) Viśvamūrti (one of universal form) (42) Trivarga (one who fulfils the three aims of life) (43) Svargasādhana (one who is the means of achieving heavenly abode) (44) Jñānagamya (one who can be realized only through perfect knowledge) (45) Dṛḍhaprajña (one of steady intellect) (46) Devadeva (lord of Devas) (47) Trilocana (three-eyed) (48) Vāmadeva (49) Mahādeva (50) Pāṇḍu (greyish in colour) (51) Parivṛḍha (master, chief) (52) Dṛḍha (firm) (53) Viśvarūpa (multiformed) (54) Virūpākṣa (one with hideous eyes) (55) Vāgīśa (lord of speech) (56) Śuci antar (pure within) (57) Sarvapraṇayasaṁvādin (one who converses lovingly with everyone) (58) Vṛṣāṅka (one marked with a bull) (59) Vṛṣavāhana (bull-vehicled) (60) Īśa (61) Pinākin (62) Khaṭvāṅgin (one armed with the iron club called Khaṭvāṅga) (63) Citraveṣa (one of variegated guise) (64) Cirantana (the ancient one) (65) Tamohara (remover of darkness) (66) Mahāyogin (67) Goptṛ (protector) (68) Brahmāṅgahṛd (one who took away a limb of Brahmā) (69) Jaṭin (having matted hairs) (70) Kālakāla (death unto death) (71) Kṛttivāsas (one having the hide of an elephant as garment) (72) Subhaga (elegant) (73) Praṇavātmaka (of the nature of Praṇava) (74) Unmattaveṣa (one having the guise of a mad man) (75) Cakṣuṣya (beneficent to the eyes) (76) Durvāsas (Ill-clad) (77) Smaraśāsana (chastiser of Smara) (78) Dṛḍhāyudha (one having strong weapons) (79) Skandaguru (venerable father of Skanda) (80) Parameṣṭhin (81) Parāyaṇa (the greatest goal) (82) Anādimadhyanidhana (one who has neither beginning nor middle nor end) (83) Girīśa (84) Giribāndhava (kinsman of the mountain i.e. Himavān) (85) Kuberabandhu (Kubera's kinsman) (86) Śrīkaṇṭha (glorious-necked) (87) Lokavarṇottamottama (the most excellent one among the castes in the world) (88) Sāmānyadeva (common lord, i.e. to Devas and to Asuras) (89) Kodaṇḍin (one armed with a bow) (90) Nīlakaṇṭha (blue-necked) (91) Paraśvadhī (one having the axe) (92) Viśālākṣa (large-eyed) (93) Mṛgavyā-

dha (deer-hunter) (94) Sureśa (lord of Devas) (95) Sūryatāpana (scorcher of the sun) (96) Dharmakarmakṣama (one competent to perform righteous rites) (97) Kṣetram (holy centre) (98) Bhagavān (lord) (99) Bhaganetrabhit (one who pierced the eyes of Bhaga) (100) Ugra (fierce) (101) Paśupati (102) Tārkṣya (identical with Garuḍa) (103) Priyabhakta (one fond of his devotees) (104) Priyaṁvada (one who speaks pleasing words) (105) Dānta (one with self-control) (106) Dayākara (merciful) (107) Dakṣa (skilful) (108) Kapardin (one having matted hairs) (109) Kāmaśāsana (chastiser of Kāma) (110) Śmaśānanilaya (one who has the cremation ground as his abode) (111) Sūkṣma (subtle) (112) Śmaśānastha (stationed in the cremation ground) (113) Maheśvara.

41-50. (114) Lokakartā (the maker of the worlds) (115) Bhūtapati (lord of the goblins) (116) Mahākartā (the great maker) (117) Mahauṣadhi (the great medicine) (118) Uttara (later one) (119) Gopati (lord of Go i.e. cow or speech) (120) Goptā (protector) (121) Jñānagamya (comprehensible through perfect knowledge) (122) Purātana (ancient one) (123) Nīti (justice) (124) Sunīti (one who dispenses good justice) (125) Śuddhātmā (pure-souled) (126) Soma (accompanied by Umā) (127) Somarata (interested in the moon) (128) Sukhī (happy) (129) Somapa (imbiber of the Soma juice) (130) Amṛtapa (imbiber of nectar) (131) Soma (moon) (132) Mahānīti (employing great policy) (133) Mahāmati (of great intellect) (134) Ajātaśatru (one whose enemy is not yet born) (135) Āloka (light) (136) Sambhāvya (one worthy of being honoured) (137) Havyavāhana (conveyer of Havya i.e. sacrificial offering) (138) Lokakāra (creator of the worlds) (139) Vedakāra (maker of the Vedas) (140) Sūtrakāra (compiler of aphorisms) (141) Sanātana (eternal) (142) Maharṣi (great sage) (143) Kapilācārya (one identifying with the great sage Kapila) (144) Viśvadīpti (illuminator of the universe) (145) Trilocana (three-eyed) (146) Pinākapāṇi (one having the Pināka in his hand) (147) Bhūdeva (lord of the earth) (148) Svastida (bestower of welfare) (149) Sadāsvastikṛt (continuous creator of welfare and prosperity) (150) Tridhāmā (having the three syllables or worlds as abode) (151) Saubhaga (fortunate) (152) Sarva (identical with all) (153) Sarvajña (omniscient)

(154) Sarvagocara (perceptible to everyone) (155) Brahmadhṛk (holder of the brahman i.e. the Vedas) (156) Viśvasṛk (creator of the universe) (157) Svarga (heaven) (158) Karṇikārapriya (one fond of Karṇikāra flowers) (159) Kavi (poet) (160) Śākha (branching) (161) Viśākha (162) Gośākha (?) (163) Śiva (164) Naika (not one) (165) Kratu (sacrifice) (166) Sama (equal) (167) Gaṅgāplavodaka (identical with water flowing in the Gaṅgā) (168) Bhāva (pure emotion) (169) Sakala (entire one) (170) Sthapati (architect) (171) Sthira (steady) (172) Vijitātmā (one who has conquered the Ātman) (173) Vidheyātmā (one with a controlled mind) (174) Bhūtavāhana (one having the goblin as vehicle) (175) Bhūtasārathi (having a goblin as his charioteer) (176) Sagaṇa (one accompanied by his Gaṇa) (177) Gaṇakārya (the work of Gaṇas) (178) Sukīrti (one of good renown) (179) Chinnasaṁśaya (one whose doubts are cleared) (180) Kāmadeva (181) Kāmapāla (protector of Kāma) (182) Bhasmoddhūlitavigraha (one who has smeared his body with Bhasman) (183) Bhasmapriya (one fond of Bhasman) (184) Bhasmaśāyin (one lying on Bhasman) (185) Kāmin (lover) (186) Kānta (lovely) (187) Kṛtāgama (proficient in Vedas) (188) Samāyukta (endowed with good qualities) (189) Nivṛttātmā (one whose Ātman has receded from the world) (190) Dharmayukta (endowed with piety) (191) Sadāśiva (192) Caturmukha[917] (four-faced) (193) Caturbāhu (four-armed) (194) Durāvāsa (one whose abode is not easily accessible) (195) Durāsada (inaccessible) (196) Durgama (very difficult of access) (197) Durlabha (difficult to get) (198) Durga (impassable) (199) Sarvāyudhaviśārada (expert in the use of all weapons) (200) Adhyātmayoganilaya (having his abode in spiritual yoga) (201) Sutantu (good supreme being) (202) Tantuvardhana (one who increases offspring).

51-60. (203) Śubhāṅga (one having splendid limbs) (204) Lokasāraṅga (one who has attained the essence of the worlds) (205) Jagadīśa (lord of the universe) (206) Amṛtāśana (one whose diet is nectar) (207) Bhasmaśuddhikara (one who purifies through Bhasman) (208) Meru (209) Ojasvin (powerful) (210) Śuddhavigraha (one of pure physical form)

917. Caturmukha—identical with the four-faced Brahmā, see p.60 note 78.

(211) Hiraṇyaretas (one with golden semen virile) (212) Taraṇi (sun) (213) Marīci (ray) (214) Mahimālaya (abode of greatness) (215) Mahāhrada (one like a great deep pool of water) (216) Mahāgarbha (of huge womb) (217) Siddhavṛndāravandita (one who is saluted by Siddhas and Devas) (218) Vyāghracarmadhara (one who wears the tiger skin) (219) Vyālin (one who possesses snakes) (220) Mahābhūta (the great element) (221) Mahānidhi (the great treasure) (222) Amṛtāṅga (one of nectarine limbs) (223) Amṛtavapu (one of nectarine body) (224) Pañcayajña (one of five yajñas) (225) Prabhañjana (violent destroyer) (226) Pañcaviṁśatitattvajña[918] (one conversant with the twentyfive principles) (227) Pārijāta (the wish-yielding divine tree) (228) Parāvara (the great one second to none) (229) Sulabha (easily accessible) (230) Suvrata (one of good rites) (231) Śūra (hero) (232) Vāṅmayaikanidhi[919] (the sole treasury of literature) (233) Nidhi (treasure-trove) (234) Varṇāśramaguru (preceptor of all castes and stages of life) (235) Varṇin (religious student) (236) Satrujit (conqueror of enemies) (237) Śatrutāpana (scorcher of enemies) (238) Āśrama (hermitage (?)) (239) Kṣapaṇa (one who dispels) (240) Kṣāma (small and lean) (241) Jñānavān (one possessing perfect knowledge) (242) Acalācala (unmoving like a mountain) (243) Pramāṇabhūta (one who has become an authority) (244) Durjñeya (very difficult to be known) (245) Suparṇa (Garuḍa) (246) Vāyuvāhana (windvehicled) (247) Dhanurdhara (one who holds the bow) (248) Dhanurveda (the science of archery) (249) Guṇarāśi (abode of Guṇas) (250) Guṇākara (mine of good qualities) (251) Anantadṛṣṭi (one of infinite vision) (252) Ānanda[920] (bliss) (253) Daṇḍa[921] (punishment (254) Damayitā (one who oppresses) (255) Dama (self-control) (256) Abhivādya (one

918. pañcaviṁśati-tattva—emboding twentyfive principles, see p. 3 notes, 11 and 12.

919. Vāṅmayaikanidhiḥ—vāṅmayasya śabda-śāstrasyaiko 'dvitīyo nidhiḥ—the sole treasure of grammatical knowledge. Śiva is the original composer of grammar. Cf. Pāṇini-Śikṣā: yenākṣara-samāmnāyamadhigamya maheśvarāt kṛtsnaṁ Vyākaraṇam proktaṁ tasmai pāṇinaye namaḥ.

920. Ānandaḥ—blissful : "ānandam brahma".

921. Daṇḍaḥ—rod of chastisement. Cf. "daṇḍo damayitām asmi" *Bhagavadgītā*—cited in *ST*.

worthy of being saluted and honoured) (257) Mahācārya (great preceptor) (258) Viśvakarman (of universal action) (259) Viśārada (adept) (260) Vītarāga (one devoid of passion (261) Vinītātman (humble soul) (262) Tapasvin (performing penance) (263) Bhūtabhāvana (creator of living beings) (264) Unmattaveṣa (one in the guise of a mad man) (265) Pracchanna (hidden) (266) Jitakāma (one who has conquered lust) (267) Jitapriya (one who has conquered pleasure) (268) Kalyāṇaprakṛti (one of auspicious nature) (269) Kalpa (wish-yielding tree) (270) Sarvaloka-prajāpati (the lord of the subject of all the worlds) (271) Tapasvin (ascetic) (272) Tāraka (redeemer) (273) Dhīmān (intelligent) (274) Pradhānaprabhu (the lord of Pradhāna or Prakṛti) (275) Avyaya (the unchanging) (276) Lokapāla (the protector of the worlds) (277) Antarhitātman (one whose Ātman is hidden) (278) Kalpādi[922] (the beginning of kalpa) (279) Kamalekṣaṇa (lotus-eyed) (280) Vedaśāstrārthatattvajña (one who is conversant with the principles and meanings of the Vedas and the scriptures) (281) Niyama (regulation) (282) Niyamāśraya (basis of regulations).

61-70. (283) Candra (moon) (284) Sūrya (Sun) (285) Śani (saturn) (286) Ketu (the planet of that name) (287) Virāma (final rest) (288) Vidrumacchavi (one having the lustre of coral) (289) Bhaktigamya (comprehensible through devotion) (290) Paramabrahman (the greatest Brahman) (291) Mṛgabāṇārpaṇa (one who discharges arrows into the deer) (292) Anagha (the sinless) (293) Adrirājālaya (one who has his residence on the king of mountains) (294) Kānta (brilliant) (295) Paramātman (the great soul) (296) Jagadguru (the preceptor of the universe) (297) Sarvakarman (one engaged in all rites) (298) Acala (the unmoving) (299) Tvaṣṭṛ (the architect of the gods) (300) Maṅgalya (Auspicious) (301) Maṅgalāvṛta (covered with auspicious things) (302) Mahātapas (of great austerities) (303) Dīrghatapas (performing austerities of long duration) (304) Sthaviṣṭha (largest, very strong) (305) Sthavira (Ancient, aged) (306) Dhruva (Firm, fixed) (307) Ahaḥ (day) (308) Saṁvatsara

922. **Kalpādiḥ— kalpasya śāstrasya ādiḥ kāraṇam —the primeval cause of sacred treatises. Cf. "śāstra-yonitvāt"—*Brahma-sūtra* —cited in *ST*.**

(year) (309) Vyāpti (pervasion) (310) Pramāṇam (means of valid knowledge) (311) Paramaṁtapaḥ (greatest penance) (312) Saṁvatsarakara (cause of the year) (313) Mantra (incantation) (314) Pratyaya (confidence) (315) Sarvadarśana (viewing everyone) (316) Aja (unborn) (317) Sarveśvara (lord of all) (318) Snigdha (affectionate) (319) Mahāretas (of great virile power) (320) Mahābala (of great strength) (321) Yogin (322) Yogya (worthv) (323) Mahāretas (of great virile power) (324) Siddha (one who has achieved (great results)) (325) Sarvādi (Cause of all) (326) Agnida (Bestower of fire) (327) Vasu (wealth) (328) Vasumanas (having mind dwelling on wealth) (329) Satya (truthful) (330) Sarvapāpahara (Dispeller of all sins) (331) Hara (332) Amṛta (Nectar) (333) Śāśvata (permanent) (334) Śānta (calm) (335) Bāṇahasta (having the hand on the arrow) (336) Pratāpavān (valorous) (337) Kamaṇḍaludhara (holding the water-pot) (338) Dhanvin (holding the bow) (339) Vedāṅga (part of the Vedas) (340) Vedavit[923] (knower of the Vedas) (341) Muni (sage) (342) Bhrājiṣṇu (shining) (343) Bhojanam (diet) (344) Bhoktṛ (the enjoyer) (345) Lokanetṛ (the leader of the worlds) (346) Dhurādhara (Bearer of burden) (347) Atīndriya (one who is beyond the pale of the sense-organs) (348) Mahāmāya (wielding great Māyā) (349) Sarvāvāsa (abode of all) (350) Catuṣpatha (a brāhmin) (351) Kālayogī (one united with Kāla i.e. time) (352) Mahānāda (of great noise) (353) Mahotsāha (of great enthusiasm) (354) Mahābala (of great strength) (355) Mahābuddhi (of great intellect) (356) Mahāvīrya (of great virility) (357) Bhūtacārin (moving among the living beings) (358) Purandara (one who pierces the cities) (359) Niśācara (walking about at night) (360) Pretacārin (one who moves among ghosts) (361) Mahāśakti (of great power) (362) Mahādyuti (of great lustre) (363) Anirdeśyavapuḥ (one whose body cannot be specifically pointed out) (364) Śrīmān (glorious) (365) Sarvahārī (the destroyer of all) (366) Amita (the unmeasured) (367) Gati (the goal) (368) Bahuśruta (one with much of learning) (369) Bahumaya

923. Veda-vit—Vedānāṁ vit jñānaṁ yasmāt—one who is the source of the Vedic knowledge. Cf. "yo Brahmāṇam vidadhāti pūrvaṁ yo vai Vedāṁs ca prahiṇoti tasmai"—cited in *ST*.

(full of many things) (370) Niyatātman (of controlled Ātman) (371) Bhavodbhava (source of origin of the world) (372) Ojaskara (cause of prowess) (373) Tejaskara (cause of splendour) (374) Dyutikara (one who diffuses light) (375) Nartaka (the dancer) (376) Sarvakāmada (the bestower of all cherished desires).

71-80. (377) Nṛtyapriya) (one who is fond of dancing) (378) Nṛtyānṛtya (dance of dances (?)) (379) Prakāśātman (of the nature of lustre) (380) Pratāpana (one who scorches) (381) Buddhākṣara (one who has understood the syllable) (382) Spaṣṭākṣara (of clear syllables) (383) Mantra (mystic syllable) (384) Sammāna (one of great honour) (385) Sārasamplava (of flooded essence) (386) Yugādikṛt (one who makes the beginning of the yugas) (387) Yugāvarta (cause of the repetition of the yugas) (388) Gambhīra (majestic) (389) Vṛṣavāhana (bull-vehicled) (390) Iṣṭa (one who is liked, worshipped) (391) Viśiṣṭa (the distinguished) (392) Śiṣṭeṣṭa (one who is fond of the disciplined) (393) Śarabha (the fabulous animal whose form Śiva assumed) (394) Śārabha (? one who has caused Sarabha) (395) Dhanuḥ (bow) (396) Apāṁnidhi (storehouse of waters) (397) Adhiṣṭhānam (the basic support) (398) Vijaya (victory) (399) Jayakālavid (one who knows the time of victory (400) Pratiṣṭhita (well-established) (401) Pramāṇajña (one who is conversant with the means of valid knowledge) (402) Hiraṇyakavaca (one having golden coat of mail) (403) Hari (identical with Viṣṇu) (404) Virocana (one who increases appeal) (405) Suragaṇa (one having Devas as his attendants) (406) Vidyeśa (lord of vidyā) (407) Vibudhāśraya (support of the learned) (408) Bālarūpa[924] (one having the form of a boy) (409) Balonmāthin (one who subdues others by means of his strength) (410) Vivarta (one who transforms himself) (411) Gahana (Abstruse) (412) Guru (weighty) (413) Karaṇam (Instrument) (414) Kāraṇam (cause) (415) Kartṛ (maker) (416) Sarvabandhavimocana (one who releases others from all bondages) (417) Vidvattama (highly

924. **Bālarūpaḥ—in the form of a boy.** *ST.* **cites a legend from the** *Mbh.* **(Droṇaparva) :**

पुराणि दग्धवन्तं तं दे ी याता प्रवीक्षितुम् ।
बालमङ्कगतं कृत्वा स्वयं पञ्चशिखं पुनः ॥

learned) (418) Vītabhaya (devoid of fear) (419) Viśvabhartṛ (the overlord of the universe) (420) Niśākara (moon) (421) Vyavasāya (energy) (422) Vyavasthāna (one with perseverance) (423) Sthānada (the bestower of (good) abodes) (424) Jagadādija (one born at the outset of the universe (425) Dundubhi (one who has the wardrum) (426) Lalita (delicate) (427) Viśva (universe) (428) Bhavātman (the soul of the world) (429) Ātmani saṁsthita (one stationed in the ātman) (430) Vīreśvara (lord of the heroes) (431) Vīrabhadra (432) Vīrahā (slayer of heretic persons) (433) Vīrabhṛd (one who sustains heroes) (434) Virāṭ (supreme being) (435) Vīracūḍāmaṇi (the crest-jewel of heroes) (436) Vettā (the knower) (437) Tīvranāda (one whose sound is poignant) (438) Nadīdhara (supporter of the river) (439) Ājñādhāra (support of behests) (440) Triśūlin (trident-bearing) (441) Śipiviṣṭa[925] (one who has penetrated the rays) (442) Śivālaya (abode of auspiciousness) (443) Vālakhilya (identical with the sages of that name) (444) Mahācāpa (wielding a great bow) (445) Tigmāṁśu (having hot rays) (446) Avyayanidhi (everlasting treasure) (447) Abhirāma (charming) (448) Suśaraṇa (perfect refuge) (449) Subrahmaṇya (perfectly conducive to the attainment of Brahman) (450) Sudhāpati (lord of the nectar) (451) Maghavān (Indra) (452) Kauśika (of the family of Kuśika) (453) Gomān (possessing cows) (454) Viśrāma (rest) (455) Sarvaśāsana (chestiser of everyone) (456) Lalāṭākṣa (having an eye in the forehead) (457) Viśvadeha (one having cosmic bodies) (458) Sāra (essence) (459) Saṁsāracakrabhṛt (one who holds the wheel of mundane existence) (460) Amoghadaṇḍin (one whose punishment is never futile) (461) Madhyastha (stationed in the middle) (462) Hiraṇya (golden) (463) Brahmavarcasī (one who has the brahminical splendour).

81-90. (464) Paramārtha (the greatest object) (465) Paramaya (identical with the greatest) (466) Śambara (hunter) (467) Vyādhaka (hunter) (468) Anala (fire) (469) Ruci (taste) (470) Vararuci (having excellent taste) (471) Vandya

925. Śipiviṣṭaḥ—śipayo raśmayas teṣu praviṣṭaḥ—pervading the rays of the sun. Cf. शिपयो रश्मयो मताः । तत्र प्रवेशाद्विश्वेशः शिपिविष्ट इहोच्यते ॥ —*Viṣṇu-sahasra-nāma-bhāṣya.*

(worthy of being saluted) (472) Vācaspati (lord of speech) (473) Aharpati (lord of the day) (474) Ravi (sun) (475) Virocana (sun) (476) Skanda (477) Śāstā (ruler) (478) Vaivasvata (pertaining to the sun) (479) Jana (people) Ajanma (unborn) (480) Yukti (cogent reason) (481) Unnatakīrti (of lofty renown) (482) Śāntarāga (one whose passion has subsided) (483) Parājaya (Defeat ?) (484) Kailāsapati (lord of Kailāsa) (485) Kāmari (enemy of Kāma) (486) Savitā (sun) (487) Ravilocana (having sun as the eye) (488) Vidvattama (highly scholarly) (489) Vītabhaya (devoid of fear) (490) Viśvahartā (destroyer of the universe) (491) Anivārita (unrestricted) (492) Nitya (permanent) (493) Niyata-kalyāṇa (one who is invariably auspicious) (494) Puṇyaśravaṇa (hearing about whom is meritorious) (495) Puṇyakīrtana (glorifying whom is meritorious) (496) Dūraśravas (one who hears from far off) (497) Viśvasaha (one who endures everything) (498) Dhyeya (worthy of being meditated upon) (499) Duḥsvapnanāśana (one who destroys evil dreams) (500) Uttāraka (redeemer) (501) Duṣkṛtihā (destroyer of evil actions) (502) Durdharṣa (one who cannot be attacked) (503) Duḥsaha (unable to bear) (504) Abhaya (one who grants fearlessness) (505) Anāndi (beginningless) (506) Bhūḥ (the earth) (507) Bhuvaḥ Lakṣmīḥ (fortune of the earth) (508) Kirīṭin (having a crown) (509) Tridaśādhipa (overlord of Devas) (510) Viśvagoptā (protector of the universe) (511) Viśvabhartā (ruler of the universe) (512) Sudhīra (perfectly bold) (513) Rucirāṅgada (having a beautiful shoulderlet) (514) Janana (one who causes birth) (515) Janajanmādi (one who is the cause of the birth, etc. of people) (516) Prītimān (one who has pleasure) (517) Nītimān (endowed with justice) (518) Naya (of good policy) (519) Viśiṣṭa (most distinguished) (520) Kāśyapa (sage of that name) (521) Bhānu (sun) (522) Bhīma (terrible) (523) Bhīmaparākrama (one whose exploit is terrible) (524) Praṇava (525) Saptadhācāra (one whose rites are of seven types (?) (526) Mahākāya (of huge body) (527) Mahādhanu (having a great bow) (528) Janmādhipa (overlord of birth (?)) (529) Mahādeva (530) Sakalāgamapāraga (Master of all Āgamas) (531) Tattvātattvavivekātman (one who naturally discriminates between the real and the unreal) (532) Vibhūṣṇu (one who is desirous of shining well (533) Bhūtibhūṣaṇa (having sacred ashes as ornament) (534) Ṛṣi (sage) (535) Brāhmaṇavid (conversant with the Brāhmaṇa texts) (536) Jiṣṇu (victorious) (537) Janmamṛtyujarātiga (one who is beyond birth, death and old age) (538) Yajña (539) Yajñapati (lord of the yajñas) (540) Yajvā (one who sacrifices) (541) Yajñānta (one who is the end of yajña) (542) Amoghavikrama (one whose exploit is never futile) (543) Mahendra (544) Durbhara (one who is difficult to control and boss over) (545) Senī (one who has armies) (546) Yajñāṅga (a part of the yajña) (547) Yajñavāhana (Yajña-vehicled) (548) Pañcabrahmasamutpatti[926] (the source of origin of the five brahmans) (549) Viśveśa (lord of the universe) (550) Vimalodaya (one whose rise is devoid of impurities).

91-100. (551) Ātmayoni (source of origin of the Ātman) (552) Anādyanta (having neither a beginning nor an end) (553) Ṣaḍviṁśat (the twentysixth principle) (554) Saptalokadhṛk (one who holds the seven worlds) (555) Gāyatrīvallabha) one who is the lover of Gāyatrī) (556) Prāṁśu (tall) (557) Viśvāvāsa (Abode of the universe) (558) Prabhākara (cause of bright light) (559) Śiśu (infant) (560) Girirata (one who loves the mountain) (561) Samrāṭ (emperor) (562) Suṣeṇa (having good army) (563) Suraśatruhā (destroyer of the enemies of Devas) (564) Amogha (one who is never futile) (565) Ariṣṭamathana (one who suppresses evil maladies) (566) Mukunda (567) Vigatajvara (one who is free from ailments) (568) Svayaṁjyotiḥ (one who is self luminous) (569) Anujyotiḥ (subsequent luminary) (570) Ātmajyoti (light of the Ātman) (571) Acañcala (one who is not fickle) (572) Piṅgala (tawny-coloured) (573) Kapilaśmaśru (one whose moustache is tawny (574) Śāstranetra (having the scripture as his eye) (575)Netratraya (having three eyes) (576) Atanu (unembodied) (577) Jñānaskandha (wise with perfect knowledge) (578) Mahājñānī (highly learned one) (579) Nirutpatti (having no birth) (580) Upaplava[927] (identical with

926. pañca-brahma-samutpattiḥ—pañca-brahmanām sadyojātādīnām utpattir yasmāt—the source of the origin of five Brahmans, viz. Īśāna, Tatpuruṣa, Aghora, Vāmadeva, and Sadyojāta, representing the five elements: ether, air, fire, water and earth.

927. Upaplavaḥ—Rāburūpaḥ *ST*. of the form of Rāhu. Cf. "upaplavaḥ Saiṁhikeyaḥ" —*Viśva*.

calamity) (581) Bhava (source of origin of the world) (582) Vivasvān (sun) (583) Āditya (sun) (584) Yogācārya (preceptor of the yoga system) (585) Bṛhaspati (preceptor of the gods) (586) Udārakīrti (one of elegant fame) (587) Udyogī (one who endeavours) (588) Sadyogī (good yogin) (589) Sadasambhava (the unborn and existing being) (590) Nakṣatramālī (having a garland of the stars) (591) Rākeśa (lord of the moonlight, i.e. moon) (592) Sādhiṣṭhāna (having a foundation) (593) Ṣaḍāśraya (having the support of the six) (594) Pavitrapāṇi (having the Pavitra in the hand) (595) Pāpāri (enemy of sins) (596) Maṇipūra (navel?) (597) Manogati (having the movement of the mind) (598) Hṛtpuṇḍarīkāsīna (one occupying the lotus-like heart) (599) Śukla (white) (600) Śānta (calm) (601) Vṛṣākapi (602) Viṣṇu (all-pervasive) (603) Grahapati (lord of the planets) (604) Kṛṣṇa (605) Samartha (competent) (606) Anarthanāśana (one who destroys miseries) (607) Adharmaśatru (enemy of sin) (608) Akṣayya (inexhaustible) (609) Puruhūta (one who is frequently invoked) (610) Puruṣṭuta (one who is frequently eulogised) (611) Brahmagarbha (born of the womb of Brahman) (612) Bṛhadgarbha (having a huge womb) (613) Dharmadhenu (cow of piety) (614) Ḍhanāgama[928] (the augment of wealth) (615) Jagaddhitaiṣin (well-wisher of the universe) (616) Sugata (having good movement) (617) Kumāra (young man) (618) Kuśalāgama (one who brings about happiness) (619) Hiraṇyavarṇa (golden coloured) (620) Jyotiṣmān (luminous) (621) Nānābhūtādhāra (supporter of the different kinds of living beings) (622) Dhvani (sound) (623) Aroga (devoid of ailment) (624) Niyamābhyakṣa presiding deity of observances) (625) Viśvāmitra (626) Dvijottama (the most excellent among brahmins) (627) Bṛhatjyoti (having a large light) (628) Sudhāmā (having good abode) (629) Mahājyoti (having a great light) (630) Anuttama (excellent one) (631) Mātāmaha (maternal grandfather) (632) Mātariśvā (wind) (633) Nabhasvān (vaporous air) (634) Nāgahāradhṛk (one wearing serpent-necklaces).

928. **Dhanāgamaḥ—dhanasya āgamaḥ yasmāt *ST*. who is the source of attainment of wealth. Cf.**

"घनं चातृप्तिपर्यन्तं शिवपूजाविधेः फलम् ।

101-110. (635) Pulastya (636) Pulaha (637) Agastya (638) Jātūkarṇya (639) Parāśara (identical with these sages) (640) Nirāvaraṇa-dharmajña (one conversant with Dharma devoid of Āvaraṇa (covering) (641) Viriñca (Brahmā) (642) Viṣṭaraśravas (having his own ears as abode i. e. quick in hearing) (643) Ātmabhū (self-born) (644) Aniruddha (unchecked) (645) Atri (sage of that name) (646) Jñānamūrti (having perfect knowledge of body) (647) Mahāyaśas (having great renown) (648) Lokacūḍāmaṇi (the crest-jewel of the worlds) (649) Vīra (hero) (650) Caṇḍaparākrama (of fierce exploit) (651) Satyaparākrama (of truthful exploit) (652) Vyālākalpa (one having serpents for ornaments) (653) Mahākalpa (having costly ornaments) (654) Mahāvṛkṣa (great tree) (655) Kalādhara (one having the digits) (656) Alaṁkariṣṇu (one who is desirous of adorning) (657) Acala (unmoving) (658) Rociṣṇu (shining) (659) Vikramottama (excellent in exploit) (660) Āśuśabdapati (the lord of the word "quick" [?]) (661) Vegin (having velocity) (662) Plavana (floating) (663) Śikhisārathi (having fire as the charioteer) (664) Asaṁsṛṣṭa (unjoined) (665) Atithi (guest) (666) Śakrapramāthin (subjugator of Śakra) (667) Pāpanāśana (destroyer of sins) (668) Vasuśravas (having riches as ears ?) (669) Kavyavāha (carrying Kavya offerings) (670) Pratapta (one who is heated much) (671) Viśvabhojana (having the universe as food) (672) Jarya (that which becomes old) (673) Jarādhiśamana (one who dispels the agony due to old age) (674) Lohita (mars) (675) Tanūnapāt (fire) (676) Pṛṣadaśva (wind, air) (677) Nabhoyoni (source or origin of the sky) (678) Supratīka (having good symbol) (679) Tamisrahā (dispeller of darkness) (680) Nidāgha (summer) (681) Tapana (sun) (682) Megha (cloud) (683) Pakṣa (a fortnight) (684) Parapurañjaya (conqueror of other people's city) (685) Mukhānila (having wind in the mouth) (686) Suniṣpanna (one that has been evolved well) (687) Surabhi (sweet-smelling) (688) Śiśirātmaka (one of cool nature) (689) Vasanta (spring) (690) Mādhava (691) Grīṣma (summer) (692) Nabhasya (month of Bhādrapada) (693) Bījavāhana (one who carries seeds) (694) Aṅgiras (695) Muni Ātreya (sage Ātreya) (696) Vimala (pure) (697) Viśvavāhana (having universe as vehicle) (698) Pāvana (one who purifies) (699) Purujit (conqueror of many) (700)

Śakra (701) Trividya (having three Vidyās) (702) Naravāhana (having human beings for vehicles) (703) Manas (mind) (704) Buddhi (intellect) (705) Ahaṁkāra (ego) (706) Kṣetrajña (individual soul) (707) Kṣetrapālaka (protector of fields) (708) Tejonidhi (store of splendour) (709) Jñānanidhi (store of knowledge) (710) Vipāka (fruitful) (711) Vighnakāraka (cause of obstacles) (712) Adhara (lower) (713) Anuttara (having no successor) (714) Jñeya (one who should be known) (715) Jyeṣṭha (eldest) (716) Niḥśreyasālaya (abode of salvation) (717) Śaila (mountain) (718) Naga[929] (tree) (719) Tanu (body) (720) Doha (milking) (721) Dānavāri (enemy of the Dānavas) (722) Aridama (suppressor of enemies).

111-120. (723) Cārudhī (of charming intellect) (724) Cārujanaka (charming father) (725) Viśalya (having no torment) (726) Lokaśalyakṛt (the tormentor of the worlds) (727) Caturveda[930] (the four Vedas) (728) Caturbhāva (the four types of emotions) (729) Catura (clever) (730) Caturapriya (one fond of clever people) (731) Āmnāya (scripture) (732) Samāmnāya (traditional repetition) (733) Tīrtha (holy centre) (734) Deva (lord) (735) Śivālaya (abode of auspiciousness) (736) Bahurūpa (having many forms) (737) Mahārūpa, (having great forms) (738) Sarvarūpa (having all forms) (739) Carācara (the mobile and immobile being) (740) Nyāyanirvāhaka (one who fulfils justice) (741) Nyāya (justice) (742) Nyāyagamya (comprehensible through logic) (743) Nirañjana (unsullied) (474) Sahasramūrdhā) (thousand-headed) (745) Devendra (lord of Devas) (746) Sarvaśastraprabhañjana (one who breaks all weapons) (747) Muṇḍa (skull) (748) Virūpa (hideous) (749) Vikṛta (deformed) (750) Daṇḍin (having a staff) (751) Dānta (having selfcontrol) (752) Guṇottama (excellent in good qualities) (753) Piṅgalākṣa (tawny-eyed) (754) Haryakṣa (lion) (755) Nīlagrīva (blue necked) (756) Nirāmaya (devoid of ailments) (757) Sahasrabāhu (thousand-armed) (758) Sarveśa (lord of all) (759) Śaraṇya (one worthy of being sought refuge

929. Nagaḥ—Śrīśailādirūpaḥ ST. Of the form of Śrīśaila and others. Cf. श्रीशैलशिखरं दृष्ट्वा पुनर्जन्म न विद्यते ।

930. Caturvedaḥ—Cf. one whose breath constitutes the four Vedas Cf. "yasya niśśvasitaṁ Vedāḥ". —cited in *ST*.

under) (760) Sarvalokabhṛt (one who supports all the worlds) (761) Padmāsana (lotus-seated) (762) Paramajyoti (Great light) (763) Parāvaraparam phalam (one yielding the great fruit of Para and Avara (great and small benefits of life) (764) Padmagarbha (lotus-wombed) (765) Mahāgarbha (great wombed) (766) Viśvagarbha (having the universe in the womb) (767) Vicakṣaṇa (clever) (768) Parāvarajña (one conversant with Para and Avara) (769) Bījeśa (the lord of the seeds) (770) Sumukha (having pleasing face) (771) Sumahāsvana (having a loud voice) (772) Devāsuraguru (Preceptor of Devas and Asuras) (773) Devāsuranamaskṛta (one who is bowed to by Devas and Asuras) (774) Devāsura-mahāmātra (high official of Devas and Asuras) (775) (Devāsuramahāśraya (the great support of Devas and Asuras) (776) Devādideva (the first Deva of all Devas) (777) Devarṣi (the sage of Devas) (778) Devāsura-varaprada (one who bestows boons on Devas and Asuras) (779) Devāsureśvara (lord of Devas and Asuras) (780) Divya (divine) (781) Devāsura-maheśvara (great lord of Devas and Asuras) (782) Sarvadevamaya (identical with all Devas) (783) Acintya (one who cannot be thought of) (784) Devatātmā (having the deities within) (785) Ātmasambhava (born of himself) (786) Īḍva (one worthy of worship) (787) Anīśa (having no Īśa above) (788) Suravyāghra (a tiger among Devas) (789) Devasiṁha (a lion among Devas) (790) Divākara (sun) (791) Vibudhāgravaraśreṣṭha (the most excellent among the learned) (792) Sarvadevottamottama (the greatest among the entire groups of Devas) (793) Śivajñānarata (one engaged in the knowledge of Śiva) (794) Śrīmān (glorious) (795) Śikhiśrīparvatapriya (one fond of the mountain Śikhiśrī).

121-130. (796) Trayastambha (having three columns) (797) Viśiṣṭāmbha (having distinguished waters (?)) (798) Narasiṁhanipātana (one who struck down Narasiṁha) (799) Brahmacārin (religious student) (800) Lokācārin (one moving amidst the worlds) (801) Dharmacārin (one performing pious deeds) (802) Dhanādhipa (lord of wealth (803) Nandin (804) Nandīśvara (805) Nagna (naked) (806) Nagnavratadhara (one who observes the holy rite of being naked) (807) Śuci (pure) (808) Liṅgādhyakṣa (presiding deity of the liṅgas) (809) Surādhyakṣa (presiding deity of Devas) (810) Yugādhyaksa (presiding deity of the yugas) (811) Yugāvaha (one causing the yugas) (812) Svavaśa (one submissive of himself). (813) Sarvaśa (one giving happiness unto all) (814) Svargasvara (one whose voice is above heaven) (815) Svaramaya (one identical with notes) (816) Svana (sound) (817) Bījādhyakṣa (presiding deity of the seeds) (818) Bījakartā (the maker of the seeds) (819) Dhanakṛt (maker of wealth) (820) Dharmavardhana (increaser of piety) (821) Dambha (haughtiness) (822) Adambha (one devoid of haughtiness) (823) Mahādambha (one of great haughtiness) (824) Sarvabhūtamaheśvara (great lord of all living beings) (825) Śmaśānanilaya (one whose abode is in the cremation ground) (826) Tiṣya (Kali age) (827) Setu (bridge) (828) Apratimākṛti (one whose features are unrivalled) (829) Lokottara (one greater than all the worlds) (830) Sphuṭāloka (one whose lustre is clear) (831) Tryambaka (three-eyed) (832) Nāgabhūsaṇa (having serpents as ornaments) (833) Andhakāri (enemy of demon Andhaka) (834) Makhadveṣin (enemy of sacrifice) (835) Viṣṇukandharapātana (one who struck down the head of Viṣṇu) (836) Vītadoṣa (one devoid of defects) (837) Akṣayaguṇa (one of inexhaustible good qualities) (838) Dakṣāri (enemy of Dakṣa) (839) Pūṣadantahṛt (one who took away the tooth of Pūṣan) (840) Dhūrjaṭi (having the burden of the matted hairs) (841) Khaṇḍaparaśu (842) Sakala (with attributes) (843) Niṣkala (without attributes) (844) Anagha (sinless) (845) Ādhāra (support) (846) Sakalādhāra (support of all) (847) Pāṇḍurābha (having greyish lustre) (848) Mṛḍa (849) Naṭa (actor) (850) Pūrṇa (full) (851) Pūrayitā (one who fills) (852) Puṇya (meritorious) (853) Sukumāra (very tender) (854) Sulocana (having good eyes) (855) Sāmageya (worthy of being sung about with Sāman mantras) (856) Priyakara (one who does pleasing things) (857) Puṇyakīrti (of meritorious renown) (858) Anāmaya (free from ailments) (859) Manojava[931] (as speedy as the mind) (860) Tīrthakara

931. **Manojavaḥ—*ST*. disjoins manojavaḥ as mano ajavāḥ, i.e. manasaḥ ajavo yasmin. Cf. "yato vāco nivartante aprāpya manasā saha"—*TA*.8.4.1; 9.1. *TU*. 2.4.1; 9.1.**

(maker of holy centres) (861) Jaṭila (one with matted hair) (862) Jīviteśvara (lord of life) (863) Jīvitāntakara (one who causes end to life) (864) Nitya (permanent) (865) Vasuretas (having wealth as semen virile) (866) Vasupriya (one fond of wealth) (867) Sadgati (the goal of the good) (868) satkṛti (having good actions) (869) Sakta (attacked) (870) Kālakaṇṭha (black-necked) (871) Kalādhara (bearer of digits) (872) Mānī (honourable) (873) Mānya[932] (worthy of being honoured) (874) Mahākāla (875) Sadbhūti (having good prosperity) (876) Satparāyaṇa (having the good one as the greatest resort) (877) Candra (moon) (878) Sañjīvana (enlivening) (879) Śāstṛ (ruler) (880) Lokagūḍha (hidden in the worlds) (881) Amarādhipa (the overlord of the immortal ones).

131-140. (882) Lokabandhu (kinsman of the worlds) (883) Lokanātha (lord of the worlds) (884) Kṛtajña (grateful) (885) Kṛtibhūṣaṇa (a jewel among gifted ones) (886) Anapāyī (having no distress) (887) Akṣara (imperishable) (888) Kānta (shining) (889) Sarvaśastrabhṛtāṁvara (the most excellent one among all warriors) (890) Tejomaya (full of splendour) (891) Dyutidhara (having lustre) (892) Lokamāya (having Māyā spreading over the worlds) (893) Agraṇī (the leader) (894) Aṇu (the atom) (895) Śucismita (of pure smiles) (896) Prasannātman (one delighted in the mind) (897) Durjaya (one who is unconquerable) (898) Duratikrama (one who cannot be transgressed) (899) Jyotirmaya (luminous) (900) Nirākāra (having no shape) (901) Jagannātha (lord of the universe) (902) Jaleśvara (lord of the waters) (903) Tumbavīṇī (having the lute called Tumbavīṇa) (904) Mahākāya (having a huge body) (905) Viśoka (devoid of sorrow) (906) Śokanāśana (destroyer of grief) (907) Trilokātman (the soul of the three worlds) (908) Trilokeśa (lord of the three worlds) (909) Śuddha (pure) (910) Śuddhi (purity) (911) Adhokṣaja (Viṣṇu) (912) Avyaktalakṣaṇa (one who has the unmanifest as the characteristic sign) (913) Avyakta (unmanifest) (914) Vyaktāvyakta (one who is manifest and unmanifest) (915) Viśāmpati (lord of subjects) (916) Varaśīla (of excellent conduct) (917) Atulavara (of incomparable boons) (918) Mānī

932. Mānyaḥ—mānayituṁ yogyaḥ *ST.* worthy of honour.

(honourable) (919) Mānadhana (having honour as wealth) (920) Maya (921) Brahmā (922) Viṣṇu (923) Prajāpāla (protector of the subjects) (924) Haṁsa (swan) (925) Haṁsagati (having the gait of the swan) (926) Yama (927) Vedhas (creator) (928) Dhātṛ (929) Vidhātṛ (930) Attṛ (devourer) (931) Hartṛ (destroyer) (932) Caturmukha (four-faced) (933) Kailāsaśikharāvāsī (one whose residence is on the peak of the Kailāsa) (934) Sarvāvāsī (having everything as his residence) (935) Satām gati (goal of the good) (936) Hiraṇyagarbha (gold-wombed) (937) Hariṇa (Deer) (938) Puruṣa (939) Pūrvajapitā (ancestral father) (940) Bhūtālaya (abode of the living beings) (941) Bhūtapati (lord of the goblins). (942) Bhūtida (bestower of prosperity) (943) Bhuvaneśvara (lord of the worlds) (944) Saṁyogin (having union) (945) Yogavid (knower of the yogas) (946) Brahmā (947) Brahmaṇya (conducive to the attainment of Brahman) (948) Brāhmaṇapriya (one fond of brahmins) (949) Devapriya (fond of Devas) (950) Devanātha (lord of Devas) (951) Devajña (knower of Devas) (952) Devacintaka (one thinking about Devas) (953) Viṣamākṣa (having deformed eyes) (954) Kalādhyakṣa (presiding deity of Kalās) (955) Vṛṣāṅka (bull-emblemed) (956) Vṛṣavardhana (one who increases piety) (957) Nirmada (one devoid of pride) (958) Nirahaṁkāra (one devoid of arrogance) (959) Nirmoha (Devoid of delusion) (960) Nirupadrava (harmless) (961) Darpahā (destroyer of pride) (962) Darpita (proud) (963) Dṛpta (haughty) (964) Sarvaṛtuparivartaka (one who changes (revolves) in all the seasons) (965) Sahajihva (having congenital tongue) (966) Sahasrārci (having thousand rays) (967) Snigdha (affectionate) (968) Prakṛtidakṣiṇa (one who is to the right of Prakṛti.)

141-150. (969) Bhūtabhavyabhavannātha (one who is the lord of the past, present and future) (970) Prabhava (source of origin) (971) Bhrāntināśana (destroyer of wrong notions) (972) Arthānartha (one who is beneficial and maleficent) (973) Mahākośa (having great treasure) (974) Parakāryaikapaṇḍita (one who is the sole clever scholar in others tales) (975) Niṣkaṇṭaka (one free from thorns) (976) Kṛtānanda (one who is blissful) (977) Nirvyāja (one who has no false pretext) (978) Vyājamardana (one who suppresses sham) (979) Satyavān (truthful) (980) Satyakīrtistambhakṛtāgama (one who is well learned and who has established truthful renown) (981) Akampita (unshaken) (982) Guṇagrāhin (one who takes good qualities) (983) Naikātmā naikakarmakṛt (one who is not a single soul and who does not perform single task alone) (984) Suprīta (one who is well pleased) (985) Sumukha (one whose face is good) (986) Sūkṣma (subtle) (987) Sukara (one having good hands) (988) Dakṣiṇānila (southern wind) (989) Skandha-Skandhadhara (shoulder and bearer of shoulders) (990) Dhurya (one who carries burdens of responsibility) (991) Prakaṭa-Prītivardhana (one who increases pleasures manifestly) (992) Aparājita (undefeated) (993) Sarvasaha (enduring everything) (994) Vidagdha (clever) (995) Śarvavāhana (having all vehicles) (996) Adhṛta (one who is not held) (997) Svadhṛta (one who is held by himself) (998) Sādhya (one who can be achieved) (999) Pūrtamūrti yaśodhara (one whose form is pūrta i.e. good social services and one who is famous (1000) Varāhaśṛṅgadhṛk (one who wears the horn of the boar) (1001) Vāyu (wind) (1002) Balavān (powerful) (1003) Ekanāyaka (sole leader). (1004) Śrutiprakāśa (one having the lustre of learning) (1005) Śrutimān (learned) (1006) Ekabandhu (sole kinsman) (1007) Anekadhṛk (holder of many things) (1008) Śrīvallabhaśivārambha (lover of fortunes' auspicious venture) (1009) Śāntabhadra (one who is calm and auspicious) (1010) Samañjasa (proper) (1011) Bhūśaya (lying on the ground) (1012) Bhūtikṛt (one who causes prosperity) (1013) Bhūti (prosperity) (1014)) Bhūṣaṇa (ornament) (1015) Bhūtavāhana (having the goblins for his vehicle) (1016) Akāya (having no body) (1017) Bhaktakāyastha (one who is stationed in the body of the devotees) (1018) Kālajñānī (one knowing the time) (1019) Kalāvapuḥ (having the digits for his body) (1020) Satyavrata (one of truthful rites) (1021) Mahātyāgī (great renouncer) (1022) Niṣṭhā (stability) (1023) Śāntiparāyaṇa (interested in peace) (1024) Parārthavṛtti (one whose activities are for the sake of others) (1025) Varada (Bestower of boons) (1026) Vivikta (isolated) (1027) Śrutisāgara (ocean of learning) (1028) Anirviṇṇa (one who is not dejected) (1029) Guṇagrāhī (one who takes up good qualities) (1030) Kalaṅkāṅka (one who is marked with a strain) (1031) Kalaṅkahā (one who dispels stains) (1032) Svabhāvarudra (one who is naturally fierce) (1033) Madhyastha (one who is stationed in the middle) (1034) Śatrughna (destroyer of enemies) (1035) Madhyanāśaka (destroyer of the middle) (1036) Śikhaṇḍī (having a tuft) (1037)Kavacī (having a coat of mail) (1038) Śūlī (having a trident) (1039) Caṇḍīmukti (liberator of Caṇḍī) (1040) Kuṇḍalin (having earrings) (1041) Mekhalin (having girdle) (1042) Kavacin (having coat of mail) (1043) Khaḍgin (having a sword) (1044) Māyin (wielder of Māyās) (1045) Saṁsāra sārathi (charioteer of the worldly existence).

151-158. (1046) Amṛtyu (having no death) (1047) Sarvadṛk (having vision everywhere) (1048) Siṁha (lion) (1049) Tejorāśi (mass of splendour) (1050) Mahāmaṇi (having a great jewel) (1051) Asaṁkhyeya (indescribable) (1052) Aprameyātmā (the Ātman that cannot be realized) (1053) Vīryavān (powerful) (1054) Kāryakovida (skilful at his task) (1055) Vedya (one who could be known) (1056) Vedārthavid (one who knows the meaning of the Vedas) (1057) Goptā (protector) (1058) Sarvācāra (one having all conducts) (1059) Munīśvara (lord of sages) (1060) Anuttama (one who has no one to excel him) (1061) Durādharṣa (one who cannot be attacked) (1062) Madhura (sweet) (1063) Priyadarśana (one who is pleasing to look at) (1064) Sureśa (lord of Devas) (1065) Śaraṇam (one who is refuge of others) (1066) Sarva (identical with all) (1067) Śabda-Brahman (verbal brahman) (1068) Satāṁ gati (the goal of the good) (1069) Kālabhakṣa (one who eats kāla i.e. time) (1070) Kalaṅkāri (enemy of stigma) (1071) Kaṅkaṇīkṛtavāsuki (one who has made Vāsuki his bangle) (1072) Maheṣvāsa (one having great bow) (1073) Mahībhartā (lord of the earth) (1074) Niṣkalaṅka (devoid of stigma) (1075) Viśṛṅkhala (free from fetters) (1076) Dyumaṇi (jewel of the firmament) (1077) Taraṇi (sun) (1078) Dhanya (blessed) (1079)Siddhida (bestower of siddhis) (1080) Siddhi-sādhana (the means of achieving siddhis) (1081) Nivṛtta (one who has turned back) (1082) Saṁvṛta (one who is surrounded) (1083) Śilpa (fine arts) (1084) Vyūḍhoraska (broad-chested) (1085) Mahābhuja (having long arms) (1086)

Ekajyoti (single luminary) (1087) Nirātaṅka (devoid of agony) (1088) Nara (human being) (1089) Nārāyaṇapriya (fond of Nārāyaṇa) (1090) Nirlepa (unsmeared) (1091) Niṣprapañcātman (ātman without extension) (1092) Nirvyagra (unexcited) (1093) Vyagranāśana (destroyer of excited state) (1094) Stavya (one worthy of being eulogised (1095) Stavapriya (one fond of eulogy) (1096) Stotṛ (one who eulogises) (1097) Vyāsamūrti (one having the form of Vyāsa) (1098) Anākula (one who is not agitated) (1099) Niravadyapadopāya (one whose position and means are not censurable) (1100) Vidyārāśi (mass of learning) (1101) Avikrama (one who has no backward gait) (1102) Praśāntabuddhi (one whose intellect is calm) (1103) Akṣudra (one who is not insignificant) (1104) Kṣudrahā (destroyer of the insignificant) (1105) Nityasundara (one who is perpetually handsome) (1106) Dhairyāgryadhurya (one who is considered chief and foremost in courage) (1107) Dhātrīśa (lord of the earth) (1108) Śākalya (the sage who arranged Ṛgveda text) (1109) Śarvarīpati (lord of the night) (1110) Paramārthaguru (a real preceptor) (1111) Dharmārthadṛṣṭi (one who has real vision) (1112) Āśritavatsalaguru (a teacher fond of those who seek refuge) (1113) Rasa (juice) (1114) Rasajña (knower of the taste) (1115) Sarvajña (omniscient) (1116) Sarvasattvāvalambana (one who supports all animals).

Sūta said :

159-161. Thus he eulogised the bull-bannered lord with his thousand names. The lord (i.e. Viṣṇu) bathed Śiva and worshipped him with lotus flowers. In order to test Viṣṇu, Maheśvara the lord of the worlds hid one of the lotus flowers intended for the worship. Viṣṇu from whom the flower was taken away thought thus, "What is this ?"

162. After realising the loss of the flower Viṣṇu plucked out his eye and devoutly worshipped the preceptor of the universe, the support of all beings. He worshipped him repeating the last name of the lord.

163. On seeing him who was in that plight, lord Śiva des-

cended from that zone of fire[933] immediately.

164-166. On seeing the lord of Devas, Viṣṇu became glad and paid obeisance to him. The lord was embellished with matted hair as if with a crown. He resembled a hundred million suns. He was divine and surrounded by clusters of flames. He was terrible with sharp fangs. He was holding the trident, axe, iron club, discus, javelin and noose. He showed gestures of granting boon and protection with his hands. He wore the hide of a tiger as his upper garment. He was adorned with Bhasman.

167. Devas including Indra rushed in and circumambulated him. The world of Brahmā shook and the earth quaked.

168. The splendour of lord Śiva burned everything within a hundred yojanas on all sides, beneath and above. There was a roar "Hā hā" on the earth's surface.

169. Glancing lovingly at Viṣṇu who stood aside with palms joined in reverence, Śaṅkara, Mahādeva said smilingly.

170. O Viṣṇu, the task of Devas has been well understood by me. I shall give you the splendid discus Sudarśana.

171. O deity of good rites, it was indeed for your welfare and for your strenuous deliberation that I assumed this form—terrific for the worlds which you have seen just now.

172. O Viṣṇu, peace and tranquillity in the battle-field is the cause of your misery. The weapon of a calm one shall also be calm. What indeed is the benefit from a calm and peaceful weapon ?

173. The weapon of a quiescent person is quiescence which is the weapon of the ascetics. To a Kṣatriya warrior there is destruction of strength due to quiescence. It increases the strength of the enemy.

174. Imagine and meditate on my unchanging form which was seen by the agitated Devas. What can be done with a weapon, O destroyer of the enemies of Devas in order to fight ?

175-176. O destroyer of the enemies of Devas, in order to fight, one shall not evince forgiveness in the battle, when weakness has passed away or not yet come in. It should not be practised towards one's own people at improper times, and when unrighteousness and calamities have disappeared. After

933. tasmāt liṅgāt, pāvakasya maṇḍalāt avatatāra *ST*. he descended from his liṅga image that had a fiery circle around it.

saying thus he gave him the discus that had the lustre of ten thousand suns.

177. The lord, the leader of the worlds, gave him an eye also resembling the lotus. Ever since then they call that deity of good holy rites "Padmākṣa" (lotus-eyed).

178. After giving the eye and discus, thus to Viṣṇu, lord Śiva touched him with his auspicious hands and said:—

179. "O excellent Viṣṇu, I am the bestower of boons. Choose the desired boons. I have been captivated by you by your devotion, to be sure."

180. On being urged thus by the lord of Devas, Viṣṇu bowed down to the lord of Devas and said "O Mahādeva, bless me with this excellent boon of devotion to you.

181-182. I do not wish for anything else, O lord, because devotees do not have any other desire."

On hearing his words the merciful lord with the moon for his ornament touched him and granted him faith. Mahādeva spoke thus to Viṣṇu the great soul.

183. O excellent Deva, you will always remain a devotee of mine. You will certainly be worthy of being saluted and worshipped by Devas and Asuras, thanks to my grace.

184-186. When Satī the daughter of Dakṣa, the goddess of Devas, with splendid eyes, reproaches her mother and father and becomes the divine daughter of Himavān, Umā by name, O Viṣṇu of good holy rites, you will give her as your sister to me at the behest of Brahmā and thus become my kinsman. You will be worthy of being worshipped in the world.

187. Ever since that time you will view me with divine feelings and delight, as though I have become your friend.

188-190. After saying this the lord Śiva vanished. Then lord Viṣṇu requested Brahmā who is on a par with the sages, in the presence of Devas:

"O lotus-born deity, the divine hymn mentioned by me is splendid. He who reads this or listens to this or narrates this to excellent brahmins will attain the benefit of having gifted away a piece of gold at every name.

191-195. His benefit shall be that of a thousand horse-sacrifices. He shall bathe Rudra with ghee, etc. by means of holy vessel or auspicious water pots, repeating the thousand names with faith. He shall thus propitiate lord Śiva. He acquires the benefit of a thousand sacrifices. He shall be worthy of being worshipped by Devas. Lord Śiva will be pleased with him." Then the lotus-eyed lord said to lord Viṣṇu "So be it." Both of them bowed down to the lord of Devas, the preceptor of the universe and went away.

Hence, O brahmins, a sinless man who worships the lord with the thousand names or who repeats the thousand names attains the greatest goal.

CHAPTER NINETYNINE

Destruction of Dakṣa's sacrifice

The sages said:

1-2. O Sūta of great intellect, the origin of the goddess has been indicated by you. Now, mention in detail her birth as the daughter of Menā after her self immolation as Sati in the previous birth and then the destruction of Dakṣa's sacrifice. How was she given to Śiva, the lord of Devas, by Viṣṇu ?

3-5. How was her marriage with him ? It behoves you to narrate all this to us now.

On hearing their words, Sūta the most excellent among the Paurāṇikas, narrated the birth of the great goddess to those noble-souled ones.

Sūta said:

It was at the outset mentioned to Daṇḍin in detail by Brahmā; it was then mentioned to Kumāra (Sanat) by him. Then it was mentioned to Vyāsa, the intelligent sage. I have heard it from him and I am now recounting it to you all in detail.

6-7. O highly blessed ones, at your entreaty I shall mention it to you after bowing down to Umā and Śiva.

She is the mother of the universe. She is named Bhagā. She isthe three-fold pedestal of the deity in the form of Liṅga.

Liṅga is the lord himself. O excellent brahmins, the creation of the universe is by both of them. Śiva in the from of Liṅga is the splendour stationed above darkness.

8. In view of the union of Liṅga and pedestal he became Ardhanārīśvara (lord with the form of a woman in one half). At the outset he created his son Brahmā the four-faced lord.[934]

9. Śiva who excels the whole universe, the lord Ardhanārīśvara, full of knowledge, granted knowledge to Brahmā.

10. The lord Śiva saw Brahmā being born. Brahmā too saw Rudra, Śaṅkara and Mahādeva.

11. On seeing the lord Ardhanārīśvara stationed there, the lotus-born deity eulogised Śiva, the bestower of the boons, by means of pleasing words.

12. The unborn lord requested the lord the soul of the universe, by saying "Divide yourself." He created the goddess from the left side of his body as his befitting wife.

13. This ancient splendid lady, viz:—Śraddhā,[935] became the daughter of Dakṣa at the behest of the lord.

14. At that time, her name was Satī. She resorted to Rudra alone as her husband. In course of time, she rebuked Dakṣa. The goddess then became the daughter of Menā.

15-20. It was due to the curse of Nārada that Dakṣa also was prompted to censure them. The haughty Dakṣa, dishonoured the lord of Umā contemptuously. When Satī came to know of this action of her father Dakṣa, by her yogic power

934. Brahmāṇaṁ vidadhe devam. Cf. yo brahmāṇaṁ vidadhāti pūrvaṁ yo devānām prathamam purastāt—cited in *ST*.

935. Śraddhā, the first wife of Śiva who afterwards became Satī the daughter of Dakṣa. {She became Pārvatī in her third birth. Cf. तस्यैवं विदुषो यज्ञस्यात्मा यजमानः श्रद्धा पत्नी —cited in *ST*. and also *Ādityapurāṇa*:

मम सृष्टिविवृद्ध्यर्थमंशेनैकेन शाश्वते ।
मम पुत्रस्य दक्षस्य पुत्री भव सुरेश्वरि ।।
एवं शक्तिभ्रुवोर्मध्यात्ससर्जात्मसमप्रभाम् ।
आदाय शिरसा शम्भो राज्ञां सा परमेश्वरी ।।
अभवद् दक्षदुहिता स्वेच्छया ब्रह्मरूपिणी ।।

she reduced her body to ashes.[936] Later she was born as goddess Pārvatī, the daughter of the lord of the mountains, and performed penance. On coming to know of this and at the instance of the son of Cyavana, the infuriated lord Bharga destroyed the extensive sacrifice of Dakṣa. The son of Cyavana was the well-known and intelligent Dadhīca. Thanks to the grace of the three-eyed lord, the leading sage conquered Viṣṇu in battle and cursed Devas along with Viṣṇu: "O Devas, your imminent destruction is by the fire originating from Rudra's anger, due to the Māyā of Śaṅkara, the great lord.

CHAPTER HUNDRED

Destruction of Dakṣa's sacrifice

The sages said:

1. How did lord Parameśvara, Maheśvara at the instance of Dadhīca, behave after conquering all of them along with Viṣṇu?

Sūta said:

2. In the great sacrifice of Dakṣa, lord Rudra burned Devas along with Viṣṇu and sages.

3. O sages of good holy rites, his Gaṇa named Bhadra was sent by the lord Parameṣṭhin distressed as he was by the unbearable pangs of separation from the goddess.

4-8. Vīrabhadra created splendid lords of Gaṇas born of his hairs. Accompanied by them the valorous Bhadra mounted the chariot of which lord Brahmā was the charioteer. He then set out to Dakṣa's sacrifice. The leaders of the Gaṇas with their different weapons followed him in aerial chariots splendid all round. The yard of the sacrifice was near Gaṅgādvāra[937] on

936. Cf. अरुद्रभागं तमवेक्ष्य चाध्वरं पित्रा च देवे कृतहेलनं विभो। अनाहृता यज्ञसदस्यधीश्वरी चुकोप लोकानिव धक्ष्यती रुषा ।। cited in *ST*.

937. Gaṅgādvāra—identical with Haradvāra is known by various names —Mokṣadvāra, Māyādvāra, etc.

the splendid and charming peak of the Himālayas. O brahmins, the famous and splendid holy centre Kanakhala[938] was that spot. This lordly Vīrabhadra was sent by Parameṣṭhin (i. e. lord Śiva) in order to destroy it. At that time there were portentous calamities indicating fear of danger to the world.

9. The mountains crumbled; the earth quaked; the winds whirled to and fro and the ocean became agitated.

10. The fires did not blaze; the sun did not shine; the planets were not illuminated. Neither Devas nor Dānavas looked pleased.

11-13. Then, in a trice, Bhadra entered the sacrificial yard accompanied by gaṇas born of his hairs. He was like a black fire. He spoke to Dakṣa of unmeasured splendour:—"O Dakṣa, I have been sent by the Pinākа-bearing lord to burn you today along with the leading sages by mere contact of mine. After saying this the leading Gaṇa burnt that sacrificial chamber.

14. The infuriated leaders of the Gaṇas uprooted the sacrificial posts and hurled them about along with the Hotṛ and Prastotṛ. They burned everything.

15-19. The lords of the Gaṇas seized them and cast them into the running current of the Gaṅgā. Vīrabhadra of great splendour and undistressed soul made the hands of Indra and other Devas stunned as they raised them. He uprooted the eyes of Bhaga sportively with the tip of his finger. With his fist he hit the teeth of Pūṣan and made them fall. He kicked the moon with the toe of his foot. He cut off the head of lord Indra. After cutting off the hands of Agni and after uprooting his tongue sportively he kicked him on his head with his leg.

20-24. He cut off the staff of Yama. He hit lord Īśāna[939] a guardian of the quarters of great strength by means of his trident. Without any difficulty he killed thirty three Devas thus. Sportingly he killed three thousand three hundred and thirty

938. Kanakhala—a holy place of pilgrimage near Haradvāra. Here the patriarch Dakṣa performed a sacrifice where Satī the wife of Śiva immolated herself.

939. Īśānam—a guardian of the quarters, Īśāna by name, who was struck by Vīrabhadra.

three Devas[940] along with the three leading Devas. He killed the leading sages too. This lord killed those Devas who stood in readiness for fighting. Lord Rudra hit them with his fist, swords, arrows and other things. Then Viṣṇu of great splendour and intensified strength lifted up his discus, and fought with Rudra. A terrible fight ensued between them. It made hairs to stand on end.

25-30. Thanks to his yogic power, innumerable and divine bodies with conch, discus and iron clubs in their hands were born of Viṣṇu. They were equal to him in lustre. Lord Vīrabhadra killed all of them by means of his iron club and hit Viṣṇu on the head. Then he sportively hit him on the chest, he fell senseless on the ground. The lord got up again and lifted up his discus to kill him. He stood there gloriously with his eyes reddened with anger. Vīrabhadra of undistressed soul stunned his terrible discus that had the lustre of black sun and which he had kept in his hand. He did not move. He stood stunned thereby motionless like a mountain.

31. The bow of the lord was attacked with three hits and it split into three. Through contact with the tips of the bits of the bow he cut off the head of the lord.

32-37. His head that was cut off fell quickly into the nether worlds wafted by the wind originating from the vital breaths of the Pināka-bearing lord. At that time the Āhavanīya fire too entered there. On seeing the great sacrificial hall utterly in disarray with the sacred vessels destroyed, sacrificial posts broken along with the arched gateway, and the great hall burned, sacrifice fled. As it fled towards the sky in the guise of a deer, Vīrabhadra seized and beheaded it. Thereafter the powerful Vīrabhadra kicked the following on their heads, viz.—Prajāpati, Dharma, Kaśyapa the preceptor of the universe, Ariṣṭanemi the leading sage with his sons, sage Aṅgiras, Kṛṣṇāśva and the renowned Dakṣa. O excellent brahmins, he cut off Dakṣa's head and burned it in the fire.

38-40 The valorous Vīrabhadra then slit off the tip of the nose of Sarasvatī of the mother of Devas with the tip of his

940. trayañ caiva. the three : Indra, Agni, and Soma.

finger. He stood in their midst, covered with glory like Śiva in the cremation ground.

In the meantime Brahmā of great splendour bowed down to him and imploringly addressed Bhadra thus: "O Bhadra, enough of your wrath. All the heaven-dwellers are already destroyed.

41-46. O deity of good holy rites, be pleased. May everybody be forgiven by you along with those born of your hairs. Thanks to the influence of Brahmā, Parameṣṭhin, he gradually calmed down. At his behest he became quiescent.

The bull-emblemed lord Śiva appeared in the firmament accompanied by his Gaṇas. On being requested by lord Brahmā, the great lord of all the worlds the bestower of everything gave back their own respective bodies to those who were killed. He gave back the head to Indra, to Viṣṇu, to Dakṣa and to the leading sages and others. He gave back the tip of the nose to the goddess Sarasvatī and to the mother of Devas. He gave back life to all those who were destroyed. He granted them boons and presents. He sportively made another face similar to the head of Dakṣa whose face had been destroyed.[941]

47-51. Dakṣa regained consciousness and got up. With palms joined in reverence he eulogised the bull-bannered lord of the chiefs of Devas. On being eulogised by him the lord of great splendour granted him different boons. He bestowed the chieftaincy of Gaṇas upon Dakṣa of undistressed activities. Devas eulogised lord Nārāyaṇa with palms joined in reverence. Brahmā and the sages severally eulogised the bull-bannered, blue-necked lord who was the chief of Devas, and the cause of the origin of Brahmā. After blessing those Devas, the supreme lord vanished.

941. The head of Dakṣa, that was smashed by Vīrabhadra, was substituted by Śiva with the head of sacrificial animal.

CHAPTER HUNDRED AND ONE

Destruction of Kāma

The sages said:

1. How did the mother goddess, the splendid Satī become the daughter of the lord Himavān? How did she attain Śiva, lord of the chiefs of Devas as her husband?

Sūta said:

2. O excellent brahmins, that excellent lady by her own will resorted to the body of Menā. By practising penance she was born as the daughter of Himavān.

3-7. The lord of the mountains celebrated her post-natal and other rites. When she attained twelfth year she performed a penance. Along with her, her younger sister of splendid face too performed the penance. Both the sisters were different entities. She was bowed to by all the worlds. The sages surrounded her and eulogised her for her penance. She was called Aparṇā and her younger sister of splendid face was called Ekaparṇā.[942] The third excellent sister was Ekapāṭalā. The supreme lord Śiva was captivated by her penance.

8. In the meantime, there was an asura of great splendour, named Tāraka. He was the son of Tāra.

9. He had three sons:—Tārakākṣa, Vidyunmālī and Kamalākṣa.

10. Their grandfather was an asura of great strength named Tāra. By means of his penance as also by the grace of lord Brahmā, he had acquired great power.

11. Tāra of great splendour conquered the three worlds consisting of the mobile and immobile beings. At the outset he conquered Viṣṇu too.

12. A fierce, thrilling fight ensued between them. It lasted a thousand divine years without intermission, both by day and night.

13. Seizing Viṣṇu along with his chariot, he hurled him a hundred yojanas away. Defeated in battle by Tāra, the Garuḍa-bannered deity Viṣṇu fled.

942. The purāṇa mentions the three daughters of the lord of the Himālayas, viz. Aparṇā, Ekaparṇā, Ekapāṭalā. The eldest Aparṇā (or Haimavatī) was married to Śiva. Cf. v-26 of this chapter.

14. Tāra, the son of Diti, acquired boons and strength a hundred times more from Brahmā. He occupied the entire universe.

15-16. The lord of the chiefs of Daityas conquered Devas along with their chief, Indra. With his Māyā he prevented Devas from functioning as lords of the worlds. Devas along with Indra were afflicted with fear. Although they were heroic they never attained peace. Afflicted with fear they never got a refuge.

17. Then the glorious lord of the immortal beings rushed to Āṅgirasa and said in the presence of Devas.

18. "O sir, the great Dānava Tāraka is the son of Tāra. We have been overpowered by him as calves by the lordly bull.

19. O highly blessed one, O Bṛhaspati, Devas whirl about here and there like birds in a cage. They have no fixed abode. In the great fight they have been defeated and are now afraid of him.

20. Due to the power of this demon, O excellent Āṅgirasa, all those weapons of ours which never failed before have now become futile.

21-24. This demon fought with Viṣṇu, O Bṛhaspati, for twenty thousand years and still he has not been killed by him. Since he has not been defeated in battle even by the powerful Viṣṇu how can people like us stand in front of him in battle?"

Thus requested by Indra, Bṛhaspati the preceptor of Devas approached lord Brahmā[943] along with the thousand-eyed Indra as well as other leaders of Devas. He spoke to him. Brahmā the dispeller of the agony of his devotees heard everything orally conveyed by him with love. Then he spoke to Bṛhaspati in the presence of Devas including Indra.

25-30 "I know your distress, O leading Devas. Still, listen now. Satī, the goddess born of Rudra's body rebuked Dakṣa[944]

943. Kuśadhvajam—i.e. Brahmā.

944. vinindya devam—Satī reproached her father for not inviting Śiva to the sacrifice and then as an expiation for her father's sin she immolated herself. The *Bhāgavata purāṇa* records her harangue addressed to her father thus: यत्पादपद्मं महतां मनोऽलिभिर्निषेवितं ब्रह्मरसासवार्थिभिः । लोकस्य यद्वर्षति चाशिषोऽर्थिनस्तस्मै भवान् द्रुह्यति विश्वबन्धवे ।। अतस्तवोत्पन्नमिदं कलेवरं न धारयिष्ये शितिकण्ठगर्हितः । जग्धस्य मोहाद्धि विशुद्धिमन्धसो जुगुप्सितस्योद्धरणं प्रचक्षते ।।

and became born as Umā the daughter of Himavān. She is bowed to by all the worlds. O excellent Devas, let her try to captivate the lofty mind of lord Rudra by means of her beauty. Through their union lord Skanda will be born who will sportingly kill the demon Tāraka. He will be known as Śaktidhara (holder of Śakti or spear), Ṣaḍāsya (six-faced), Dvādaśabhuja (twelve-armed), Senānī (commander-in-chief), Pāvaki (son of fire), Svāheya (son of Svāhā), Kārttikeya (son of Kṛttikās), Gāṅgeya (son of Gaṅgā), Śaradhāmaja (born in the abode of the forest Śara, lord Śākha, Viśākha, Naigameśa, Senāpati (commander-in-chief), Kumāra, Mahāsena (having a great army). Though he will be only a small boy, he will kill Tāraka and protect Devas."

31-33. Thus advised by Brahmā, Parameṣṭhin, Bṛhaspati of good holy rites bowed to the lord of Devas. Accompanied by Devas including Indra, he went to the peak of the mountain Meru and remembered Kāma. On being remembered by the preceptor of Devas, Kāma came along with his wife Rati. With palms joined in reverence, he spoke to Bṛhaspati sitting along with Indra, O excellent brahmins.

34-38. "O Bṛhaspati, since I am remembered by you I have come here in your presence. Tell me what I have to do." Thus, he who was summoned by Bṛhaspati spoke to him. Lord Indra too honoured the fish-emblemed god and said:—"Unite Umā happily with Śiva today whereby the bull-emblemed lord can sport with her. Take adequate steps for the same along with your wife Rati. Mahādeva, if pleased, will grant you excellent boon. He is already separated from her. On acquiring Umā the daughter of the lord of the mountain he will be delighted." On being told thus, Kāma bowed to Indra the lord of Śacī and of Devas and decided to go to the penance grove of the lord of Devas in the company of Rati.

39-46. He was accompanied also by Vasanta his comrade. He decided to join the lord with Pārvatī. Beholding Kāma laughingly, the lord stared at him contemptuously. Then the fire blazed forth from his third eye burned Kāma as he stood by his side. Rati then cried piteously. On hearing her lamentations, the bull-emblemed lord was overwhelmed by mercy. He looked at her mercifully and said:—"O gentle lady, it is true that your husband is unembodied. But at the time of dalliance he will do everything that has to be done. There is no doubt about this. When Viṣṇu of great renown becomes the son of Vasudeva as a result of the curse of Bhṛgu, when he incarnates for the welfare of worlds, the son born to him will be your husband. On hearing this, Rati the wife of Kāma, the lady of pure smiles, bowed to Rudra and went along with Vasanta with the hope of regaining her husband.

CHAPTER HUNDRED AND TWO

The penance of Umā

1-2. The bull-emblemed lord Śiva was delighted by the penance of Pārvatī the great goddess. At the instance of Brahmā, he married her for the welfare of persons in all stages of life and for his own pleasure.

3. Accompanied by the great sages—Marīci and others, the lotus-born Brahmā went to the penance-grove of Pārvatī the great goddess.

4. He circumambulated that goddess the fountain-head of the universe and said to her:—"O daughter of the mountain, why do you cause distress to the worlds by means of your penance?"

5. O mother, it was by you that the universe was created. Do not destroy it. Hold up and preserve all these worlds by means of your splendour.

6-9. Śiva is the glorious lord of all the worlds and Devas. All of us are only his servants. That great lord will woo you. O bestower of boons, O Mother, you have been created by him and surely he can never remain without you. He will be your husband.

After saying thus and bowing down to Pārvatī many times and glancing at her reverentially lord Brahmā returned. Thereafter, lord Śiva went to her penance-grove in the guise of a brahmin in order to bless her.

10. On seeing the great lord come there in the guise of a brahmin, she could recognize him as the lord through her intelligence. She bowed to the bull-bannered lord.

11. After worshipping the boon-bestowing lord who had come there in the guise of a brahmin, she eulogised him.

12-16. Preserving the traditional practice of the noble-souled mountain, the lord blessed the goddess and said laughingly. Moreover, Śiva, the lord of all Devas wanted some fun in the midst of the good elite—"O great goddess, I shall, assuming a gentle form, meet you at the celebration of your Svayaṁvara." After saying this the lord looked at her with a divine vision and went away. She too returned home. On seeing the goddess come back Himavān, along with Menā (his wife) became delighted. He embraced her in her ascetic garb and kissed her on the head. Without knowing what had been whispered to his daughter by the lord of Devas, he announced publicly to hold the Svayaṁvara celebration of his daughter.

17-22. Then all these came to attend the Svayaṁvara celebration of the daughter of the mountain lord. They were—lord Brahmā, lord Viṣṇu, lord Indra, the fire-god, the sun, Bhaga, Tvaṣṭṛ, Aryaman, Vivasvān, Yama, Varuṇa, Vāyu, Soma, Īśāna, the Rudras, sages, Aśvins, twelve Ādityas, Gandharvas, Garuḍa, Yakṣas, Siddhas, Sādhyas, Daityas, Kimpuruṣas, Nāgas, oceans, rivers, Vedas, Mantras, Sūktas, Kṣaṇas, elephants, mountains, sacrifices, planets beginning with the sun, the three thousand three hundred and thirtythree Devas and many others.

23-26. Then the daughter of the mountain, the goddess, mounted the aerial chariot Sarvatobhadra. It was a splendid car made of gold, and embellished with the jewels. She was accompanied by the Apsarases who bedecked in ornaments were singing and dancing. She was eulogised by the bards, Gandharvas, Siddhas and Kinnaras. Mālinī held the white umbrella interspersed with the rays of jewels, in honour of the bride. Sandhyā held the disc of full moon. She was surrounded by divine ladies holding chowries in their hands.

27-28. Jayā stood there holding the garland of flowers of divine trees. Vijayā held a fan and stood near the goddess.

Even as the goddess was stationed in the midst of Devas holding the flower garland, the bull-emblemed lord Mahādeva took the form of an infant just for the sake of fun. The lord slept on the lap of the goddess.

29-32. Devas saw the infant in her lap and asked her "Who is this infant here?" They were greatly agitated. Indra, the slayer of Vṛtra, lifted up his arm and brought forth his thunderbolt. The hand that was lifted, remained stunned by the will of the lord of Devas who was in the form of an infant. Indra could not hurl his thunderbolt nor could he shake his arm. Agni too stood similarly and could not hurl his Śakti.

33. Yama could not wield his staff. O leading sages, Nirṛti could not wield his sword. Varuṇa could not use his weapon Nāgapāśa (serpentine noose). Samīraṇa (wind god) could not wield the staff of his banner.

34-35. The following persons lifted up their respective weapons (but could not use them) : Soma (Moon) lifted up his iron club and stood (motionless). Dhaneśa the most excellent among staff-bearers lifted up his staff (and stood motionless). Similarly, Īśāna lifted up his sharp trident and stood motionless; the Rudras too lifted the trident; the Ādityas their threshing rod and the Vasus their Mudgara (iron-club). But all these heaven-dwellers were immediately rendered stunned and motionless by the lord.

36-37. Similarly, other heaven-dwellers too were rendered stunned by the lord of Devas. Shaking his head Viṣṇu lifted up his discus and stood ready to strike. The hair on his head became steady. He could not hurl his discus nor could he move his arms.

38. The deluded Pūṣan gnashed his teeth on glancing at the boy. The moment he was looked at by Śiva his teeth fell down.

39-40. Similarly, the lord curbed their strength, splendour and yogic power.

Now, even as those Devas who were infuriated, were stunned and rendered motionless, Brahmā who was highly dejected meditated on Śiva and understood that it was lord Īśāna lying on the lap of Umā.

41. On realising the lord Brahmā, he became surprised. He rose up immediately and saluted his feet and eulogised him.

42-47. He eulogised the lord by ancient Sāman songs, holy names and secret appellations.

"You are the creator of all the worlds. You are the instigator of Prakṛti. You are the cosmic intellect of all the worlds. You are the Ahaṁkāra (ego). You are Īśvara.

O Īśa, you alone make elements and sense-organs function. I am the ancient one formerly created out of your right side. O lord of great arms, lord Nārāyaṇa was created from your left side.

O cause of creation, this goddess Prakṛti, always adopts the form and nature of your wife and becomes the cause of the universe. O Mahādeva, obeisance to you. Obeisance to the great goddess. O lord of Devas, it was through your favour and my behest that these subjects, Devas and others, were created and deluded by your yogic power. Grant favour unto them. May they become as they were here-to-fore.

Sūta said :

48. After imploring thus to Maheśvara the lord of Devas, the lotus-born lord Brahmā spoke to Devas who had been rendered stunned and motionless.

49. O ye Devas, all of you are deluded. You have not understood Śaṅkara, your lord, who is bowed to by all of you, the lord who has come into our midst.

50. O Devas, all of you beginning with Indra including Nārāyaṇa and accompanied by the sages quickly seek refuge in lord Śaṅkara.

51. You seek refuge in Īśvara the great Ātman, your lord as well as mine. You seek refuge in the most excellent lord accompanied by the daughter of Himavān who is Prakṛti.

52. The most excellent Devas, all those who had been rendered stunned and motionless including Nārāyaṇa mentally bowed down to lord Śiva.

53. Then the three-eyed lord of Devas became pleased with them. At the instance of Brahmā, the lord made them as they were before.

54. After being pleased, the lord of Devas assumed an

exceedingly wonderful form consisting of three eyes. It dispelled all their miseries.[945]

55-59. Thanks to his brilliance, Devas including Indra, Candra (Moon), the sun, Brahmā, Sādhyas, Nārāyaṇa, Yama, and Rudra requested the lord for an eye that will enable them to see the dazzling form of the lord. The lord gave them the divine eye competent to see everything. To Bhavānī and to the mountain too he gave the excellent vision. After acquiring divine sight Devas with Indra and Viṣṇu as their leaders, including Brahmā and Indra saw the lord. Then they immediately bowed down to the lord. So also Bhavānī, the lord of the mountains, sages and Gaṇas approved of by Śiva bowed down to Mahādeva. The Siddhas, Cāraṇas, and other heaven-dwellers showered flowers.

60-63. The divine Dundubhis were sounded; the sages eulogised the lord; the chiefs of the Gandharvas sang; the Apsarases danced; the leaders of the Gaṇas rejoiced; Ambā the daughter of the lord of mountains too rejoiced. The delighted goddess placed at his feet the divine fragrant garland in the presence of the heaven-dwellers. Devas including Brahmā, Yakṣas, Nāgas and Rākṣasas shouted "Well done, well done" and made obeisance to him then and there with their heads touching the ground.

CHAPTER HUNDRED AND THREE

The glory of Śakti

Sūta said:

1. Thereafter Brahmā saluted Mahādeva with palms joined in reverence and said to Maheśvara "O lord, may the marriage be celebrated."

2. On hearing these words of Brahmā Parameṣṭhin, the lord of the Bhūtas said to Brahmā "As you please."

945. sarvadeva: ST. reads sarvadeva for sarvadoṣa. nivāraṇam—sarvadevair api draṣṭum aśakyam ST. so dazzling that it could not be visualized even by the gods.

3. O sages of good holy rites, for the marriage of Maheśa, a divine splendid city full of jewels was created by Brahmā instantaneously.

4-11. The following persons went to the place of marriage:—Aditi, Diti, Danu, Kadru, Sukālikā, Pulomā, Suramā, Siṁhikā, Vinatā, Siddhi, Māyā, Kriyā, Durgā, Sudhā herself, Svadhā, Sāvitrī the mother of Devas, Rajanī, Dakṣiṇā, Dyuti, Svāhā, Svadhā, Mati, Buddhi, Ṛddhi, Vṛddhi, Sarasvatī, Rākā, Kuhū, Sinīvālī, Anumati, Dharaṇi, Dhāraṇī, Īlā, Śacī, Nārāyaṇī, and other mothers and wives of Devas—all of them went there joyously saying "O this is Śaṅkara's marriage." Nāgas, Garuḍas, Yakṣas, Gandharvas, Kinnaras, Gaṇas, oceans, mountains, clouds, months, years, Vedas, Mantras, Yajñas, Kriyās, Hūṁkāra, Praṇava, thousands of Pratihāras (jugglers, porters), the crores of Apsarases, the divine damsels and their female attendants—all these went to the place of marriage. The rivers in the continents and the worlds of Devas assumed the forms of women and proceeded there with delighted minds.

12. The highly blessed leaders of the Gaṇas bowed to by all the worlds went there joyously saying, "O this is Śaṅkara's marriage."

13. Crores of Gaṇas and leaders of Gaṇas, having the colour of the conch came there. Kekarākṣa came with ten crores; Vidyutas came with eight crores.

14. Viśākha came with sixtyfour crores; Pārayātrika with nine crores; Sarvāntaka with six crores; the glorious Vikṛtānana too came with six crores.

15-16. The leading Gaṇa, Jvālākeśa came with twelve crores, the glorious Samada with seven crores; Dundubha with eight crores; Kapālīśa with five crores; Sandāraka with six crores; Kaṇḍaka and Kumbhaka with several crores of followers.

17. O brahmins, Viṣṭambha the leading Gaṇa and the most excellent of all came with eight crores; Pippala and Sannāda with a thousand each.

18. Āveṣṭana was accompanied by eight crores. Candratāpana came with seven crores; Mahākeśa the leader of the Gaṇas, with a thousand crores.

19. The heroic Kuṇḍī and the splendid Parvataka came

with twelve crores; Kāla, Kālaka and Mahākāla with hundred crores each.

20. Āgnika came with a hundred crores; Agnimukha with a crore. Similarly Ādityamūrdhā and Dhanāvaha came with a crore each.

21. O sages of good Mantras, Sannāma and Kumuda came with a hundred crores; Amogha and Kokila with a crore each.

22. Another Gaṇa-leader Kākapāda came with six crores; lord Santānaka with six crores; Mahābala, Madhupiṅga and Piṅgala with nine crores each.

23. Nīla, Deveśa and Pūrṇabhadra came with ninety crores; Caturvaktra of great strength with seventy crores.

24. Devas came with hundreds and thousands of crores of followers.

25. The Bhūtas came with a thousand crores; the Pramathas with three crores; Vīrabhadra with sixtyfour crores and the Romajas with crores.

26. Karaṇa came with twenty crores; the auspicious Kevala with ninety crores. So also Pañcākṣa, Śatamanyu and Meghamanyu too came thus.

27. Kāṣṭhakūṭa, Sukeśa and Vṛṣabha came with sixtyfour crores. The eternal lord Virūpākṣa also came with the same number.

28-31. Tālaketu, Ṣaḍāsya, Pañcāsya, Sanātana, Saṁvartaka, Caitra, Lakulīśa, Svayaṁprabhu, Lokāntaka, Dīptāsya, lord Daityāntaka, Mṛtyuhṛt, Kālahā, Kāla, Mṛtyuñjayakara, Viṣāda, Viṣada, Vidyuta, lord Kāntaka, the glorious lord Bhṛṅgīriṭi who was a favourite of the lord of Devas, Aśani, Bhāsaka and Sahasrapād came with sixtyfour crores. These and other leaders of the Gaṇas were innumerable and very powerful.

32. All of them had a thousand hands each; they wore matted hairs and crowns; they were embellished with the crescent moon; they were three-eyed and blue-necked.

33. They were adorned with necklaces, earrings, shoulderlets, crowns and other ornaments. They were on a par with Brahmā, Indra and Viṣṇu. They were equipped with Aṇimā and other siddhis.

34. The leading Gaṇas who usually roamed about in the

nether regions, those who stayed in all the worlds and those who resembled crores of suns, came there.

35. Tumburu, Nārada, Hāhā, Hūhū and Sāmagas came to that city taking with them their musical instruments and jewels.

36. The sages and ascetics delighted in their minds and repeated holy mantras pertaining to the marriage and other divine songs.

37-38. Thus, when people from all places had assembled, Viṣṇu himself led the daughter of the lord of the mountains into that city. She was fully bedecked and had smiles on her face. Then Brahmā spoke to Viṣṇu, Nārāyaṇa the lord of Devas, in that assembly.

39. O lord, you were born at the outset from the left side of Rudra, along with Bhavānī and other deities. I was born from his right side.

40. Indeed, Himavān the lord of the mountains was created for the purpose of sacrifice. He is my own form. This daughter of Himavān was born by the grace of Brahmā's power.

41. The lord has come here for the proper functioning of the rites laid down in the Vedas and the Smṛti texts as well as for the sake of marriage rites. Hence, the goddess is the mother of the worlds. The lord is my creator as well as yours.

42. The universe is created by the cosmic forms of this lord Rudra since the lord has the eight forms of earth, fire, water, ether, wind, moon, sun and the hotṛ.

43-45. Still, at the instance of the lord of the mountains as well as at my instance this unborn Prakṛti of white, black and red colour should be given to Śiva. You too are the Prakṛti. The alliance with the king of the mountains is conducive to your welfare as well as mine. In the Pādma Kalpa, I was born of your umbilical lotus. Hence, you are my father and an ancestor to this mountain who is a part of mine.

Sūta said:—

Thereupon, Viṣṇu, the lord of Devas said to Brahmā—"So be it."

46-47. Then Devas, sages and Śaṅkara the lord of Devas as well as scholars stood up. The lord Viṣṇu, the learned

Padmanābha bowed to them and washed the feet of the lord with his own hands. He sprinkled the water thereof on his own head as well as those of Brahmā and the lord of mountain Himavān.

48-51. "This daughter of Menā and my younger sister now belongs to you by matrimonial rite." Saying thus, he dedicated the goddess to the lord of Devas along with water. Viṣṇu too offered himself to the lord along with water. Then the excellent sages who were masters of the Vedic texts said:—"On consideration, it is indeed this lord Śiva who is the giver, the receiver of the material offered and the benefit thereof. Of course, through his Māyā has emanated the universe from him." Saying this they bowed down to him. The hair on their skins stood on end due to pleasure. The heaven-walkers—Siddhas and Cāraṇas—showered flowers on him.

52. The divine drums were sounded. The Apsarases danced. The Vedas assumed physical forms and bowed down to the great lord.

53-54. Along with Brahmā and the sages they bowed down to the lord of Umā and of Devas. The lord glanced at the bashful daughter of the snow-clad mountain. He was never satiated. She too of splendid and unblemished body was not satiated on seeing the bull-bannered lord. He spoke to Viṣṇu—"I am the bestower of boons." He too then spoke to Śaṅkara.

55-57. "Devotion to you. Be pleased." He then gave him (Hari) the title Brahmā[946] as well as instructions in Brahman (Eternal truth). Thereupon, Brahmā again spoke to the lord:—"I now offer Havis to the holy fire, officiating as a priest at the sacrifice. If you give me permission, I shall proceed with the rituals, as yet not performed, but which are still to be observed. Śaṅkara, the lord of Devas, the lord of the universe said to the lord "O excellent Deva, do as you please, whatever you like.

58-64. O Brahmā, O lord of Devas, I shall act according to your instructions."

946. Brahmākhyam—the title of Brahmā was bestowed upon Viṣṇu. Thus, Viṣṇu is sometimes designated as Brahmā Cf. अतएव ब्रह्मत्वेन विष्णोर्विष्णुपुराणादौ वर्णनं सङ्गतम् *ST.*

Thereupon, Brahmā the grandfather of the world, became delighted in his mind. He bowed to the lord, and joined the hand of the goddess to the hand of the lord. The fire-god himself was present there with palms joined in reverence. Brahmā performed the Homa duly chanting Mantras taken from the Vedic texts. The mantras had assumed physical forms and were present there. He offered the fried rice[946a] in the due order. After worshipping the brahmins brought by Viṣṇu he blessed them with different boons. He then made the lord circumambulate the holy fire thrice.[947] In the presence of Devas and men the joined hands were separated joyously. Lord Brahmā then bowed to the husband of Umā, the lord of Devas. He offered Pādya, Ācamanīya, Madhuparka[948] and a cow to the couple. Again, Lord Brahmā bowed down to Śiva and stood aside along with Devas headed by Indra.

65. The sages beginning with Bhṛgu showered gingelly seeds and whole rice grains. The sun and the rest of luminaries worshipped and eulogised the bull-bannered lord.

66. Śiva concluded the sacred Vedic rites, and imposed the fire on to the Ātman. He was thus united with her for the welfare of the worlds.

67-69. He who reads or listens to this nuptial of Rudra, or he who smilingly narrates this to brahmins who have mastered the Vedas and the Vedāṅgas, attains the chieftancy of the Gaṇas and rejoices with Śiva. Wherever this narrative is repeated and glorified by the brahmins, the lord occupies that place as long as the story continues. Hence, O brahmins, O excellent brahmins, in the course of the celebration of the marriage of leading brahmins and Kṣatriyas, the lord should be duly glorified after the worship and not otherwise. Thus excel-

946a. lājāhoma—the brother of the bride pours out of his joined hands into her joined hands fried rice-grains mixed with Śamī leaves. The bride sacrifices them with firmly joined hands, standing, while the bridegroom recites the verses. For detail, see P.G.S. 1.6. 1-2.

947. triḥ pradakṣiṇā—circumambulating the sacrificial fire thrice, from left to right so that the right side is turned towards the fire. But in the Hindu nuptial rites, as observed now-a-days, the bride and bridegroom circumambulate the fire, seven times.

948. madhuparka—It is a mixture of honey, butter, sugar, and curd offered to a guest when he first comes to the house.

lent detailed account of the marriage of Śiva-Umā should be glorified.

70-71. After the marital rites with the goddess the daughter of the lord of the Himavān, the bull-bannered lustrous lord went to the divine city Vārāṇasī, accompanied by Devas, Gaṇas and also Nandin.

72. Umā whose face beamed with delight bowed down to the bull-bannered lord who was comfortably seated in Avimukta. She asked him about the glory of that holy centre.

73-74. The lord who bore the crescent moon on his forehead recounted the greatness of the holy centre:—"O goddess of Devas, the greatness of Avimukta cannot be recounted by me in detail. This holy centre is honoured by the sages. O fair lady, how shall I tell you in detail the merits of Avimukta ?

75-81. Sinners who die here shall be liberated even in their very birth. A man dispels at Vārāṇasī the sins he has committed elsewhere. The sins committed at Vārāṇasī turn the sinner into a Piśāca and they lead him to hell.[949] It is better for men to court Piśācahood after committing thousands of sins at Vārāṇasī than to attain the position of Indra a thousand times in heaven without the pleasure of being in the city of Kāśī. No living animal is reborn if it dies in this place where the lord Viśveśvara, the lord of Oṁkāra, the lord clad in elephant's hides, is ever present. After recounting the glory of the holy centre briefly the moon-crested lord dismissed the leaders of Gaṇas and pointed out a garden to the goddess. It was here that lord Vināyaka, the deity with the face of an elephant, was born, for creating obstacles in the way of Daityas and for dispelling the same in the way of heaven-dwellers. Thus, the entire essence of the story has been narrated to you. It is a splendid story and I have narrated just as it had been heard by me by the grace of Vyāsa.[950]

949. paiśācya—according to *ST.* this hell is in preference to the rebirth. Vārāṇasyāṁ kṛtam pāpam paiśācanarakāvaham, na tu punar janmaprāpakam *ST.*

950. prasādāt—i.e. by the favour of the sage Veda Vyāsa.

CHAPTER HUNDRED AND FOUR

The eulogy of the lord

The sages said:

1. How was the elephant-faced Vināyaka, the leader of the Gaṇas, born? What is his power? O Sūta, it behoves you to narrate this to us.

Sūta said:

2. O brahmins, in the meantime, Devas including Indra and Upendra assembled together in order to create obstacles in the holy rites of Daityas.

3-6. Asuras, Yātudhānas, Rākṣasās of ruthless activities and other beings of Tāmasa and Rājasa nature on the earth worship the lord without impediment, by means of sacrifices and charitable gifts. The brahmins worship Brahmā and Viṣṇu and acquire the desired boons. In the same manner they attain everything. It is due to this, O excellent Devas, that we are able to achieve victory always. It behoves you to eulogise him in order to make him create Vighneśa the leader of Gaṇas for creating obstacles for them and for the destruction of obstacles in the way of the heaven-dwellers, for the sake of granting sons unto the women and for the achievement of holy rites unto men.

7. After saying thus to one another they eulogised the sinless lord Śiva.

"Obeisance to you the Ātman of all; to the Pināka-bearing lord, the omniscient one."

8. Obeisance to the sinless Viriñca,[951] to the deity who bestows on the goddess everything that is of consequence; to one who has no body; to one whose body is of great substance; to one who removes the physical form of Viṣṇu.

9. Obeisance to you stationed in the zone of the nectarine base in the body; obeisance to the Kāla (time) differentiated as Kṛta, etc., obeisance to the force of Kāla; obeisance to you.

10. Obeisance to one of the form of Kāla, Agni and

951. Viriñcāya—viśeṣeṇa recayati brahmāṇḍānyutpādayatīti Viriñcas tasmai *ST*. the creator of the universe.

Rudra. Obeisance to one indicated by the eight words[952] beginning with Dharma; obeisance to one whose body is sanctified by Kālī; obeisance to you the cause of Kālikā.

11. Obeisance to the great blue-necked lord, obeisance to you having the excellent vehicle; obeisance to you the lord of Ambikā; obeisance to the lord of Hiraṇya.

12. Obeisance to you Hiraṇyaretas; obeisance to the trident-bearing lord identical with all; obeisance to one holding skull, staff, noose, sword, leathern shield and goad.

13. Obeisance to the husband of the daughter of Himavān; obeisance to you whitish and golden[953] in complexion; obeisance to one whose semen is yellow in colour, obeisance to fire for the protection of Devas.

14. Obeisance to the fifth one;[954] obeisance to the bestower of boons on the Pañcayajñins;[955] obeisance to you having the five-hooded serpent for necklace; obeisance to you the five-syllabled mantra itself.

15. Obeisance to the deity whose form is worshipped in five ways by the five Kaivalya Devas; obeisance to you whose vision is on the five syllables;[956] obeisance to you greater than the greatest.

16. Obeisance to one of inexhaustible form; obeisance to one of adamantine limbs and jaws constituted by the sixteen vowels;[957] obeisance to you whose right and left hands are cons-

952. dharmādyaṣṭapadāya—the lord of the guardians (Indra, etc.) of the eight quarters.

953. pīta-śuklāya—of yellow and white complexion in the form of ardha-nārīśvara.

954. pañcamāya—one who is stationed beyond the four stages of consciousness—turīyātītāya *ST*. or one who can be realized by a system of worship comprising madya (wine), māṁsa (flesh), matsya (fish), mudrā (mystical gesticulation) and maithuna (sexual intercourse). The letter 'm' the best among the letters is variously interpreted by the right and left hand worshippers of Śakti.

955. pañca-mahāyajña: The five daily sacrifices to be performed by a house-holder constitute ब्रह्मयज्ञ, पितृयज्ञ, देवयज्ञ, भूतयज्ञ and नृयज्ञ which are defined as

अध्यापनं ब्रह्मयज्ञः पितृयज्ञस्तु तर्पणम् ।
होमो दैवो बलिर्भौतो नृयज्ञोऽतिथिपूजनम् ॥

956. pañcākṣara-dṛśe—one who sees or favours by the five-syllabled mantra 'namaś śivāya'.

957. ṣoḍaśa-svara—vide I. 17. 73-76.

tituted by the five letters beginning with '*k*' and the five letters beginning with '*c*'.

17. Obeisance to you Rudra whose right and left legs are constituted by the five letters beginning with "*ṭ*" and the five letters beginning with "*t*". Obeisance to one whose penis is constituted by the five letters beginning with "*p*" ; obeisance to one who holds seven limbs and seven constituents, lymph etc. constituted by the letters beginning with "*y*".[958]

18. Obeisance to one whose form is the Ātman ending with"*s*";[959] obeisance to one whose anger is constituted by the letter '*h*' ending with kṣa.[960] Obeisance to one whose limbs are constituted by the letters l, v, r, h, and ś; obeisance to you devoid of limbs.

19. Obeisance to one who causes sounds in the heart of all living beings; obeisance to one who is always seen by devotees in between the eyebrows; obeisance to the excessive-rayed.

20. Obeisance to one whose eyes are constituted by the sun, moon and fire; obeisance to the deity of the form of the supreme soul; obeisance to one who is stationed above the three Guṇas, obeisance to one whose feet constitute the holy centre.[961]

21. Obeisance to the essential principle of the holy centres; obeisance to you greater than the greatest; obeisance to Ṛk, Yajus and Sāman Vedas; Obeisance to Oṁkāra.

22. Obeisance to one who stays above, after creating threefold form in the Oṁkāra;[962] obeisance to the yellow one, to one dark in complexion; to the red one; to one of excessive refulgence.

23. Obeisance to one who is situated in five abodes[963] in

958. yadyaṅga—the seven letters beginning with 'y' and ending with 's'.

959. sāntātma—N.S. reads śāntātma-rūpiṇe but this reading is not supported by *ST*.

960. kṣadanta—the letter ending with 'kṣ', i.e. 'kṣ' inclusive of the preceding letter 'h'.

961. tīrtha-pādāya—tīrthaṁ saṁsāra-taraṇopāyaḥ pādo yasya sa tīrthapādaḥ *ST*. the worship of whose feet is the means of crossing the ocean of birth and death.

962. trividhaṁ rūpam—the forms Brahmā, Viṣṇu and Rudra.

963. sthāna-pañcaka—i.e. earth, water, fire, wind and ether.

five ways[964] within the Cosmic Egg and without in order; obeisance to Brahmā, Viṣṇu, to you and to Kumāra.

24. Obeisance to the lord of Umā; obeisance to you who move above all; obeisance to you of subtle form at the root; obeisance to you the gross as well as subtle.

25. Obeisance to you devoid of all conceptions; to you protected from all; to you devoid of beginning, middle and end; to you stationed in Cit.

26. Obeisance to you worshipped perpetually by Yama, Agni, Vāyu, Rudra, Varuṇa, Soma, Indra and Nirṛti and the guardians of different quarters.

27-29. Obeisance to you who are worshipped in everything and in all paths and always. Obeisance to Rudra, Rudranīla, Kadrudra Pracetas. Obeisance to the bold Maheśvara; obeisance to Śiva. O lord, O destroyer of sacrifice, of Kāma, of Yama, of Agni and of Dakṣayajña, listen. Forgive the deceptive utterances and peculiar activities pursued by the leaders of Devas as well as Asuras and those other leaders Viṣṇu and Indra.

The devotee who devoutly reads the hymn glorified by Devas the chief of whom are Indra and Agni, or who narrates this attains the greatest goal.

CHAPTER HUNDRED AND FIVE

The origin of Vināyaka

Sūta said :

1.2. After bowing to Īśvara thus, when the leading Devas stood aside, the Pināka-bearing great Īśvara, Bhava, the lord of Ambikā, granted a vision of his to those excellent Devas. With their eyes moistened due to their joy, Devas bowed to the lord with respect.

3. The lord glanced at them with visions sweet as nectar. The lord said to the leading Devas—"Welfare be to you."

964. aṇḍa-bahiḥ—as the sheath of the Cosmic Egg.

4-6. The lord of speech Bṛhaspati glanced at the lord fearlessly, bowed to him and said—O Īśa, it is with the desire for a boon that Devas have come here. You have always been unobstructedly requested by Asuras and others. You are prayed to by those who are harmful and injurious to Devas, for the achievement of their desire. Hence, bless us with a good cause of impediment to those who bring about injury to Devas. This alone is our request.

7. On hearing that, the Pināka-bearing lord of Devas, Śiva created the body of the leading Deva Gaṇeśvara.[965]

8-10. The leading Gaṇas and the lords of Devas eulogised Maheśvara, the origin of the world and the splendid dispeller of the distress of worldly existence. Then Ambikā welcomed the elephant-faced lord Gajānana the cause of the origin of the world, the wielder of the trident and noose. Siddhas and sages showered flowers. The heaven-walkers, the groups of Devas eulogised lord Maheśa the bestower of the cherished desires. The lords of Devas bowed to Gaṇeśa and Maheśa alertfully.

11. That boy emanating from both of them, the embodied form of gentleness and terrific appearance, the abode of all auspiciousness stood there and danced.

12-13. Gajānana was bedecked in wonderful garments and ornaments of various kinds. The gentle son of Maheśvara saluted his father and mother. Lord Bhava, the lord of all, himself performed the post-natal rites of his recently born son Gajānana.

14. He held him in his arms that offered gentle pleasure and happiness. Mahādeva, the preceptor of the universe, embraced him and kissed him on his head and said.

15. O my son, you are born for the destruction of Daityas and for rendering help unto Devas and brahmins the expounders of Vedas.

16. Be stationed in the heavenly path. Create impediment in the rituals of that person by whom the sacrifice had been performed without the monetary gifts on the surface of the earth.

965. Lord Śiva entered the womb of Umā to be born as Gaṇeśvara; vide, the Vedic concept that the wife becomes the mother unto her husband when the latter is born of her in the form of a son:

तज्जाया जाया भवति यदस्यां जायते पुनः । *AB*.

17. Remove the vital breaths of the person who improperly performs the rites of teaching and study of the Vedas, the commentaries thereon and the rites mentioned in them.

18. O lord, remove the vital breaths of men and women fallen off from their castes. O leading man, similarly, do unto those who are devoid of their duties.

19. O Vināyaka, it behoves you to bestow equality with you, on those men and women who worship you on all occasions.

20. O boy Gaṇeśvara, protect your devotees with all efforts. On being worshipped here and hereafter protect old people and those who are in the prime of their youth.

21. O Vighneśvara, O Gaṇeśvara, everywhere in the three worlds, you alone will undoubtedly become worthy of being worshipped and honoured.

22. O son, even when the brahmins worship me, as Nārāyaṇa or Brahmā or when they perform sacrificial rites you will be worshipped at the outset.

23. If anyone performs auspicious rite laid down in the Śrutis or Smṛtis or any worldly ceremony without worshipping you at the outset, it will be turned inauspicious.

24. O Gajānana, you are worthy of being worshipped by brahmins, Kṣatriyas, Vaiśyas and Śūdras by the offerings of splendid edibles and food-stuffs for the achievement of all Siddhis.

25. There is nothing to be achieved by Devas and others anywhere in the three worlds without first worshipping you with scents, fragrant flowers and incense.

26. Those people, those human beings, who worship you are undoubtedly to be worshipped by even Indra and others.

27. If those who seek benefits do not worship you, you will harass them through impediments, even if it be Brahmā, Viṣṇu, Indra and Devas or even I myself.

28. Then lord Gaṇapati created Vighnagaṇas (attendants of impediment). Along with his Gaṇas he bowed to the lord and stood in front of him.

29-30. Ever since then, people worship Gaṇeśvara in this world. This Gaṇeśvara created obstacles in the rituals of Daityas.

Thus, every detail connected with the nativity of Gaṇeśa, Skanda's elder brother, has been recounted to you.

He who reads this, listens to this or narrates this shall be happy.

CHAPTER HUNDRED AND SIX

Tāṇḍava dance of Śiva

The sages said :

1. We have heard about the nativity of the elder brother of Skanda. It behoves you now to tell us precisely wherefore and how Lord Śiva begins his Taṇḍava dance.

Sūta said :

2. Dāruka born in the family of Asuras attained heroism through his penance. Like the fire at the end of a yuga he killed Devas as well as brahmins.

3-7. Devas were extremely afflicted and hurt by Dāruka. They sought refuge in Brahmā, Īśāna, Kumāra, Viṣṇu, Yama and Indra. Knowing that the Asura could be killed only by a woman, he was confronted in a battle by Indra[966] and others in fine guises of women. Still they were overwhelmed by him. O brahmins, they approached Brahmā and acquainted him with everything. Accompanied by Brahmā they approached the lord of Umā. With Brahmā at the forefront, they eulogised him. Approaching the lord of Devas and bowing to him in diverse ways Brahmā said :—"O lord, the demon Dāruka is a terrible fellow. We have been defeated by him at the outset. It behoves you to protect us by killing Dāruka who is destined to be killed by a lady.

8. On hearing this submission of Brahmā the lord who destroyed the eyes of Bhaga, said laughingly to the goddess, the daughter of the mountain-lord.

966. **For brahmādyaiḥ read śakrādyaiḥ. The former reading does not suit the context.**

9. O splendid and good-looking lady, I am now requesting you for the welfare of the worlds to slay Dāruka who is destined to be killed by a lady.

10. On hearing his words, the goddess[967] entered the body of the lord, she being desirous of taking birth from the lord of Devas.

11. She entered the lord of Devas the most excellent Deva only in part.[968] But Brahmā and Devas such as Indra and others did not know this.

12. On seeing the splendid daughter of the lord of the mountains stationed by the side of the lord as before, even the omniscient four-faced lord Brahmā was deluded by her Māyā.

13. Having entered the body of the lord of Devas, Pārvatī made her own body out of poison in the neck of the lord.

14. On coming to know of this the enemy of Kāma (i. e. Śiva) created Kāli the blue-necked goddess with matted hair from his third eye.

15. When the black-necked goddess was born the glory of victory too originated. Now Bhavānī and Parameśvara were sure to inflict defeat over the demon.

16. On seeing Kālī who resembled fire and whose black neck was embellished with poison, taking her origin, Devas and Siddhas, the chief of whom were Viṣṇu, Brahmā and Indra, fled, due to fright.

17. Similarly, an eye manifested itself in the forehead, the exalted contour of the crescent moon on the head, the terrible poison in the neck, the sharp and the terrible trident in the arm and the ornaments in their respective places.

18. Along with the goddess were born the lords of Siddhas as well as Piśācas who wore divine garments and who were bedecked in ornaments.

19. At the behest of Pārvatī, the great goddess slew the demon Dāruka who used to attack and kill the chiefs among Devas.

20. O leading brahmins, by virtue of impetuosity, and the fire of anger, the entire universe became agitated.

967. jagato'raṇiḥ—the source of creation.

968. ekāṁśena—svakīya-ṣoḍaśa-bhāgena *ST.* by her sixteenth part.

21. Bhava assumed the form of a boy due to his power of Māyā and stationed himself in the cremation ground full of corpses and ghosts. Īśvara, then cried in order to quaff the fire of her anger.

22. O brahmins, on seeing the boy, who was actually Īśāna the goddess was deluded by his Māyā. She took him, kissed him on his head and suckled him at her breasts.

23. Along with her breast-milk the boy quaffed up her warth also and he became the protector of the holy centres.

24. He assumed eight[969] physical forms for his manifestation as the intelligent protector of holy centres. Thus, her excessive anger was ceased by that boy.

25-28. In order to propitiate her, the delighted trident-bearing lord of Devas performed the tāṇḍava dance at dusk, along with the ghosts and leaders of goblins. After quaffing the nectar-like dance of Śiva upto the throat [i.e. after enjoying the dance of Śiva very much] Parameśvarī danced in the midst of ghosts, happily along with yoginīs. Devas all round, including Brahmā, Indra and Viṣṇu, bowed to and eulogised Kālī and then prayed to the goddess Pārvatī. Thus, the Tāṇḍava of the trident-bearing lord has been briefly mentioned to you. Others[970] are of the opinion that the Tāṇḍava of the lord is due to the Bliss of yoga.

CHAPTER HUNDRED AND SEVEN

The story of Upamanyu

The sages said:

1. O Sūta, it behoves you to recount now how the chieftancy of the Gaṇas was acquired from Maheśvara by Upamanyu. How was the milk-ocean also obtained by him ?

969. mūrtayo'ṣṭau—*ST*. adds: tāstu Kāśyām prasiddhāḥ; the eight forms of Bhairava are represented by their respective images in Vārāṇasī.

970. apare—Sanakādayaḥ *ST*. the sages Sanaka and others.

Sūta said:

2. When the three-eyed lord went away after creating[971] Kālī thus, Upamanyu worshipped him by performing penance and acquired the benefit of worship.

3-7. O excellent brahmins, there was a sage known as Upamanyu. He was as refulgent as Kārttikeya.[972] Once while playing about in the hermitage of his maternal uncle, he got only a small quantity of milk while his uncle's son drank a good quantity of excellent milk malicioulsy. On seeing him drinking milk as much as he pleased, Upamanyu spoke to his mother. "O mother, O highly blessed mother, O ascetic woman, give me cow's sweet milk, which should be hot and not too little in quantity. I am bowing down to you."

Sūta said:

Thus fondly requested, the mother earnestly embraced her son. O brahmins, recalling again and again to his mind the milk, the highly refulgent Upamanyu lamented to her and said—"Give me, give me milk".

8-9. That sweet-voiced lady ground some seeds she had gathered by gleaning one by one. She then stirred the grounded paste with water and then lovingly called her son gently and said, "Come, come on, my dear son". The distressed lady embraced the boy tenderly and gave him the artificial milk she had prepared.

10. O excellent brahmins, on drinking the artificial milk given by his mother the boy became dejected and said, "O mother, this is not milk".

11. On observing this she became unhappy. With her hands she wiped her son's lotus-like wide eyes. She kissed him on the head and said:—

12. There is a river full of jewels within the range of heaven and nether worlds. Those who are unfortunate, being devoid of devotion to Śiva do not perceive it.

13. Such persons do not obtain kingdom, heaven, salvation and the diet of milk. They do not achieve pleasing things unless Bhava is satisfied with them.

971. upālabhya—utpādya *ST*. having created.

972. Kumāra iva—Skanda-sadṛśaḥ ST. as Karttikeya.

14. Everything results from the grace of Bhava and not from the grace of other deities. Those who are devoted to other deities are miserable, confused and bewildered.

15-18. Whence can we get milk? We have not worshipped Mahādeva. O son, only that can be achieved, which has been gifted after exalting Śiva and not by exalting Viṣṇu or any other lord.

On hearing the words of his mother, Upamanyu of great refulgence, despite his being a boy, bowed down to his mother who was piteously miserable, and said:—"O highly blessed lady, eschew your sorrow. If there exists Mahādeva anywhere, sooner or later I shall obtain the milk ocean."

Sūta said :

After bowing to her and saying thus, he began to get ready to perform penance.

19. The mother then said to him, "Perform the splendid penance perfectly". On being permitted by her he performed a very severe penance.

20. He went to the mountain Himavān. With great attention and concentration he took in only wind as food. Due to his penance the universe became agitated.

21-24. The excellent Devas bowed down to Viṣṇu and mentioned everything to him. On hearing their words lord Viṣṇu thought, "What is this ?" On deep consideration he re-realized the cause. With a desire to see Maheśvara, he hastened to the Mandara mountain. On seeing the lord, he joined his palms in reverence, bowed down to him and said:—"O lord, a certain brahmin boy known as Upamanyu has, for the sake of milk, burnt everything by means of his penance. Curb him." On hearing their petition, the Pināka-bearing lord resolved to go there in the guise of Indra.

25. Having assumed the form of Indra the king of immortal beings, he went to the penance grove of the sage riding on the white elephant. He was accompanied by Devas, Asuras, Siddhas and Nāgas.

26. Indra was accompanied by Śaci and he mounted the elephant. The sun held the fan in his left hand and the white umbrella in the other.

27. With his white umbrella, lord Sadāśiva who had assumed the form of Indra and was accompanied by Umā [in the form of Śacī] shone like the Mandara mountain with the disc of the moon above it.

28. Having assumed the form of Indra like this, the lord went to the hermitage of Upamanyu in order to bless him.

29-30. "Today my hermitage[973] has been sanctified since Indra, the lord of Devas and of the universe, has come here along with the sun god". O excellent sages, so said Upamanyu, on seeing lord Śiva in the guise of Indra. He bowed down his head.

31. On seeing that the brahmin boy after saying thus, stood aside with palms joined in reverence, lord Śiva in the guise of Indra said in a majestic tone.

32. "O highly intelligent sage of good holy rites, O elder brother of Dhaumya, I am delighted with you for your penance. Tell me the boon you wish to choose. I shall give you all desired things."

33. The excellent sage who was thus urged by Indra, said with palms joined in reverence:—"I choose devotion to Śiva."

34. On hearing the words of the sage, Lord Īśāna himself in the guise of Indra said excitedly as if he was angry.

35. "O celestial sage, you do not know me, the lord of Devas. I am Indra the overlord of the three worlds, bowed to by all Devas.

36. O brahmin sage, be my devotee. Worship me always. I shall give you everything. Welfare unto you. Leave off Rudra devoid of attributes".

37. On hearing the words of Indra that rent his ears, Upamanyu said thus after repeating the splendid five-syllabled mantra : Oṁ namaḥ śivāya.

38. "I think some base Daitya has come here in the guise of Indra, in order to create obstacles in my holy rites. It cannot be otherwise.

39. Every quality has been mentioned by you while engaged in censuring Bhava. Incidentally, the state of his being devoid of attributes has been extolled.

973. pāvitaś cāśramaḥ. We have adopted the N.S. reading.

40. Of what avail is much talk? I know that I have committed a great sin in my previous birth. For I am compelled to hear the censure of Bhava.

41. On hearing the censure of Bhava, one must kill the person who censures, immediately and cast off his body at the very instant. He shall thereby go to the world of Śiva.

42. He, who plucks out the tongue of the person who is engaged in censuring Śiva verbally, uplifts twentyone generations of his family and goes to the world of Śiva.[974]

43. O' base one, let alone my desire for milk. I shall leave off my body after killing you by the missile of Śiva.

44. Undoubtedly what had been mentioned by my mother was true. The lord has not been worshipped by us in the previous birth."

45. After saying this boldly to the lord, Upamanyu the knower of mantras resolved to kill Indra by means of the Atharva missile.

46. The sage of great refulgence took a handful of Bhasman from the receptacle. Then, he discharged the Atharva missile against him and roared.

47. The sage of great brilliance, the unchanging soul meditated on the lord, invoked the Dhāraṇā of Agni, and got ready to burn his body like the dry fuel.

48. When the brahmin boy attempted this, the lord, the destroyer of the eyes of Bhaga, prevented him by means of the missile of Soma.

49. The Atharva missile of that sage that resembled Kālāgni was withdrawn by Candraka (moon) missile at the instance of Nandin.

50. Then lord Parameśvara assumed his own form with the crescent moon at his crest and showed himself to the brahmin.

51-52. All round the boy, the following appeared, viz:—thousands of milk currents, the milk ocean, the ocean of curd, the ocean of ghee, the ocean of fruits, the ocean of various edibles and food-stuffs and mountains of Apūpas.

53. The merciful lord looked smilingly at the smiling daughter of the mountain. He then sympathetically looked at

974. Mark the sectarian attitude of this purāṇa.

Upamanyu who was surrounded by his kinsmen. The lord then said:

54. See, O dear Upamanyu. Enjoy all pleasure as you desire in the company of your kinsmen. O highly blessed one, This Pārvatī is your mother.

55-56. You have been adopted as my son now. Hence, this ocean of milk, the ocean of honey, the ocean of curds, the ocean of rice soaked in ghee, the ocean of fruits and lambatives, the ocean of edibles and foodstuffs and also mountains of baked pies.

57. O sage, your father is Mahādeva who is the father of the worlds. Undoubtedly your highly blessed mother is the mother of the universe.

58. Immortality is bestowed upon you. So also the perpetual chieftancy of the Gaṇas. Choose your boons; you shall not hesitate in this matter. I shall give you whatever you ask for.

59. After saying thus, Mahādeva lifted him with his hands. Lord Bhava kissed him on the head and handed him to the goddess.

60. O excellent brahmins, on seeing her son the delighted goddess, the daughter of the mountain gave him yogaiśvarya (the prosperity of the yoga) and the Brahmavidyā (the esoteric doctrine of Brahman).

61. After attaining the boon from her, and the perpetual bachelorhood he eulogised Mahādeva with words choked with delight.

62. With palms joined in reverence he bowed down again and again to the lord. He chose boons with eyes devoid of Rajas Guṇa.[975]

63-64. O lord of the chiefs of Devas, bless me with unswerving devotion unto you. O Mahādeva, may I have faith and perpetual nearness to you. On thus being requested by him the smiling lord Śaṅkara offered the brahmin the cherished desire. Thereafter the lord vanished there itself.

975. virajekṣaṇam—virajeṣu eva ikṣaṇaṁ yasya tam *ST.* one who looks after the affairs of only those who are given to benevolent activities.

CHAPTER HUNDRED AND EIGHT

Glory of the Pāśupata-Vrata

The sages said :

1. This elder brother of Dhaumya was seen by Kṛṣṇa, son of Vasudeva, of unafflicted activities. From him he acquired the divine holy rite of Pāśupata.

2. O Sūta, how was the knowledge acquired from him by the intelligent Kṛṣṇa ? It behoves you to recount this story that destroys all sins.

Sūta said:

3. Although the eternal lord had incarnated of his own accord as the son of Vasudeva, yet he despised human form and so performed purificatory rites for the body.

4. For obtaining sons the lord wanted to perform penance. He went to the hermitage of Upamanyu and saw that sage there.

5. O brahmins, on seeing Upamanyu, the elder brother of Dhaumya, Kṛṣṇa circumambulated him three times and bowed to him respectfully.

6. By the mere sight of that intelligent sage all the impurities of Kṛṣṇa originating from the body as well as physical activities perished.

7-8. O leading brahmins, repeating the mantras beginning with "Agnih" and "Vāyuḥ" in due order, Upamanyu of great lustre dusted him with Bhasman. With a delighted mind the sage gave him the perfect divine knowledge pertaining to Paśupati. O brahmins, it was due to the favour of the sage that Kṛṣṇa became initiated honourably in the divine rite of Paśupati.

9. By means of penance he saw lord Maheśvara at the end of a year. On seeing the lord accompanied by Ambā[976] and the Gaṇas he obtained a son known as Sāmba who was unbewildered.

976. Sāmbam—ambayā saha; pārvatī-sahitam *ST*. accompanied by the mother goddess Pārvatī.

10. Ever since then, all the divine sages of unimpeded holy rites and all the devotees of Paśupati surrounded Kṛṣṇa and stood by him.

11-14. I shall recount another holy rite that bestows perpetual salvation upon all living beings. The devotee shall make a gold girdle, a shaft-receptacle or support, a gold block spherical in shape and a fan with a handle. Then the man or woman shall make an ink-pot and a pen. He shall gather a knife or scissors and a vessel. The devotee shall dust his body with Bhasman and give these articles to a devotee of Paśupati. He shall dedicate a golden, silver or copper vessel in accordance with his capacity. He shall then worship the yogins.

15. All these persons shall be liberated from their sins along with the members of their families. They will go to the divine region of Rudra. No doubt need be entertained in this respect.

16. Hence, by means of charitable gifts a householder is liberated from the bondage of worldly existence. If one makes charitable gifts to yogins, Śiva becomes pleased quickly.

17. If a person desires salvation, he shall make charitable gifts of kingdom, son, riches, horse, a vehicle or all his possession.

18. One shall strenuously attempt to achieve the fixed goal through his physical body that is uncertain and un-fixed. The excellent and eternal Pāśupata vrata is the cause of redemption from the ocean of worldly existence.

19. Thus everything has been succinctly mentioned to you. He who reads this or listens to this undoubtedly goes to the world of Śiva.

CHAPTER ONE

The greatness of Nārāyaṇa

The Sages said:

1. By what is Kṛṣṇa[1] the lord of the chiefs of all Devas, satisfied? O Sūta, it behoves you to mention this as you are conversant with all topics.

Sūta said:

2. O leading brahmins, formerly the great sage Mārkaṇḍeya[2] of great splendour was asked by Ambarīṣa[3] (the same question). I shall recount it precisely.

Ambarīṣa said:

3. O sage Mārkaṇḍeya, you are the master of all virtuous rites. O sage of great intellect, you are an ancient one and an expert in the teachings of the Purāṇas.

4. O highly intelligent sage of good holy rites, what is the most excellent one among the holy divine rites for the devotees of Nārāyaṇa? Recount it.

5. On hearing his words, Mārkaṇḍeya stood up. With the palms joined in reverence, he remembered lord Nārāyaṇa, the unchanging Kṛṣṇa, Acyuta, and said.

Mārkaṇḍeya said:

6-8. O king, listen duly to what I say. The remembrance of Nārāyaṇa, his worship, the devoted obeisance to him,—every one of these holy rites is on a par with the horse-sacrifice. Janārdana is that excellent Puruṣa who is the only Being who

1. Kṛṣṇa—son of Vasudeva and the eighth incarnation of Viṣṇu. He is said to be a devotee of Śiva.

2. Mārkaṇḍeya—an ancient sage, son of Mṛkaṇḍu. He is the reputed author or narrator of the *Mārkaṇḍeya Purāṇa*.

3. Ambarīṣa—a descendant of Manu Vaivasvata and son of Nābhāga celebrated for his devotion to Viṣṇu.

is the greatest soul. Brahmā and all other beings are born of him. Based on this fact I shall recount the chief Dharma as seen and understood by me.

9-12. Formerly, in the Tretāyuga, there was a certain brahmin named Kauśika who was perpetually engaged in singing Sāmans and was devoted to Vāsudeva. He thought of him always whilst seated or taking food or lying down on the bed. He frequently sang songs of his noble activities. After reaching the holy centre or the excellent shrine of Viṣṇu he used to sing in praise of Viṣṇu by means of exquisite songs wherein the beating of the time, the intonation and the regulated rise and fall of the sounds contributed to make them sweet. He sang in different tunes pleasing to the ears, in diverse ways. He followed the path of devotion and subsisted solely on alms voluntarily offered by the people.

13. On seeing him singing thus in praise of the lord a certain brahmin Padmākṣa, gave him cooked rice.

14. Kauśika of great refulgence partook of the rice with the members of his family. In great delight he continued to sing in praise of lord Viṣṇu.

15-16. The brahmin Padmākṣa continued to listen to the songs although he went out of the house now and then. After the lapse of some time, seven of the disciples of Kauśika came there. They were born of the families of brahmins, kings and vaiśyas. They were pure and they excelled one another in wisdom and learning. They were devoted to Vāsudeva.

17-20. To them also, Padmākṣa served cooked rice. Perpetually accompanied by his disciples, Kauśika was delighted in his mind. In a holy centre of Visṇu he sang in praise of Viṣṇu and stayed there. There was a certain vaiśya Mālava. He was devoted to Viṣṇu. With a delighted mind he used to offer him garlands of lights perpetually. His chaste wife Mālavī used to scrub the environs of the holy shrine and smear cowdung all round. She used to sit beside her husband listening to the excellent music.

21. For hearing the songs in praise of Viṣṇu fifty excellent brahmins of extolled holy rites came there from Kuśasthala.[4]

4. Kuśasthala or Kuśasthalī, is the same as Dvarakā, near the extreme western promontory. It was the capital of the country Ānarta in the peninsula of Gujarat. It is also one of the seven names of Ujjayinī. Cf. Sk. v. 1. 26. 45.

22. They were wise and learned. They were conversant with the real meaning of what they learnt. Carrying out the tasks of the noble-souled Kauśika, they stayed there listening to his songs.

23. The ability of Kauśika to sing sweetly became well known. On hearing about it, the king Kaliṅga[5] came there and spoke in these words:

24. "O Kauśika, accompanied by your attendants sing in praise of me. O ye people of Kuśasthala, you too hear the same.

25-30. On hearing it, Kauśika said to the king in an appeasing tone:—"O great king, neither my tongue nor my words eulogise any one other than Viṣṇu. They do not speak in praise of even Indra."

When this was said, his seven disciples, viz—Vasiṣṭha, Gautama, Hari, Sārasvata, Citra, Citramālya and Śiśu spoke to the king in the same way as Kauśika did.

The disciples from Kuśasthala who were devoted to Viṣṇu also spoke thus to the king:—"O king these ears of ours do not wish to hear about anyone other than Viṣṇu. We will hear the songs of his praise and never the eulogy of any other."

On hearing this, the king became angry and spoke to his servants:—"Sing, ye, so that these brahmins may hear about my renown. When it is being sung about all round how can it be that they do not hear it?"

31-33. The servants who were ordered thus sang excellent songs about the king. Those brahmins whose way was blocked, became sad after the songs were over.

On realising the inclination of the king, Kauśika and other brahmins plugged one another's ears by means of wooden pikes.

"This king has compelled his servants to sing obstructing us as he stands by his own songs of praise". Saying thus, the brahmins of regular observances cut off the tips of their tongues with their own hands.

34-36. Then the infuriated king confiscated their riches and banished them from his kingdom. Thereupon, they went to the north. In due course of time they courted death. On seeing them come, Yama (God of death) was bewildered as

5. Kaliṅga—here, name of a king.

to what should be done. At that time, O king Ambarīṣa, Brahmā spoke to the chiefs of Devas: "comfortably accommodate Kauśika and other brahmins today.

37. Welfare unto ye all. If you wish to retain your Deva-hood bring those persons here who perpetually worship Viṣṇu by means of music."

38-39. The guardians of the quarters who were thus ordered, shouted "O Kauśika" again and again. Some of them cried "O Mālava, O Mālava." Others shouted "O Padmākṣa, O Padmākṣa". They approached them, seized them and carried them to the world of Brahmā by the aerial path. Those Devas reached the world of Brahmā within a Muhūrta.

40. On seeing Kauśika and others, Brahmā the grandfather of the worlds greeted them. He honoured them by welcoming them.

41. O excellent king, on seeing what Brahmā did Devas became excessively grave. There was great commotion among them.

42-50. Lord Brahmā forbade the excellent Devas. He took Kauśika and other sages and hurried to the world of Viṣṇu, with great devotion to Vāsudeva. Lord Viṣṇu was surrounded by Devas. Lord Nārāyaṇa, the lord of the path of knowledge, was being served by the splendid Siddhas who resided in the Śvetadvīpa.[6] They were devotees of Viṣṇu with great mental concentration and purity. They had four divine arms. They were on a par with Nārāyaṇa. They were equipped with the characteristic signs of Viṣṇu. They were brilliant and devoid of sins. He was served by those great people numbering eighty thousand. as also by people like us (i. e. Mārkaṇḍeya) and by Nārada, Sanaka and other sinless souls. He was also served by different beings all round. Celestial women too served him. He was seated on a Bhadra Pīṭha (holy seat) in the middle of an aerial chariot that had a thousand doors, that extended to a thousand Yojanas in length. It was divine, bright as well as set with jewels. It was spotlessly

6. **Śveta-dvīpa—It has not been possible to identify this is land. Colonel Wilford has attempted to identify it with Britain. See *H.M.* p. 153.**

pure and splendid with exquisite, diverse workmanship. Viṣṇu glanced benignantly at them who were engaged in worldly affairs[7] (?) Kauśika and others surrounded the lord at that time. He came, prostrated and eulogised the garuḍa-bannered lord. Glancing at him, lord Viṣṇu, Nārāyaṇa said "O Kauśika." With great pleasure he addressed them in due order.

51. There was a great shout of victory when this wonderful event took place. The lord, the soul of the universe, said to Brahmā—"O Brahmā, listen to what is to be mentioned by me.

52. These brahmins who were the residents of Kuśasthala endeavoured for the welfare of everyone. They were engaged in achieving what had to be accomplished by Kauśika.

53. They are engaged in listening to my glory. They are equipped with the knowledge of reality. They are not devoted to any other deity. May they all become Devas named Sādhyas.

54. Offer them entry to places near me as well as to other auspicious places, for ever"

After saying this, lord Viṣṇu said to Kauśika.

55. O brahmin of great intellect, accompanied always by your own disciples, be my attendant.[8] Attain the chieftancy of all my attendants and always remain with me.

56-57. Lord Viṣṇu spoke thus to Mālava and Mālavi : "O Mālava, stay as you please in my world, along with your wife as long as this world lasts. Assume a divine form. Be a glorious lord. Listen to the songs of my praise."

58-59. Lord Viṣṇu said to Padmākṣa, "Become the lord and the bestower of riches. Come to me in due course and visit me. Then happily rule over your kingdom."

After saying thus, lord Viṣṇu spoke to Brahmā.

60. Thanks to the songs of Kauśika, my yogic slumber is over. Accompanied by his disciples he eulogises me in the shrines dedicated to me.

61-67. He was banished from the kingdom by the cruel king Kaliṅga. He cut off his tongue and resolved thus, "I

7. loka-kārya-prasaktānām—according to *ST.* it refers to Devas who look after the welfare of the people.

8. digbandhaḥ—samīpavartī *ST.* a technical term meaning an attendant or a body-guard.

will never eulogise anyone other than Viṣṇu." He has now attained my world. These brahmins who regularly practise observances, who are my devotees and who are highly renowned plugged their ears by means of pikes. They resolved thus:— "We will never hear anything other than the glory of Viṣṇu." These brahmins have attained Deva-hood and my proximity. Accompanied by his wife, Mālava scrubbed and cleaned my holy centre. He decorated my shrines with clusters of lights. He used to worship me perpetually. He regularly listened to the songs of my glorious deeds. Hence, he has attained my eternal and massive world. This Padmākṣa gave food to the noble Kauśika. Hence, he has become the lord of riches and attained my proximity. So said Viṣṇu in that assembly, Viṣṇu who is worshipped by the entire world.

68-71. At that instant, there came Lakṣmī the consort of Viṣṇu, slowly and smilingly. She was bedecked in ornaments of diverse kinds. She was accompanied by experts in the science of instrumental music and by those who were conversant with the function of the lute. They were charming in the use of sweet words. They sang in praise of Lakṣmī. She was surrounded by thousands and crores of ladies. On seeing her arrive, the chieftains of the attendants, who were as huge as mountains and who wielded iron clubs like Bhuśuṇḍī[9] and Parigha[10] threateningly admonished Brahmā and other Devas as well as sages making them recede to give way to her. They were delighted in their tasks.

72. All of us (i. e. Mārkaṇḍeya and others) went out along with Brahmā and Devas. At that very time, Tumburu[11] the excellent sage was called.

73-75. He entered and stood near the goddess and the lord. Comfortably seated there, he sang exquisitely and played on the lute with delight. The excellent sage was worshipped by them and honoured with divine ornaments studded with jewels and splendid garlands. Tumburu was delighted, as also the other sages and Devas.

9. bhuśuṇḍī—a kind of weapon, perhaps fire-arms. It is probably a contraction of bhuja-śatru-muṇḍī (or śatru-bhuja-muṇḍī), that which cuts the arm of the enemy.

10. parigha—a club studded with iron.

11. Tumbaru—a Gandharva, proficient in music.

76-82. O king, the destroyer of enemies,[12] sage Nārada saw Tumburu depart after being duly honoured. On seeing the hospitable reception accorded to Tumburu by Viṣṇu, Nārada was overwhelmed with grief affecting his eyes and heart. In the height of his grief he began to worry and ponder over, "By what means will I gain access to Viṣṇu in the presence of the goddess? Alas! it has been attained by Tumburu. Fie upon me the stupid fellow of confounded mind. I have been driven out of the presence of Viṣṇu by the attendants. Where shall I go? How can I live? Alas! a wonderful feat has been achieved by Tumburu". Thinking thus, the brahmin sage performed penance for a thousand years according to divine reckoning. He did not even breathe. Reflecting on the hospitable reception to Tumburu, he meditated on Viṣṇu. He repeatedly cried though he was a scholar and said, "Fie upon me." O king, listen to what Viṣṇu did in this regard.

CHAPTER TWO

The glory of Viṣṇu

Mārkaṇḍeya said:

1. Thereafter, lord Nārāyaṇa, the soul of the universe gave everything to Nārada and made him equal to Tumburu in due course of time.

2. He made Nārada the leading sage like this. This incident happened formerly. The singing of Nārāyaṇa's songs again and again is an excellent thing.

3. Viṣṇu who is propitiated with songs, grants excellent renown, wisdom, refulgence, satisfaction and abode as it happened to Kauśika.

4-5. Viṣṇu granted excellent Siddhi to Padmākṣa and others. Hence, O king, the following should be performed by you in the holy centre of Viṣṇu in particular, viz.—worship,

12. arindama—vocative case. It is addressed to Ambarīṣa to whom the story is being narrated.

singing, dance, the instrumental music and other festivities. O king, this should be always performed by you along with the persons who are the devotees of Viṣṇu.

6-9. This must always be heard. Viṣṇu should always be praised. The scholar who undertakes songs, dances, narratives and discourses on Viṣṇu in the holy centres of Viṣṇu with devotion acquires the memory of previous births, intellect, awareness at the time of death and identity with Viṣṇu. O leading king, this is true.

O king, what you have asked me has been recounted to you. What more shall I tell you ? O most excellent one among the persons who maintain holy rites, tell me.

CHAPTER THREE

Achievement of the Science of Music by Nārada

Ambarīṣa said:

1. O Mārkaṇḍeya of great intellect, by what means did the highly blessed, saintly lord Nārada acquire the musical lore ?

2. At what time did he attain equality with Tumburu ? Tell me all these things. O highly intelligent one, you are omniscient.

Mārkaṇḍeya said:

3. This matter has been heard by me from Nārada of divine vision. This Nārada of great intellect and of great refulgence mentioned it to me himself.

4-6a. The saintly lord performed penance for a thousand divine years without breathing and recollecting the honour and gravity of Tumburu. He, as the repository of all penances, performed a severe penance. Then, Nārada the great sage heard in the firmament the divine unembodied wonderful words uttered in a loud voice :

6b-11a. "O leading sage, wherefore do you perform the terrible penance ? If your mind is interested in music go and see Ulūka on the mountain on the northern bank of the Mānasa lake.[13] He is known as Gānabandhu one devoted to music. Go quickly and see him. You will acquire proficiency in music." Nārada who was the best among the eloquent people became excessively surprised on being told thus. He approached Ulūka on the mountain on the northern bank of the Mānasa lake. All round him were seated Gandharvas, Kinnaras, Yakṣas and Apsarases. They were trained by that master and had acquired musical lore. All those who were seated there had exquisite sweetness of tone. They were happy and joyous. Then glancing at Nārada, Ulūka said after duly prostrating to him and worshipping him with greetings.

12-22. "O highly intelligent one, why have you come here? O brahmin, what has to be done by me? Tell me what I shall do to you?"

Nārada said :

O leading Ulūka of great intellect, listen to everything precisely. I shall recount all the antecedents of mine, all the wonderful things that occurred in the past. O scholar, in the previous yuga, Viṣṇu accompanied by Lakṣmī set me aside though I stood near him. Delightedly he invited Tumburu and listened to his excellent songs. Brahmā and other Devas were banished from their abodes. Kauśika and others of unswerving behaviour seated themselves (near) Viṣṇu for singing. With their songs they propitiated Viṣṇu and attained the chieftancy of the Gaṇas and they were happy. Due to this, I became dejected. I have come here to perform penance. What is given by me by way of charity, what is offered by way of Homa, what is heard or learnt by me—all these do not merit even a sixteenth fraction of the path of music associated with the glory of Viṣṇu. Pondering over this, O brahmin, I performed a terrible penance for a thousand divine years for that purpose. Thereafter, O Ulūka, I heard an aerial voice pertaining to you viz.—"O divine sage, if you have any interest in music, go to Ulūka. O brahmin, ere long you will know". On being urged

13. Mānasottara-śaile—on the mountain to the north of the Mānasa lake in the country of Gandharvas.

thus I have come to you. What shall I do? O unchanging one, I am your disciple. Protect me."

Ulūka said :

23. O Nārada of great intellect, listen to what befell me formerly. It is very wonderful and splendid and it will dispel my sins.

24-28. Formerly, there was a righteous king known as Bhuvaneśa. He performed a thousand horse-sacrifices and ten thousand Vājapeyas. That king gifted away millions and crores of cows, gold pieces, clothes, chariots, elephants, horses and virgins to brahmins. He ruled over the earth making people in his kingdom sing in praise of himself and preventing from singing about others. He proclaimed thus:—"If any one sings in praise of Viṣṇu or anyone else, he will be killed by me. The great Being is worthy of being worshipped by the Vedas. May women sing about me, perpetually and everywhere. May the bards sing only about me."

29-33. Having ordered thus, the king of great refulgence ruled over the kingdom. Very near the capital of that king there was a brahmin known as Harimitra. He was a devotee of Viṣṇu and was devoid of all Dvandvas (mutually clashing opposites.) He used to frequent the banks of rivers and worship the idol of Viṣṇu. He offered sweet rice cooked in milk, sweet pies, etc. to Viṣṇu with ghee and curds in plenty. After duly bowing down with his mind dedicated to Viṣṇu he sang in praise of him with exquisite beating of time and due intonation. He was endowed with excess of devotion and his innermost mind dwelt on Viṣṇu. Once upon a time, spies came there at the behest of the king.

34. They spoiled his activities of worship all round. They arrested the brahmin and informed the king duly.

35. Then the wicked king rebuked the excellent brahmin, confiscated his riches, and exiled him from his kingdom.

36-37. The Mlecchas[14] seized the idol of Viṣṇu and went

14. mlecchāḥ—The term *mleccha* has a bearing on the date of this Purāṇa. Mlecchas were wild ferocious tribes, such as Huns, whose acts of violence caused vast devastations and destructions and struck terror in the social life of the country. Like the cattle-lifting Paṇis of the Ṛgvedic age, they are mentioned here as stealers of the images of Devas.

off. Thereafter, on the lapse of a great deal of time, that king who had been honoured in the world passed away. He was afflicted with hunger and dejected. In his grief he said to Yama :

38. O lord Yama, even though I have come up to the heaven, I have hunger and thirst always. What is the sin committed by me ? What shall I do ?

Yama said :

39-40. Sin has been committed by you in regard to Harimitra and his worship of Vāsudeva. O king, due to that sin, the ailment of hunger has descended on you. It was due to delusion as a result of ignorance, that this great sin has been committed by you to Harimitra the devotee of Vāsudeva.

41-44. O lord of men, your charitable gift, including sacrifice, etc. has perished. You called off Harimitra of great intellect who was singing about the lord with his musical instruments and seized his wealth and the presents offered by him in the worship of Vasudeva. These articles were looted by your servants. At your behest they committed sins. O excellent king, excepting the glory of lord Viṣṇu nothing else should be sung about by a brahmin in the course of his musical activity. Hence, a great sin has been committed by you. All your heavenly worlds have perished. Now, go to the mountain cavity.

45-47. You must continuously bite and eat your own body cast off by you previously. In your hunger you must eat your own body even as you are stationed in the great hell until this manvantara concludes. When the manvantara passes off in due course of time you will attain human birth on the earth.

Ulūka said:

After saying thus, Yama who was conscious of everything vanished there itself.

48. Being eulogised by the chiefs of the Gaṇas, the glorious Harimitra went to the world of Viṣṇu on an aerial chariot, taking along with him the groups of his kinsmen, there.

49. The king Bhuvaneśa, continued to stay in the mountain crevasse eating his own skin. Still he was overwhelmed with hunger and thirst.

50-56. I saw the king there. He told me everything. After seeing him and understanding everything, I approached Harimitra who was proceeding ahead on an aerial chariot sparkling like the sun, surrounded by the immortal beings. I attained excellent longevity by the grace of Indradyumna. It was due to him, O sage of good holy rites, that I could see Harimitra. Thanks to the power of his prowess, my mind turned towards music. O sage, I sat among the Kinnaras for sixty thousand years practising the art of music. My tongue was blessed and it was rendered clear. Then, I learnt music. Within twice that period I attained perfection in the art. By that time ten manvantaras had elapsed. I became a preceptor of music. Gandharvas and others came there. Kinnaras approached me as their preceptor. O sage of great penance, musical lore cannot be acquired by means of penance.

57-63. Hence, you shall acquire music from me along with proper hearing of the notes. The sage who was advised thus bowed down to Ulūka and sang. Hear that, O excellent sage, and bow down to Vāsudeva.

Mārkaṇḍeya said:

On being urged thus by Ulūka, the sage Nārada learned the art of music in accordance with the procedure of learning. At that time, Ulūka said—"Be devoid of shyness now".

Ulūka said:

One shall eschew all shyness during sexual intercourse, while singing, when playing the game of dice, while conducting discourse in an assembly, when carrying out business transactions, while taking food, when hoarding wealth, and in calculating income and expenses.

One should never sing with bent body, nor while being shrouded under blankets, etc. While singing, undue manual gestures should be eschewed, mouth should not be opened too wide nor should the tongue be stretched out. One should not sing with the hands lifted up or with the eyes turned upwards. While singing, one should not survey one's own body nor stare at another man.

64. It is not proper to clap at the buttocks while rising up nor should there be laughter, anger and shaking of limbs. Memory shall not be diverted elsewhere.

65. O sage of great intellect, in the practice of music these trends are not recommended. Beating of time, O sage, is impossible with a single hand.

66. Practice of music shall not be pursued by one overwhelmed with hunger, thirst or fear; nor shall it be conducted in darkness. These and similar things shall not be indulged in the practice of music.

Mārkaṇḍeya said:

67. That saintly lord Nārada, who was advised thus, learned and practised music for the period of a thousand divine years adhering to those characteristics and injunctions laid down by his teacher Ulūka.

68. Thereafter, he became richly endowed with the knowledge in the varieties of musical notes. He became an expert in playing on lutes and other instruments. He became conversant with all notes and tunes in the gamut.

69. The excellent sage perfectly understood the hundreds and thousands of different tunes. He mastered thirtysix thousand notes with their minute differences.

70. Gandharvas and Kinnaras who were associated with the sage were perfectly delighted with his singing.

71-75. After acquiring the art of music, the sage said to Ulūka:—"O preceptor of intellect, the destroyer of ignorance,[15] you are an expert in the art of music. Having approached you I have become richly endowed with the art. What shall I do for you?

Ulūka said :

O Brahmin, in the course of a day of Brahmā, there are fourteen Manus. After their reign, O great sage, the dissolution of the three worlds takes place. The tenure of my life lasts till that period. I have blessedness till then. O excellent sage, whatever you have contemplated in your mind shall be my teaching fee.

15. dhvāṅkṣa-śatru. The musician sage Ulūka is represented as an owl, the enemy of crows (dhvāṅkṣas). Or dhvāṅkṣasya andhakāramayasya ajñānasya śātayitā—the remover of ignorance.

Nārada said:

"O preceptor of great intellect, hail unto you. When this kalpa passes and merges into another you will become Garuḍa, be favourable to me. I shall go now.

Mārkaṇḍeya said :

After saying this, Nārada went to Viṣṇu.

76-77. He sang songs in praise of Viṣṇu in the Śveta continent. After listening to that, lord Viṣṇu said to Nārada—"O Nārada, still you are not better than Tumburu. I shall tell you the time when you will become better.

78-79. Having resorted to Ulūka you have become perfectly familiar with topics of music. In the course of the twenty-eighth cycle of four yugas of Vaivasvata Manu I shall be born in the family of the Yadus towards the end of Dvāpara age, O sage of great intellect, I will be born of Devakī and Vasudeva with the name of Kṛṣṇa.

80. At that time you will approach me and remind me duly. Then and there, I shall make you fully endowed with the art of music.

81-83. I shall make you equal to Tumburu, nay even excelling him. Till then learn and teach this art among Devas and Gandharvas. After saying this, Viṣṇu vanished there itself. Thereafter, the celestial sage of divine refulgence became devoted to Vāsudeva. Bedecked in ornaments Nārada the store-house of austerities became engrossed in playing on his lute.

84-85. With his lute resting on his shoulders, the righteous sage wandered over all the worlds, viz. the worlds of Varuṇa, Yama, Agni, Indra, Kubera, Vāyu and Īśa. The sage who was proficient in playing on lute sang in praise of Viṣṇu after going to the assemblies of these guardians of quarters.

86-88. Here and there, he was duly worshipped by the Gandharvas and Apsarases. Once upon a time, he went to the world of Brahmā. There were two Gandharvas Hāhā and Hūhū. They were adepts in the art of vocal and instrumental music. The divine Gandharvas were the bards of Brahmā. In their company, the excellent sage of great refulgence sang in praise of Lord Viṣṇu. He was duly honoured by Brahmā.

89. After bowing down to Brahmā, the grandfather of the worlds Nārada wondered over the worlds, as he pleased.

90. After the lapse of a great deal of time, the sage went to the abode of Tumburu taking his lute with him. Seated, there, he began to sing.

91. On seeing the seven notes[16] Ṣaḍja etc. stationed there, the saintly lord went out hurriedly.

92. The sages of great intellect learned and taught this art in different places. The great sage became exhausted thereby.

93. Though he was an expert in the science of music he sat staring at the presiding goddess of the seven notes. But they did not descend upon the lute-strings while he played on them.

94-95. Thereafter on the mountain Raivataka[17] the great sage bowed down to Kṛṣṇa and told him about what Nārāyaṇa in Śvetadvīpa had told him formerly in respect to the excellence in the art of music. On hearing this, Kṛṣṇa spoke to Jāmbavatī smilingly and joyously.

96-98. "O gentle lady, teach this excellent sage the art of playing on lute in accordance with the Śāstraic injunctions" Saying to Viṣṇu laughingly, "As you say", she taught the sage Nārada. When a year was completed he approached Viṣṇu once again, bowed down to him and stood in front of him. Viṣṇu then said—"Go near Satyā (Satyabhāmā) and acquire due training."

99-102. "As you say", saying thus, the sage bowed down to Satyabhāmā and began to sing. The scholarly sage was trained by her. When a year was completed, the sage went to the abode of Rukmiṇī, on being directed by Viṣṇu. The excellent sage was addressed thus by the maid-servants and other ladies—"Although you have been singing for a long time, you do not understand the notes properly.

16. ṣaḍjādyāḥ –seven notes of the musical gamut. Cf.

निषादर्षभगान्धारषड्जमध्यमधैवताः ।
पञ्चमश्चेत्यमी सप्त तन्त्रीकण्ठोत्थिताः स्वराः ॥

17. Raivataka or Raivata, a mountain near Dvārakā. F.E. Pargiter (MP. p. 289) identifies it with the Baradā hills. Cf. Arch. Surv. of W. India by J. Burgess, Kāthiawaḍ, pp. 12, 15, 84 and 154. Pargiter holds that like the Himavat, Vindhya, and other ranges, which are often spoken of in the singular, Raivata denotes a group of ranges.

Then, with very great effort the sage was trained by the gentle lady Rukmiṇī for a period of three years. The sage then sang when the presiding ladies of Svaras attained harmonious blend with the strings.

103. Then, Lord Kṛṣṇa, the incomprehensible soul, himself called the great sage and taught him the excellent art of music.

104. Thereby the excellent sage surpassed Tumburu. The celestial sage thereupon danced in joy after duly bowing down to Viṣṇu.

105. Viṣṇu laughed and said:—"O great sage, you now know everything. With due and perfect knowledge sing in my presence.

106. What you have been seeking has been attained by you. Hence, sing in praise of me along with the sage Tumburu.

107-109. Thus urged, Nārada acted accordingly. When Kṛṣṇa worshiped Rudra the leader of the worlds, the sage sang in praise of Śiva at the behest of Viṣṇu. He sang in the company of Rukmiṇī, Satyā and Jāmbavatī as well as Kṛṣṇa. O excellent king, he had become by this time an expert in the seven primary notes.[18]

O leading sages, thus the gradual acquisition of the art of music[19] by the sage Nārada has been mentioned to you.

110-112. O king, a brahmin who sings the glory of Vāsudeva befittingly attains the world of Viṣṇu. One who sings in praise of Rudra will be more excellent. Otherwise, one will fall into the hell. A person singing in praise of any one else will also fall into the hell.

One who is devoted to Viṣṇu mentally, verbally and physically, one who sings about him and one who hears his glory shall attain him. Hence, they know that he is the greatest lord.

18. śruti-jāti-viśāradaḥ—expert in music.

19. geyam—science of music.

CHAPTER FOUR

The description of a devotee of Viṣṇu

The sages said :—

1. O highly intelligent one, tell us, what are the characteristics of those persons who are devoted to Vāsudeva and who are called Vaiṣṇavas, devotees of Viṣṇu?

2. O Sūta, the most excellent one among those who know all topics, recount all this to us. What does the lord the conceiver and creator of living beings do unto them ?

Sūta said :

3. Formerly, the sage Mārkaṇḍeya was asked by Ambarīṣa the same topic as has been mentioned by you now. I shall precisely recount the same to you.

Mārkaṇḍeya said :

4. O king, listen. What you ask me is pertinent. Nārāyaṇa is present there where the devotee of Viṣṇu stays.

5. Viṣṇu is remembered as their diety everywhere. When he is being eulogised, a Vaiṣṇava invariably feels an emotional thrill.

6-7. He who is delighted on seeing persons endowed with devotion of Viṣṇu, and those who perform rites laid down in Śrutis and Smṛtis is eulogised as a Vaiṣṇava. On seeing them his body shivers and perspires. Drops of tears are seen in his eyes. A Vaiṣṇava does not wear more clothes than what are needed for his body's protection.

8. On seeing a devotee of Viṣṇu coming, the Vaiṣṇava, standing face to face, performs obeisance as though towards Vasudeva himself.

9-10. He should be known as the devotee, he will be victorious in the three worlds who speaks with forbearance even on hearing harsh words. He who puts on scents, fragrant flowers etc. on his head thinking that every thing belongs to Viṣṇu is known as Vaiṣṇava.

11-13a. Endowed with affection he shall perform only auspicious rites in the holy centre of Viṣṇu. He shall worship the idol of Viṣṇu perpetually with a purified soul. He shall then be known as a devotee of Viṣṇu. Mentally, verbally and physically he is devoted to Nārāyaṇa for ever. Indeed, he is a great Bhāgavata devotee of the lord.

13b-14a. He who offers food and duly propitiates another devotee of Viṣṇu in accordance with his ability, is really a Vaiṣṇava.

14b-16a. If a scholar devoted to Viṣṇu accepts the food from anyone with a delighted mind, that food is undoubtedly one that goes into the mouth of Viṣṇu. Viṣṇu the soul of the Universe, the favourite of his devotees, becomes more pleased than from his own worship, when he sees the same being done to his devotee.

16b-21. On seeing a Vaiṣṇava who is devoted to Viṣṇu and who has burned all his sins, even Devas become afraid. They bow down to him before proceeding on their own ways. Listen to an ancient anecdote that demonstrates prowess of a devotee of Viṣṇu. On seeing the son of Bhṛgu who was a devotee and a Vaiṣṇava who had buried his sins, Yama stood up with palms joined in reverence and bowed to him. Hence, a man shall devoutly worship Vaiṣṇavas in the same manner as they worship Viṣṇu. He undoubtedly attains nearness to Viṣṇu. A devotee of Viṣṇu surpasses thousands of other devotees. A devotee of Rudra is far better than thousands of other devotees of Viṣṇu. There is certainly no one greater than the devotee of Rudra in this world. Hence, by all means one shall worship a Vaiṣṇava or a devotee of Rudra for achieving virtue, love, wealth and salvation.

CHAPTER FIVE

The anecdote of Śrīmatī

The sages said :

1. Ambarīṣa, a descendant of Ikṣvāku, ruled over the earth. He was extremely devoted to Vāsudeva and he always followed the behests of Viṣṇu.

2-4. O Sūta of great intelligence, we have heard this much in brief but it behoves you now to recount all this in detail.

It is well known in the world that the discus of Viṣṇu perpetually warded off fear from enemies and ailments of that great soul of righteous conduct. O excellent one, recount the story of Ambarīṣa wholly. O Sūta, we wish to know precisely his greatness, majestic dignity and excellent devotion. It behoves you to narrate it.

Sūta said :

5. O leading sages, may the story of the intelligent Ambarīṣa be heard. The glory of Ambarīṣa is extremely destructive of all sins.

6. The beloved wife of Triśaṅku,[20] the mother of Ambarīṣa was resplendent with all characteristic attributes. She was perpetually endowed with purity.

7-13a. Her name was Padmāvatī. She worshipped Nārāyaṇa, the great Ātman who was in his yogic slumber, who lay on the couch of Śeṣa, who was the source of origin of the lotus of the Cosmic Egg, who is called Kālarudra in view of his tamas quality, who is Kanakāṇḍaja (i.e. born of the golden Egg i.e. Brahmā) in view of his rajas quality and who is Viṣṇu the omnipresent lord bowed to by all Devas in his Sattva quality.[21] She worshipped the lord for ever mentally, physically and verbally. She wreathed the garland herself and offered them to the lord. She ground the scents, etc. into paste; offered incense and other articles; scrubbed and smeared the ground and cooked Havis all by herself. She was zealous and eager in doing all these things. The chaste lady continuously uttered the names Nārāyaṇa, Ananta, etc. With her innermost conscience devoted to him the pure queen worshipped Viṣṇu for ten thousand years with scents, flowers, etc.

13b-15. She always propitiated highly blessed devotees of Viṣṇu, devoid of all sins, by giving charitable gifts, and honouring them with riches and jewels. Once that blessed lady had concluded her fast on the Dvadaśī day and was lying asleep in

20. For detail, See *H.M.* pp. 288, 289.

21. The verse occurs in 1.1.22, 1.6.30. The same idea is expressed in the *Brahmāṇḍa Purāṇa* (*Prakriyā Pāda*. 4.6).

सत्त्वं विष्णू रजो ब्रह्मा तमो रुद्रः प्रजापतिः ।

front of lord Viṣṇu along with her husband. Then lord Nārāyaṇa, Puruṣottama spoke to her.

16-17. O gentle lady, O lustrous lady, tell me. What boon do you wish from me? On seeing the lord thus generous she said—"May my son be a Vaiṣṇava. May he be an Emperor of great refulgence, pure and engrossed in his duties."

Viṣṇu said, "So be it," and gave her a fruit.

18. On waking up she saw the fruit and mentioned everything to her husband. In great delight and with her mind directed towards the lord she ate the fruit.

19-20. Then, in due course of time, she gave birth to a son destined to make the family flourish. He was devoted to Vāsudeva. He maintained a good conduct. He was richly endowed with auspicious characteristics, and had curly hairs that resembled small wheels. On seeing the son born the father performed all holy rites.

21-22. The lord became well known in the world as Ambarīṣa. The glorious lord was crowned king when his father passed away. He entrusted the kingdom to the care of his ministers and became a sage. He performed a severe penance repeating the names of lord Nārāyaṇa for a thousand years.

23-27a. He meditated on lord Puruṣottama as follows:—He is stationed in the middle of the lotus of the cavity of his heart, coming there from the middle of the solar sphere. He has four arms holding the conch, discus, iron club and the lotus. He is as resplendent as pure gold. He is identical with Brahmā, Viṣṇu and Śiva. The lord is endowed with all ornaments and wears yellow robes. The lord has the scar Śrīvatsa on his chest. Thereupon, lord Viṣṇu, the soul of the universe, eulogised by all Devas, bowed to by the worlds, made Garuḍa resemble Airāvata of unimaginable splendour and rode on it. He came to the place of penance seated on it in the guise of Indra. He then spoke thus to the excellent king.

27b-30. "Welfare unto you. I am Indra. What boon shall I grant you? I am the lord of all the worlds. I have come down to help you."

Ambarīṣa said :

I have not meditated upon you while performing penance. Nor do I wish for anything given by you. O Indra, you will comfortably go back. My lord is Nārāyaṇa. I bow down to that lord of the universe. O Indra, go away. Do not do anything to distract my mind."

Thereupon, Lord Viṣṇu laughed and resumed his own form.

31-32. Viṣṇu the soul of everyone shone like another blue mountain, on Guruḍa. He had the sword, the bow Śārṅga, the iron club and the discus in his arms. He was eulogised by Devas and Gandharvas all round. The delighted king bowed to and eulogised the Guruḍa-bannered lord.

33-38. "O lord, O lord of the worlds, O my lord, be pleased. O Kṛṣṇa, O Viṣṇu, O lord of the Universe, bowed to by the worlds, you are the primordial lord; you have no beginning. You are the eternal Puruṣa; you are lord Viṣṇu the incomprehensible lord. You are Govinda, the lotus-eyed lord. You are born of the body of Maheśvara. A lotus is grown up from your umbilicus. You sojourn the skies.[22] You stride over the firmament; you are the Kapālin carrying the kavya[23] offerings. You are the wind-god conveying the havya[24] offerings. You are the primordial lord delighted in holy rites. You are the great Ātman stationed within the Ātman. O Govinda, I have resorted to you. O son of Devaki, be victorious. O lord. be victorious, O lord of the Universe, O lotus-eyed one, save me. I have no other goal but you. You alone are my refuge."

Sūta said:

Lord Viṣṇu then spoke to him:—"O king of good holy rites what is it that you have resolved to do? I shall give you everything. You are my devotee. I am always fond of devotion. Hence, I have come here to give you whatever you seek"

Ambarīṣa said :

39-42. O lord of the worlds, O excessively blissful one. There is this perpetual idea in my mind. Just as you are devoted to Bhava the great Ātman, the lord of Devas so also may I be perpetually devoted to you mentally, verbally and

22. khagamaḥ—khe hṛdayākāśe 'gamyate yogibhiḥ prāpyate iti khagamaḥ *ST*. one who is realized by the yogins in their hearts.

23-24. kavya and havya are the offerings made to the manes and Devas. The sacrificial fire wherein these offerings are made is called kavyavāha because it carries offerings to the manes as well as gods.

physically. O lord Viṣṇu, I shall be yours. I shall make the universe devoted to you and protect the earth. I shall propitiate the excellent Devas by performing sacrifices and worships. I shall protect the devotees of Viṣṇu and extirpate the enemies. I am afraid due to the distressful danger from worldly affairs. Hence, my mind dwells in you.

The lord said :

43-44. May it be as you please. This rare discus Sudarśana has been acquired by me through the grace of Rudra. It will continuously dispel the evil effects of curses of the sages and similar calamities. It will also destroy all enemies and ailments. After saying this the lord vanished.

Sūta said :

45-50. Then the king bowed down to the direction the lord had gone. He was extremely delighted. He entered his city Ayodhyā[25] and ruled from there. He employed brahmins and other castes in their respective duties. He was devoted to Viṣṇu. Delighted in his heart he protected the pious devotees of Viṣṇu. He performed hundreds of horse-sacrifices and Vājapeyas[26] and protected this earth surrounded by the seas. Viṣṇu stayed in every house. The chanting of the Vedas rose up from every house. So also the sound of names of Viṣṇu and the sound of sacrifices. While that leading king was ruling over the kingdom, the earth was free from famine; grass and plants grew in plenty. The subjects were devoid of ailments for ever. They were rid of all harassments.

51-52. Ambarīṣa of great refulgence protected the earth. As he remained thus, he had a lotus-eyed daughter renowned as Śrīmatī and endowed with all good attributes. She was as splendid as the divine Māyā. She attained the age when she should be given in marriage.

53. At that time the glorious sage Nārada and the highly intelligent Parvata[27] came to the kingdom of Ambarīṣa.

25. Ayodhyā—It is situated on the Sarayu river in Avadha near Faizabad, U.P.

26. Vājapeya—one of the seven forms of the Soma-sacrifice offered by kings or Brahmins aspiring to the highest position, and preceding the Rājasūya and the Bṛhaspati-sava.

27. Parvata—a sage, often associated with Nārada.

54. On seeing the two sages come Ambarīṣa of great refulgence bowed down and worshipped them.

55-56. On seeing that girl playing about like the lightning streak amidst clouds the saintly lord Nārada smilingly asked—"O king, who is this highly blessed girl comparable to the daughters of Devas. She is resplendent with auspicious signs. Tell me, O king, the most excellent one among virtuous persons.

The king said:

57. "O lord, this is my daughter Śrīmatī. The splendid girl has attained the age when she should be given in marriage. I am in search of a bridegroom.

58. On being told thus, O brahmins, the leading sage Nārada desired her. O excellent sages, the sage Parvata too loved her.

59. Nārada the righteous soul called the king secretly and said, "Give your daughter unto me."

60-64. The saintly lord Parvata too made the same request. Thereupon, the righteous king was frightened. He bowed down to both of them and said, "O Sirs, both of you woo my daughter. How can I do this? O Nārada of great intellect, O saintly lord Parvata, listen to what I say. If this splendid daughter of mine chooses one of you, I shall give him my daughter. Otherwise I am helpless." After saying "So be it" they said—"We shall come again tomorrow." The leading sages, who were devoted to Viṣṇu and who were the wisest of the wise went away delighted in their minds.

65. After going to the world of Viṣṇu Nārada the most excellent among sages bowed down to Viṣṇu and said:—

66. O lord, hear me. I shall tell you in secret. O lord of the worlds, obeisance to you.

67. Then lord Viṣṇu the soul of the universe smilingly said to the sage, "Say". The sage then said to him.

68. King Ambarīṣa is a glorious king who follows you. His daughter is a beautiful girl with large eyes and her name is Śrīmatī.

69-72. Desirous of marrying her I went to him. Now listen to my words. This glorious sage Parvata is your devotee of great austerities. He too desires her. O lord, the king Ambarīṣa of great refulgence said thus to us—"If this girl chooses one of you, endowed with handsome features I shall give her unto him."

As the king said thus I too said "So be it. O king, I will come to your abode tomorrow morning." So saying I came away. O lord of the universe, I have come to you and it behoves you to do what is pleasing to me.

73. O lord of the Universe, if you wish to do what is pleasing to me kindly manage it in such a way as to make Parvata's face appear like that of a monkey.

74. "So be it" said Viṣṇu the slayer of Madhu,[28] smilingly—"O gentle one, I shall do what is desired by you. Go back now."

75. When he was assured thus, the delighted sage bowed to Viṣṇu. Considering himself blessed he went to Ayodhyā.

76. When that excellent sage had gone Parvata the great sage was delighted. He bowed down to Viṣṇu and told him secretly.

77. After submitting his mission he said—O lord of the universe, please make the face of Nārada appear like that of the dark-coloured monkey Golāṅgūla.

78-80. On hearing that, lord Viṣṇu said—"I shall do what is desired by you. Hurry down to Ayodhyā. Let not Nārada know my understanding with you." Saying "Let it be so," he too went away.

On knowing that the two excellent sages had come, the king decorated Ayodhyā with flags and festoons. He embellished it with flowers and fried grains scattered about.

81. The portals of the houses were sprinkled with water. The bazaars and the highways were watered well. The city was fumigated with fragrant essences.

82. After decorating the city the king embellished the Assembly hall with splendid scents, incenses and jewels of diverse kinds.

83. It was rendered splendid by means of garlands and festoons. It was decorated with jewel-studded columns. Elegant

28. Madhu-sūdana—the destroyer of Madhu, an Asura, brother of Kaiṭabha. For the story, see *Mārkaṇḍeya*.

cushioned seats with exquisite coverings were placed all round.

84. After making these arrangements the leading king took the girl with him and entered the hall. She was richly bedecked in all ornaments. She appeared like Śrī with her large beautiful eyes.

85. Her waist was so slender that it could be measured with a single hand. She was smooth and glossy in five[29] of her limbs. Her face was remarkably splendid. Divinely resplendent like that Śrīmatī came into the hall surrounded by ladies.

86. The assembly hall of the king was richly elegant with choicest jewels and excellent gems of diverse kinds. The seats were arranged decently. Garlands and festoons were neatly tied. The elite of the society entered it and shone brilliantly.

87. The noble son of Brahmā, the saintly lord of great soul, the most excellent among the knowers of Brahman, the great sage Nārada well-versed in the threefold lore came there accompanied by Parvata.

88. On seeing that they had come, the king was in a great flutter of the mind. Offering them illustrious seats he worshipped both.

89. Both of them were great Siddhas and celestial sages. Both of them were excellent among those who were endowed with perfect knowledge. The noble souls, the excellent sages seated themselves and waited for the girl.

90. At the outset the king bowed down to both and then he addressed his splendid daughter, the renowned lady with eyes resembling the petals of a lotus.

91. O gentle lady, offer this garland to one of these two after bowing down to him duly, whosoever it may be, whom you mentally choose as your bridegroom.

92-96a. On being urged thus, the splendid-eyed bride took up the divine golden garland in her arms. Surrounded by the ladies in attendance she came to the place where those noble sages were sitting. On glancing at the excellent sages, Parvata and Nārada she saw that they had the faces of monkeys. Seeing the face of Golāṅgūla monkey the girl was a bit frightened and excited in her mind. She stood trembling like a plantain tree in a storm. The king then said to her—"O dear one,

29. pañca-snigdhām—delicate in five limbs.

what are you going to do? O splendid lady, offer the garland to any one of these two."

96b-103. The frightened girl said to her father—"These two are human apes. I do not see the excellent sages, either Nārada or Parvata. But in between them I see a handsome youngman less than sixteen years in age. He is richly bedecked in all ornaments. He resembles the Atasi[30] flower. He is elegant with long arms, large eyes and moon-like lustre.[31] His hips and neck are marked with lines. His eyes are large and reddish. He shines brilliantly with two remarkable eyebrows that by and large resemble a bent bow. Clear-cut threefold curly hairs are manifest in his umbilical region. The belly is splendidly manifest. He is clad in goldcoloured robes. His nails are raised up and resemble gems. The hands are shaped like lotuses. His face and eyes resemble lotuses. His nose is splendid. He is lotus-hearted and lotus-navelled. He is perfectly enveloped in glorious splendour. Looking at me he is smiling broadly with the rows of teeth resembling the buds of Kunda flowers. He is standing stretching his right hand towards me. The hairs on his head are splendid. It is him that I see. The king then spoke to her as she stood there trembling like the tender stem of the plantain tree with her mind all in a flutter "O dear one, what are you going to do?"

104. When this was spoken, sage Nārada who began to doubt, asked, "O girl, how many hands has he? Tell me precisely."

105-110. The bride with pure smiles said—"I see a pair of arms."

Parvata then asked her—"O splendid lady, what do you see on his chest? Tell me. What do you see in his hands?"

The bride then spoke to him, "I see a garland exquisite in its five-fold forms on his chest. In his hand I see the bow and the arrows."

On being replied to thus, the excellent sages looked at each other. They thought thus in their minds. "This is a deception of some one. The wielder of Māyā and the culprit is Viṣṇu himself. How can a newcomer make our face like this in the

30. atasī—flax, saṇa, Beṅgalā 'sun' used as hemp, crotolaria Juncea.

31. Defective reading.

manner of that of a Golāṅgūla monkey ?" So thought Nārada. Parvata too began to worry thus mentally:—"How is it that I have attained the form of a monkey ?"

111-116. Then the king bowed down to Nārada and Parvata and said—"What is this intellectual confusion that has been brought abo ut by both of you? Both of you, please be quiet as befitting those who seek the hand of a bride."

On being told thus, the excellent sages spoke to the king furiously. "It is you who cause this delusion, not we, by any means. Let this girl choose one of us. Let there be no delay."

Thereupon the young lady again bowed down to her favourite deity. On looking up she saw, as before, the handsome young man standing between them honourably attentive. He was bedecked in all ornaments and resembled the Atasī flower. His hands were long; his limbs supple and well-developed, his eyes extended as far as his ears. On seeing him she offered the garland unto him. Thereafter, the girl was never again seen by anybody.

117-119. A tumult arose : "What is this ?" said everyone in surprise: Viṣṇu has taken her away to his abode. This excellent lady Śrīmatī was born as a result of penances performed formerly for attaining him. She has now gone to Viṣṇu."

The two leading sages who had thus been hoodwinked[32] became extremely dejected. They hastened to the abode of Viṣṇu.

120. On seeing that they had come, lord Viṣṇu said to Śrīmatī:—"The excellent sages have come. Hide yourself here."

121. Saying "So be it", the gentle lady smilingly did so. Nārada bowed down in front of Viṣṇu and said to him.

122. "Indeed you have done what is pleasing to me and Parvata ! Certainly, O Viṣṇu, it is you who have abducted the bride.

123. With your intellect you have deluded us and cheated us, O excellent lord." On being told thus, lord Viṣṇu closed his ears with his hands and said:—"What is this being uttered by you two ?

124-126. Oh! is this emotion of love a course of conduct for sages ?"

32. dhikkṛtau—tiraskṛtau, i.e., rejected (by Śrīmatī).

On being told thus, the sage Nārada replied, whispering into his ear:—"How is it that my face resembled that of a Golāṅgūla monkey ?" The lord whispered back into his ear:—"O learned one, I have turned Parvata too into a monkey. It is for your own pleasure that your face was made to resemble that of a Golāṅgūla and not otherwise.

127. Parvata two spoke similarly and the lord replied to him in the same manner. Then Viṣṇu spoke within the hearing of both.

128-135. "I have done what is pleasing to you both. I can truthfully say so." Nārada, the righteous soul then said—A person armed with a bow stood between us. Who was it ? Did not he abduct her ?"

On hearing it, Viṣṇu spoke to the excellent sages:—"There are many excellent noble men wielding Māyā. I am always armed with my discus. I remain for ever with my four arms. O excellent sages, to be sure not having seen Śrīmatī there I have not desired her. Indeed, this is known to you both."

On being told thus, the sages became mentally delighted. They bowed down to the lord and said:—"O lord of the universe,what is your fault in this matter ? It is the wickedness of that king alone. He has wielded Māyā."

Having said this, Nārada and Parvata left that place. They went to Ambarīṣa and cursed him. Nārada and Parvata said, "Wherefore have we come here ? After inviting us why have you given your daughter to another person ? Why had you a recourse to deception ? Hence, darkness, sorrow will attack you.

136-137. For the same reason you will not know your ownself precisely."

When the curse was uttered thus, a mass of darkness rose up. Thereupon, the discus of Viṣṇu appeared instantly on behalf of the king. Frightened of the discus the terrible darkness rushed against the two sages.

138-144. Thereupon, the frightened great sages began to run with fear creeping up all their limbs. On seeing the discus and the inaccessibly terrible tamas closely behind them they hastened their steps saying "Alas ! We have acquired the bride !"

Distressed in their fright they ran as far as the Lokāloka[33] mountain. They shouted in their excess of fear—"Save us, Save us" to Viṣṇu. They went to the world of Viṣṇu and said:—"O Nārāyaṇa O lord of the universe, O Vāsudeva, O Hṛṣīkeśa, O Padmanābha, O Janārdana, save us, O lotus-eyed one. O Puruṣottama, you are our lord." Thereupon, the glorious lord Nārāyaṇa who cannot be properly thought of, the lord with the mark of Śrīvatsa scar,[34] stopped the discus as well as the Darkness with the desire to bless his devotees.

"Ambarīṣa is my devotee. So also are these excellent sages. I must do what is wholesome and beneficial to him as well as to them both now."

The excellent lord, the glorious lord Viṣṇu called them. Delighting them with his words lord Viṣṇu said—"Both of you listen to these words of mine.

145-149. The curse of the sages shall not be otherwise. Nor should the boon granted by me to the king for his protection. A glorious and virtuous king Daśaratha will be born[35] as the famous son of the great-grandson of the son of Ambarīṣa. I will be born as his eldest son Rāma. There my right hand will be Bharata. Śatrughna will be my left hand. This Śeṣa will be born as Lakṣmaṇa. There you come to me. Now you leave the king alone: you leave off the excellent sages also", so said Viṣṇu.

Tamas (darkness) who was addressed thus was destroyed instantaneously.

150-152. The discus that was warded off remained as before. The two excellent sages who were rid of their fear bowed down to Viṣṇu and came out with great dejection. They said to each other, "From now onwards till our death we shall never woo a girl." After taking this vow the sages became purely devoted to yoga and meditation. They remained celibates for ever.

33. Lokāloka—it is a fabulous belt of mountains bounding the outermost of the seven seas and dividing the visible world from the regions of darkness.

34. Śrīvatsa-lāñchanaḥ—Viṣṇu having curls of hair or a peculiar mark on his breast.

35. bhavati—bhaviṣyati. The present tense is used for the past tense to denote a near future. Cf. वर्तमानसामीप्ये वर्तमानवद्वा Pāṇini—*Aṣṭādhyāyī*.

153-159. After ruling over the earth king Ambarīṣa went to the world of Viṣṇu along with his attendants and kinsmen. In order to know Ambarīṣa and the two leading sages Rāma became an Īśvara unaware of his own Ātman after being born as the son of Daśaratha. Looking at Viṣṇu, the excellent sages Bhṛgu and others said:—"Māyā should not be practised against scholars. After a long time, Nārada and Parvata realised the activity of Viṣṇu and became devotees of Rudra.

Thus, everything has been mentioned to you, viz. the greatness of Ambarīṣa as well as the deceptive practice of Māyā of Viṣṇu.

The man who reads, listens to or narrates this tale shall eschew Māyā and attain the world of Rudra. This is holy and highly sacred. It has been recounted by the Vedas. One who reads this in the morning and evening will attain identity with Viṣṇu.

CHAPTER SIX

The origin and activities of Alakṣmī

The sages said:

1-7. O Lomaharṣaṇa, the Māyā of the intelligent Viṣṇu, the lord of Devas has been listened to. How did Jyeṣṭhā (deity of Misfortune) originate from Viṣṇu the lord of Devas. It behoves you to recount it to us factually.

Sūta said:

In order to delude the universe, the glorious lord Viṣṇu who has neither beginning nor end and who is the lord of the universe, created this twofold aspect in the universe. Viṣṇu created one set consisting of brahmins, Vedas, Vedic virtues and Padmā—Śrī. The lord of great refulgence made another set consisting of Jyeṣṭhā, Alakṣmī, the base men excluded from the Vedic sphere as well as sin. It was after creating Alakṣmī at the outset that Viṣṇu created Padmā afterwards. Therefore, Alakṣmī is Jyeṣṭhā (the elder), O excellent brahmins. At the outcome of nectar after the terribly potent poison, the inauspicious Jyeṣṭhā was born. So it is heard. Thereafter Śrī—Padmā was born who later become Viṣṇu's wife.

8-14. A brahminical sage Duḥsaha married the inauspicious Jyeṣṭhā after seeing her fully stabilised mentally. Accompanied by her the delighted sage wandered all round the world. O brahmins, wherever there was a loud chanting sound of the names of Viṣṇu and Śiva the great Ātman, wherever there was a loud sound of the Vedic mantras, wherever these was the column of smoke rising from sacrifices and wherever there were people with their limbs smeared with Bhasman, the deity of mislortune was extremely frightened. She used to close her ears and run about here and there. On seeing Jyeṣṭhā behaving thus, sage Duḥsaha became confused and bewildered. Accompanied by her he went to the forest. In the terrible forest he performed a great penance. Saying "I will not perform the penance" the girl Jyeṣṭhā roamed about from house to house. The pious sage, the leading yogin, devoted to the practice of yoga and perfect wisdom saw the noble Mārkaṇḍeya coming there.[36] Bowing down to the great sage, Duḥsaha said :

15-18. O saintly lord ! this wife of mine will not stand me by any means. O brahminical sage, what shall I do with this wife ? Where shall I enter and where shall I not enter ?

Mārkaṇḍeya said:

O Duḥsaha listen; this inauspicions lady is called everywhere thus—Akīrti (Ill-repute), Alakṣmī (misfortune), Atulā (unbalanced, incomparable) and Jyeṣṭhā (the eldest). By no means enter those places where noble souls, devoted to Viṣṇu, following the Vedic path, as well as the devotees of Rudra who have dusted and smeared their bodies with Bhasman are present always.

19-23. By no means enter the precincts of the parks, cowpens, wealth and abodes of those delighted Brahmins, Kṣatriyas, Vaiśyas and Śūdras who repeat the names and prayers of the lord as follows:—O Nārāyaṇa, O Hṛṣīkeśa, O Puṇḍarīkākṣa, O Mādhava, O Acyuta, O Ananta, O Govinda, O

36. tatra—mohakāle *ST*. when he was in delusion.

Vāsudeva, O Janārdana, O Rudra, O Rudra, obeisance, obeisance to Śiva; obeisance for ever to Śaṅkara the extremely auspicious one; O Mahādeva, obeisance to the consort of Umā, to the lord of gold; obeisance to you with golden arms; obeisance to the bull-emblemed lord; O Nṛsiṁha, O Vāmana, O incomprehensible one, O Mādhava.

24. Viṣṇu's discus which is very terrible with clusters of flames and which resembles a thousand suns dispels their inauspiciousness for ever.

25-26. Avoid that house wherein there is Svāhākāra[37] and Vaṣaṭkāra[38] and go elsewhere. Eschew from a distance the places where there is a loud chanting of the Sāman hymns and where people engrossed in repeating the Vedic hymns, devoted to their daily rituals and engaged in worshipping Vāsudeva are ever present.

27-30. Avoid the houses where the holy rite of Agnihotra is performed, where the Liṅga is worshipped and where the idols of Vāsudeva and Caṇḍika are present. Avoid persons devoid of all sins and move away from them. Avoid persons who worship Maheśvara by means of Nitya[39] (obligatory) and Naimittika[40] (conditional) yajñas, O Duḥsaha and go elsewhere along with this lady; you must eschew those persons by whom brahmins well-versed in Śrutis, cows, preceptors, guests and the devotees of Rudra are always worshipped.

Duḥsaha said:

O excellent sage, mention to me those places where I can enter without fear at your instance.

Mārkaṇḍeya said :

31-37. Devoid of fear and accompanied by your wife you shall enter the house where husband and wife are at logger heads and where brahmins well-versed in the Vedic lore as well as cows, preceptors and guests are never present. Without

37. svāhākāra—an exclamation used in offering oblations to the gods (with dat.); "Indrāya svāhā, Agnaye svāhā."

38. Vaṣaṭkāra—an exclamation used in offering oblations to the gods, (with dat. of the deity); Indrāya vaṣaṭ, Agnaye vaṣaṭ.

39-40. nitya-naimittika—obligatory and casual (sacrificial rites).

the least tinge of fear enter that place where Rudra the lord of Devas, Mahādeva the lord of the three worlds is despised. O dear one, accompanied by your wife, enter the houses of the following :—Where there is no devotion to Vāsudeva; where Sadāśiva is not present; Japa, Homa, etc. are not performed; Bhasman is not kept in the house; where there is no worship of Rudra on ceremonious occasions and particularly on Caturdaśī (fourteenth) and Aṣṭamī (eighth) days of the dark halves; where people are devoid of Bhasman during the Sandhyās (at dawn and dusk); where they do not worship Mahādeva on Caturdaśī (fourteenth) days; where they are devoid of the names of Viṣṇu; where they associate with wicked men. Accompanied by your wife you shall enter the houses of even those brahmins who are deluded and wicked and who do not repeat thus—"Obeisance to Kṛṣṇa, to Śiva, to Śarva, to Parameṣṭhin".

38. Accompanied by your wife you shall enter those places where there is no loud chanting of the Vedic mantras, where there is no worship of preceptors and where the people are devoid of rites relating to their ancestors.

39. Devoid of fear and accompanied by this lady, always enter the house where every night there is mutual quarrel among the inmates.

40. Fearlessly enter that place where there is no worship of Liṅga, where men do not perform japa and where devotion to Rudra is censured.

41. In the company of your wife enter that house where there is no guest well-versed in the Vedic lore, where there is no preceptor and where there is no Vaiṣṇava nor cows present.

42. With your wife, you delightedly enter that place where people eat foodstuffs without giving anything to children who keep on watching the same.

43. Always enter that place where people do not worship Mahādeva or Vāsudeva nor perform sacrifices duly.

44. Enter that house or realm where people are engaged in sinful activities, are deluded, have no mutual mercy and remain lethargic.

45. Approach that house where the housewife never keeps

secret[41] and destroys domestic felicity and is never worthy of praise. Always stay there with a delighted mind.

46-51. Accompanied by your wife enter that place where there are thorny trees, where there is the winding creeper of Niṣpāva[42] and where there is Brahmavṛkṣa.[43] If the following trees grow in the houses enter them accompanied by your wife Agastya[44] tree, Arka[45] plant, Bandhujīva,[46] Karavīra[47] in particular, Nandyāvarta[48], Mallikā,[49] the creeping plant Kanyā[49a] Drohi[50] Jaṭī,[51] the black[52] plantain[53] trees, Tāla,[54] Tamāla,[55] Bhalāta,[56] Tintiḍīkhaṇḍa,[57] Kadamba,[58] Khadira,[59] Nyagrodha,[60] Aśvattha,[61] Cūta,[62] Udumbara[63] and Panasa.[64] If there is a

41. prākārāgāravidhvaṁsā—or one who does not preserve the sanctity of the house, i.e. one who wanders at will, a characterless woman.

42. Niṣpāva-vallarī—known as Pāvaṭā *ST*.

43. Brahma-vṛkṣa—pālāśa. Butea Frondosa.

44. Agastya—Agasti Grandiflora.

45. Arka—Calotropis Gigantea, the larger leaves are used for sacrificial ceremonies.

46. Bandhujīva—known as putrajīva.

47. Karavīra—Oleander, a species of soma.

48. Nandyāvarta—known as Tagara.

49. Mallikā—Jasminum zambac.

49a. Kanyā—known as Aparājitā; Vallī known as Ajamodā. ST. takes these as two different herbs.

50. Drohi—a specie of Neema tree.

51. Jaṭi—known as Jaṭāmāṁsī.

52. Bahulā—the Indigo plant.

53. Kadalī—the plantain tree.

54. Tāla—the palmyra Palm, the mod. Tāl. Fans are made from its large fan-like leaves.

55. Tamāla—It grows in the mountainous districts in India.

56. Bhallāta or Bhallātaka—the nut tree. Beng. Bhel. It grows in the mountainous parts of India, with large particles of small greenish yellow flowers.

57. Tintiḍi—the Tamarind tree.

58. Kadamba—a tree having orange-coloured fragrant blossoms. Nauclea Cadamba.

59. Khadira—Acacia Catechu, mod. Khair or Khayar.

60. Nyagrodha—the Baniyan Ficus Indica. It belongs to the Kṣīra-Vṛkṣas. Its fibres descend from its branches to the earth and there take rool and form new stems.

61. Aśvattha—the holy fig tree, Ficus, Religiosa.

62. Cūta – the mango tree.

63. Udumbara—the tree Ficus Glomeratā.

64. Panasa—the jack tree, mod. Kanthāl.

Nimba[65] tree in any park or house housing crows, enter that in the company of your wife. If there is a Daṇḍinī[66] or a Muṇḍinī[66a] enter that place along with your wife.

52-56. Accompanied by your wife enter that house where there is a single maid-servant, three cows, five buffaloes, six horses or seven elephants. With your wife enter the house of that person whose household deity is Kālī, Ḍākinī,[67] of the form of a ghost[68] or Kṣetrapāla (guardian of the holy centre). Freely enter the house wherein there is the idol of a Buddhist mendicant[69] (a buddhist anchorite)[70] or the statue of Buddha.[71] That house where the tongues of the inmates do not utter the name of Viṣṇu when going to bed, or taking up a seat, or moving about in the course of their activities such as taking food etc., is indeed yours. Enter that house along with your wife.

57-61. Together with your wife enter that place where there are persons engaged in heretic activities, people excluded from the sacred rites laid down in the Vedas and Smṛtis, persons devoid of devotion to Viṣṇu, persons who censure Mahādeva, atheists and knaves. Accompanied by your wife enter the abode of the persons who do not believe in the superiority of the Pināka-bearing lord and who remember him only as an ordinary deity. It is only the wicked who do not say that Brahmā, Viṣṇu and Indra the ruler of Devas are all born by the grace of Rudra. Foolish persons of confounded mind would say that the glow-worm and the sun are on a par. They would say that Brahmā, Viṣṇu and Indra are equal to lord Śiva. Even if their houses are full and flourishing, enter them without fear and enjoy yourself along with this lady.

65. Nimba—the Neemb tree. Azadirachta Indica (its fruit is very bitter in taste).

66-66a. daṇḍinī muṇḍinī—this is not clear. It may refer to an image of staff-handed and bald Śiva considered to be inauspicious.

67. ḍākinī—an image of a female imp. attending Kālī (feeding on human flesh).

68. pretarūpā i.e. śākinī—an image of a female attendant on Durgā, supposed to be a demoness.

69. bhikṣu bimbam—an image of a religious mendicant who subsists entirely on alms.

70. Kṣapaṇakam (bimbam)—an image of a religious mendicant who wears no garment.

71. Bauddham bimb am—an image of Buddha.

62-65. Enter the abode of those stupid persons of deluded minds who eat cooked rice by themselves and who are devoid of ablution and other auspicious rites. Enter their houses. Enter the abode of that woman who falls off from the ideal of cleanliness, who is devoid of purificatory rites of the body and who is continuously engaged in eating all kinds of foodstuff. Enter the houses of men who have dirty faces, who wear dirty clothes; whose teeth are full of dirt though they are householders; who do not wash their feet; who lie down and who take their food at dusk.

66b-68. Enter the abodes of men who are engaged in gluttony; who are addicted to too much of drinking; who are foolishly engrossed in gambling and arguing. Enter the houses of those who misappropriate the wealth of brahmins; who perform sacrifices on behalf of undeserving persons; who partake of the cooked rice served by Śūdras; who are addicted to drinking; who are sinners and who relish flesh-eating and who are enamoured of other men's wives.

69b-75. Enter the houses of those who indulge in sexual intercourse by day; who are not engaged in worship on festival days and who enjoy sexual union at dusk In the company of your wife, enter the houses of those who cohabit through the anus like a dog or other animals or those who indulge in sexual intercourse under water. Enter the houses of those who carnally approach a woman in her menses, or a Cāṇḍāla woman or a virgin. Enter the houses of those who indulge in sexual intercourse in a cowpen. Of what use is much talk? Enter the houses of those who are excluded from their daily duties or those who are bereft of devotion to Rudra. Along with your wife enter the houses of those who smear their penis with powdered horns,[72] petty or divine medicinal herbs and then cohabit with women causing the heat of the vaginal passage.

Sūta said :

After saying this, the glorious brahmin sage resembling Brahmā wiped his eyes and vanished there itself. Duḥsaha also went to the above-mentioned places.

72. **śṛṅgaiḥ—kṛtrima-puṁścihnaiḥ *ST*. artificial male organs.**

76. In the company of his wife the leading sage went particularly to the abodes of those engaged in despising Viṣṇu, the lord of Devas.

This is the deity remembered as Jyeṣṭhā.

77-78. Once Duḥsaha said to her thus:—"You stay here in this hermitage on the banks of the lake. I will be entering the Nether worlds. After finding out a spot for our residence I will return to you again." On being told thus, she said:

79-81. "O blessed one, what shall I eat? Who will give oblation unto me?"

On being asked thus the sage said : "Do not enter the houses of those women who worship you with oblations, flowers and incense."

After saying this, he entered the nether worlds through a crevasse. Even now the sage remains submerged under the watery bed. The deity of inauspiciousness remains outside villages and mountains perpetually.

82. Casually, Viṣṇu, the lord of the chiefs of Devas, the overlord of the three worlds, was seen by her along with Lakṣmī. Alakṣmī said to Janārdana :

83. "O lord of long brawny arms, my husband has gone unto the crevasse after abandoning me. O lord of the universe, I am devoid of a leader and support. Give unto me the means of sustenance. Obeisance be to thee."

Sūta said :

84. Lord Viṣṇu, the lord of Devas, the husband of Lakṣmī, the slayer of Madhu, laughed and said to her.

Lord Viṣṇu said :

85-87. "Yours indeed is the wealth of those persons who censure Rudra the sinless deity, Śarva, Nīlalohita, Śaṅkara; Ambā the daughter of the Himavān, the mother of all the worlds and my devotees. Even if my devotees censure Mahādeva and worship me they are stupid and unfortunate. Their wealth belongs to you. It is at his behest and due to his grace that Brahmā and I exist.

88-92. Those who cause my enmity after despising my devotees are not my devotees even if they worship me. They are arrogant persons who seem to be my devotees. Yours indeed is their wealth, abode, field and meritorious deeds such as worship and digging wells and the like."

Sūta said :

After saying thus, Viṣṇu left Alakṣmī and went away with Lakṣmī. Lord Viṣṇu then performed the Japa of Rudra mantra for the sake of realizing the destruction of Alakṣmī.

Hence, O leading sage, perpetual oblation shall definitely be offered to her by the devotees of Viṣṇu by all means. O brahmins, she should always be worshipped by women by means of oblations of different kinds.

He who reads, listens to or recounts this narrative of Alakṣmī to excellent brahmins, will become sinless and fortunate. He is sure to attain salvation.

CHAPTER SEVEN

The twelve-syllabled Mantra

The sages said :

1-2. By repeating which mantra is the creature liberated from worldly fears ? How does he become free from sins and attain salvation ? By what Japa does he eschew Alakṣmī ? How does a man become the abode of Lakṣmī (good fortune) ? O Sūta, it behoves you to recount this.

Sūta said :

3. For the benefit of all the worlds I shall mention succinctly everything that had been formerly mentioned by Brahmā to the noble-souled Vasiṣṭha.

4-8. May all listen to my words after bowing down to Viṣṇu who is the lord of Devas, who is unborn, who is all-pervading, who is the eternal Kṛṣṇa, Acyuta, who dispels all sins, who is pure, who bestows liberation on the expounders of

Brahman.[73] He who is a scholar, he who performs meritorious deeds shall always repeat the names of Nārāyaṇa after making obeisance to him mentally, verbally and physically. One shall remember lord Viṣṇu while sleeping, walking, taking food, standing, keeping awake, opening or closing the eyes. O brahmins, he shall remember the eternal lord repeating the words—Namo Nārāyaṇāya (Obeisance to Nārāyaṇa). He who inspires edibles, beverages and lambatives by reciting the mantra "Namo Nārāyaṇāya" touches it and then partakes of it, attains the greatest salvation.

9-14. He gets rid of all sins and attains the goal of the good. The deity who is mentioned by me as Alakṣmī, the wife of Duḥsaha, undoubtedly departs, on hearing the word "Nārāyaṇa". O sages of good holy rites, Lakṣmī, who is the beloved wife of Viṣṇu, Kṛṣṇa the lord of Devas, resides in his body, house, abode and field. After looking up all the sacred texts, after pondering over them again and again this is the outcome that Nārāyaṇa should always be meditated upon. Of what avail are the multifarious mantras unto him, of what avail are the numerous holy rites unto him? The mantra "Namo Nārāyaṇāya" (obeisance to Nārāyaṇa) is the means for achieving all objects. Hence, one shall repeat the mantra "Namo Nārāyaṇāya" on all occasions. O leading brahmins, he goes to the world of Viṣṇu along with his kinsmen. O excellent sages, listen to another mantra of the lord of Devas.

15-16a. This mantra had been learned and practised by me formerly. It is the means of achieving the essence of the Vedas. It is an ancient one consisting of twelve syllables and twelve forms. I shall tell you, in brief, the greatness of the same.

16b-18. There was a certain brahmin of great intellect. He performed penance and with very great difficulty procreated a son. In due course he performed all consecratory rites on his behalf. At the proper time he invested him with the sacred thread. He taught him but the son did not utter

73. mokṣadam brahma-vādinām *ST*. that which renders salvation to those who know the Vedas. This excludes the possibility of salvation for those not conversant with the Vedas.

anything[74]. His tongue did not throb at all. The excellent brahmin became dejected.

19-20. But Aitareya (the son of brahmin) invariably uttered the name Vāsudeva.[75] His father married another lady duly and procreated many sons who learned the Vedas and became richly endowed with learning. They were honoured by everyone.

21-23. Aitareya's mother became excessively sad and dejected. She said :—"Richly accomplished sons who have mastered the Vedas and ancillary subjects and who are honoured and worshipped by brahmins delight their mother. But you a shapeless[76] son are born to me, a women devoid of good luck. My death would have been far better. On being told thus, he (Aitareya) went out to the sacrificial hall.

24. When he entered there the mantras did not come out from the mouth of the brahmins. As long as Aitareya stayed there the brahmins continued to be deluded.

25-27. But when Aitareya uttered Vāsudeva, their voices came out. Those brahmins bowed down and worshipped Aitareya. Then the yajña continued and Aitareya concluded it by means of wealth and other things. In the end with great concentration he repeated the Vedas along with their ancillaries in the Vidatha Assembly of priests. O brahmins, Brahmā and other brahmins eulogised him.

28-33. Siddhas and Cāraṇas moving about in the firmament showered flowers. O excellent brahmins, after concluding the yajña thus, Aitareya worshipped his mother and went to the abode of Viṣṇu. Thus, the greatness of the twelve-syllabled mantra has been recounted wholly. It destroys the great sins of those who read and listen to this. The man who repeats this unchanging twelve-syllabled mantra continuously attains the divine, incomparable great region of Viṣṇu even if he follows a sinful conduct. He who is interested in the twelve-syllabled mantra surely attains the greatest abode. There is

74. Jihvā na spandate—his son would not utter any other syllable than 'Vāsudeva' the name of Śrīkṛṣṇa.

75. Vāsudeva i.e. either the complete twelve-syllabled mantra "Oṁ namo bhagavate Vāsudevāya" or merely Vāsudeva, a part of this mantra.

76. nirākṛtiḥ i.e. having no personality or distinctive characteristics.

no doubt, O sages of good holy rites, that noble-souled men maintaining their own holy rites and devotedly following Vāsudeva attain the divine abode.

CHAPTER EIGHT

The eight-syllabled Mantra

Sūta said :

1-7. O excellent brahmins, the eight-syllabled[77] mantra viz. "Oṁ namo Nārāyaṇāya" and the twelve-syllabled[78] mantra, viz. "Oṁ namo Bhagavate Vāsudevāya" are the greatest mantras of the great Ātman. O brahmins, the six-syllabled[79] mantra, viz. "Oṁ namaḥ Śivāya" connotes the entire meaning of all the Vedic passages. This mantra is the means of achieving all objects. The divine five-syllabled mantra "Śivatarāya" is very auspicious. So also is the mantra "mayaskarāya" [(obeisance) to one who brings about excellence], The mantra of seven syllables, viz. "Namaste Śaṅkarāya" is the mantra of Rudra, the Puruṣa (in conjunction with) Pradhāna. O excellent brahmins, Brahmā, lord Viṣṇu, Devas including Indra and the sages worship Śaṅkara, the lord of the chiefs of Devas with these mantras. They worship Śiva, the source of origin of Brahmā, and the consort of Umā, the lord of Devas (with these mantras). They say continuously namaḥ Śivāya, namaste Śaṅkarāya, mayaskarāya, Rudrāya and Śivatarāya. By repeating these (mantras) a brahmin is instantaneously liberated from the sins of brahmin-slaughter, etc.

8-12. Formerly, in the Meghavāhana kalpa of Brahmā[80] the great Ātman, in the third manvantara, in the Tretā yuga

77. aṣṭākṣaraḥ—the eight-syllabled mantra : Oṁ namo Nārāyaṇāya.

78. dvādaśākṣaraḥ—the twelve-syllabled mantra : Oṁ namo bhagavate Vāsudevāya.

79. ṣaḍakṣaraḥ—the six-syllabled mantra : Oṁ namaś Śivāya.

80. brahmaṇaḥ—paramātmanaḥ śivasya *ST*. of the transcendental lord Śiva.

there was a certain powerful brahmin Dhundhumūka. That kalpa is called Meghavāhana because Viṣṇu the lord of Devas assumed the form of a cloud and performed penance in propitiation of Mahādeva, the hide-clad lord, Rudra. Thanks to his high reverence for Rudra, he performed penance leaving off the intake and expiration of even breath. He was overwhelmed and dejected due to too much of burden. He submitted his problem to the blue-necked lord. The lotus-eyed lord performed penance and as a result acquired wonderful strength from Śaṅkara the great Ātman.

13-14. In that Meghavāhana kalpa, due to the curse of a sage the son of Dhundhumūka became wicked. Formerly, Dhundhumūka had been deluded by his wife. He was too much attracted by her. A foetus was procreated by him in her with his mind drawn by lust.

15. It was on the Amāvasyā day, during the day time in the course of Rudra muhūrta[81] that his pregnant wife was enjoyed by him.

16-20. Her name was Viśalyā. With great strain, she gave birth to a son, O excellent sages, in Rudra muhūrta aspected by Saturn. He became an unlucky omen unto his father and mother as well as unto himself. The excellent sages Mitra and Varuṇa,[82] O brahmins, said to Dhundhumūka in secret that he was a wicked son. Vasiṣṭha said—"Although he is base and wicked, this son of yours will be liberated from sins by the prowess of Bṛhaspati (Jupiter). O excellent brahmins, Dhundhumūka became dejected on seeing the son in such a plight. He himself performed the postnatal and other rites for him. Thereafter, he taught him the Vedas.

21. O sages of good holy rites, everything was perfectly learnt by the son of Dhundhumūka. His marriage was performed and he became interested in serving his father.

22-23. O excellent sages, in the height of his arrogance this son of Dhundhumūka sought a Śūdra woman and enjoyed her like his wife by day and by night sitting with her in the same

81. rudra-daivate—presided over by Rudra. Each muhūrta has a presiding deity.

82. Mitrāvaruṇa-nāmānau—in this context Mitra and Varuṇa refer to certain sooth-sayers.

seat and lying with her in the same bed. The base brahmin the son of Dhundhumūka, of wicked intellect, eschewed the great path of virtue.

24-30. Wine was drunk by him along with her for the excitement of his lust. But, O excellent brahmins, for some vague reason that inauspicious Śūdra woman was killed by that sinner. Thereupon his father, mother and the legal wife of the wicked son of Dhundhumūka were killed by her brothers. O sages of good holy rites, those brothers-in-law were also killed by the king. Thus her and his families were destroyed in an instant. The son of Dhundhumūka went here and there in the course of his sporting activities. Somehow, he saw an excellent sage engaged repeating Rudra's names. At the outset he obtained the Pāśupata mantra of lord Maheśvara. After attaining the five-syllabled mantra and the six-syllabled mantra he repeated them a hundred thousand times severally. He performed the divine holy rite in accordance with the injunctions for a period of twelve months. In the course of that kalpa he passed away and was welcomed by Yama.

31-36. O sages of good holy rites, his mother, father, brothers-in-law, and the fortunate wife were redeemed. The chaste lady remained smiling. Along with them he got into an aerial chariot. He was eulogised by Devas including Indra. He attained the chieftancy of the Gaṇas and became a favourite of Rudra. Hence, merit is increased ten million times due to the eight-syllabled and twelve-syllabled mantras. No doubt need be entertained in this respect. Hence, he who continuously repeats these mantras in accordance with the injunctions laid down before[83] and in combination with the mantra of Śakti attains the greatest goal. This excellent story has thus been entirely mentioned to you. He who reads, listens or recounts it to excellent brahmins goes to the world of Brahmā.

83. prāguktena—here the reference is to the eightyfifth chapter, Part I.

CHAPTER NINE

The holy rite of Pāśupata

The sages said :

1-3. O Sūta, the divine and auspicious holy rite of Paśupati had been performed formerly by Devas. It had been performed by Brahmā himself and by Kṛṣṇa of unimpaired activity. Similarly, it was performed by the fallen brahmin, the son of Dhundhumūka. How could they attain salvation after performing the Pāśupata rite ? How is lord Pasupati propitiated ? It behoves you to recount this to us. We are very much eager to hear it.

Sūta said :

4-10a. Formerly, the son of Brahmā[84] of great renown was liberated from the curse of Rudra the lord of Devas. He came here from the Desert-land.[85] Eschewing the physical body of a camel[86] at the bidding of Brahmā and by the grace of Rudra, O excellent sages, he went to Nandin the son of Śilāda and bowed to him in accordance with the injunctions. On the ridge of Meru, the excellent sage listened to the discourse on the excellent virtue. After bowing to Nandin, he again and again asked him about the holy rite pertaining to Maheśvara. How is lord Paśupati propitiated ? It behoves you to recount everything to us. Then he said everything. The saintly lord Kṛṣṇa Dvaipāyana Vyāsa, heard everything from Sanatkumāra. After hearing it from Vyāsa, I relate it to you. May all listen to my words after bowing to Maheśvara.

Sanatkumāra said :

How is lord Paśupati ? Who are Paśus ? By what bonds are they bound ? How are they liberated ?

84. brahmaputraḥ—son of Brahmā, Sanatkumāra.
85. Maru-deśāt—from the desert country, not specified.
86. uṣṭra-deham—his body as camel.

Śailādi said:

10b-15a. O Sanatkumāra, I shall recount everything precisely to you, the tranquil devotee of Rudra and of auspicious mind.

All creatures from Brahmā to the immovables are Paśus of the intelligent lord. They are subject to worldly existence. Since he is their lord, he is known as Paśupati. The unchanging, all-pervading Parameśvara, who is the creator and who has neither a beginning nor an end binds souls by means of Māyā. He alone is their saviour on being served by the path of perfect knowledge.[87] No other saviour of those who are bound by the bonds of Ignorance is sought after or found.

15b-19. The twentyfour principles are the bonds of Parameṣṭhin. Śiva alone binds Paśus by means of these twentyfour bonds.[88] On being worshipped by Jīvas (individual souls) Śiva alone releases them from the bonds. The same lord on being served, releases them from the bondages constituted by the ten sense-organs that originate from the Inner mind. The lord releases the souls from the bonds of tanmātras. The lord binds those who are enamoured of worldly pleasures by means of bonds constituted by the objects of senses. By service unto Paramesvara, the souls become devotees immediately. The root "bhaj" means service.

20 22. Hence, the idea of greatest service is indicated by the word Bhakti. After binding the Individual souls, from Brahmā to the blade of grass, by means of the three-fold bonds of the form of Guṇas, Maheśvara himself causes the effect. On being worshipped by the Paśus by the steady path of devotion he releases them instantaneously. Serving by means of words, mind and body is called Bhakti. It is competent to snap all bonds through the effects in view of its being the cause.

23-27. They know the following as mental service:—viz., pondering upon the attributes of Śiva such as "He is truthful" "He is all-pervasive" etc., and the thought about his assumpion

87. jñāna-yoga—yoga of Knowledge. Cf. "jñānād eva Kaivalyam" —cited in *ST*.

88. Twenty-four tattvas (vide I. 28. 7-9; II. 15. 24, 25) are the noose that binds the individual soul (jīva).

of forms.[89] Bold self-possessed persons know that the repetition of Praṇava, etc. is the verbal service. The Prāṇāyāma, etc. are mentioned by good men as the physical service. Thus is the bondage of all embodied beings by means of the bonds of merit and sin. Lord Śiva, Parameśvara alone is the person who releases them. The twentyfour principles are mentioned as the activities and attributes of Māyā. They are called sensual objects. Through the bondage they bind the individual soul. The embodied souls who are tied by them are liberated only through devotion to Śiva.

28. By means of the fivefold bonds called Kleśas,[90] Śaṅkara binds the Paśus. On being served well by means of devotion, he alone is their redeemer.

29. O foremost ones among the biped beings, the five Kleśas (distresses) that have become bonds are Avidyā. (ignorance) Asmitā (egotism), Rāga (lust), Dveṣa (hatred) and Abhiniveśa (instinctive clinging to the worldly enjoyments).

30. Scholars call Avidyā that is stationed in five-fold[91] forms by the names Tamas, Moha, Mahāmoha, Tāmisra and Andhatāmisra.

31. O leading sages, the glorious Śiva liberates all those jīvas from Avidyā. There is no other redeemer.

32-33. Those who are devoted to yogic practices call Avidyā as Tamas (darkness); Asmitā as Moha (delusion); Rāga (lust) as Mahāmoha (great delusion); Dveṣa (hatred) as Tāmisra (darkness); Abhiniveśa and Mithyā jñāna (misconception) as Andhatāmisra (blinding darkness).

34. There are eight[92] types of Tamas. Moha is also eight-

89. Exercising supremacy over Viṣṇu who is the lord of Māyā (delusion), devotion is competent to remove all effects caused by Delusion.

90. pañca kleśāḥ. For detail, see below v-29 ff.; also Patañjali: 'अविद्याऽस्मितारागद्वेषाभिनिवेशाः पञ्च क्लेशाः—*Yogasūtra*.

91. fivefold avidyā. The use of the term avidyā for kleśa is confusing. Yaugic philosophers have used avidyā as synonymous with Kleśa. In fact, avidyā is one of the five Kleśas, identical with tamas and classified into eight categories.

92. tamas=avidyā. It is eightfold : (i) unmanifest Prakṛti, (avyakta), (ii) intellect (mahat), (iii) ego (ahaṁkāra), and five subtle elements (pañca tanmātrās).

fold.[93] The different divisions of Mahāmoha are ten[94] in number.

35. The wise have said that Tāmisra and Andhatāmisra have eighteen[95-96] subdivisions.

36-38. The relationship[97] of lord Śiva with Avidyā cannot be one that is past or one that is yet to come. Nor can it be ever due to hatred, as he is immanent. There cannot be any relationship with Abhiniveśa (instinctive desire to cling to worldly pleasures) for the lord who is beyond the pale of Māyā, and who is worthy of being resorted to, and who is the greatest Ātman.

39. In all the three periods of time Śiva who is beyond Avidyā cannot have kinsmanship with Māyā by means of activities, be they efficient or inefficient.

40. There cannot be contact with the Māyā of Śiva the bestower of auspiciousness in all the three periods of time through the development of actions.

41. Śiva who is the greatest being of the nature of enlightenment and bliss is incapable of being affected by pleasures and sorrows that perish and continue to be present in the three periods of time.

42. Mahādeva, the self-born lord of intellect, is unafflicted by fates and fortunes present in the three periods of time.

43. The lord who is the slayer of the god of Death is untouched by the impressions of rites that are present in the three units of time. He is also unaffected by the impressions of enjoyment.

44. Lord Parameśvara is the greatest of the special Male beings. He is not connected with sentient and insentient beings. He is beyond the entire universe.

93. moha=asmitā. It is eightfold : it consists of eight powers of supremacy, animā, etc.

94. mahāmoha=rāga. It is tenfold ; Five subtle elements are divided into divya (divine) and adivya (non-divine).

95. tāmisra=dveṣa. It is eighteenfold. Herein tenfold mahāmoha is added to the eightfold siddhis.

96. andhatāmisra=abhiniveśa (bhaya). It is eighteenfold. It includes five divine (divya) and five non-divine (adivya) tanmātrās along with eightfold siddhis.

97. avidyayā sambandho na. Lord Śiva has no relation with ignorance. *ST.* explains aṅganivāsinaḥ as sarvāntar-yāmirūpiṇaḥ--all-pervading.

45. Perfect knowledge and excellences are seen in the world as one excelling the other. Learned men say that Śiva is the most auspicious one excelling all.

46. He alone was the primordial expounder of the scriptural lore to the Brahmās born during the subsidiary creations[98] and who are confined and limited by time.

47. He is the preceptor of all preceptors who are confined and limited by time. He is devoid of all limitations of time. He is the lord of all.

48. This kinsmanship is without a beginning. He is beyond perfect knowledge and excellence. He is naturally perfectly pure.

49-50. Since he has no purpose of his own, the real purpose of all the activities of Parameśvara is blessing others. Praṇava is the word that expresses Śiva, the great Ātman. The word Praṇava is superior to the word Śiva, Rudra, etc.

51-52. Undoubtedly that perfection shall become accessible—the same perfection as is obtained when people repeat Praṇava even when they repeat the names of and meditate upon him who is expressed by the Praṇava syllable. By virtue of his compassion towards all, the great Pāśupata yoga, the basic tenet of perfect knowledge, has been mentioned strenuously by the lord of Devas.

53-54. Yājñavalkya said: O Gārgī, it is the supreme being that the non-yogins[99] call gross but, in fact, that is eternal and wonderful lord; one that is not long, not red, that has no head that has no setting, hence, that has a lasting taste,[100] that has no contact, no smell, no juice, no eyes, no ears, neither speech nor mind,[101] no brilliance, no proof [or magnitude], no (worldly) happiness, no name, no race, no death, no age, no ailment;

98. Cf. yo brahmāṇaṁ vidadhāti pūrvam—cited in *ST*.

99. *ST*. construes—Gārgi, ayoginaḥ yadakṣaraṁ sthūlam abhivadanti (tad brahma), the imperishable Brahma which the non-yogins call gross that Brahma is in fact......

100. punārasam—nityānandarasarūpam *ST*., comprised of the eternal flavour of joy. Cf. 'raso vai saḥ'—cited in *ST*.

101. avāṅmanaḥ. Cf. yato vāco nivartante aprāpya manasā saha TA 8.4.1; 9.1; Tu. 2.4.1; 9.1.

that is nectarine, that is expressed by the word Om, that is immortal, that has neither a predecessor nor a successor, that is endless and non-external. It eats something. It does not eat anything (?) One shall know the great lord Paśupati by the Pāśupata yoga. It is by this that there is the most excellent opportunity to realize the lord.

55. Make the lamp of Oṁkāra and seek the lord of the house who is subtle and who is stationed in the beginning and within. Restrain the most powerful organic wind that stays at the door [i.e. the pores] of the body and the leader of the sense-organs (i.e. mind). For what reason do you nurture fear by means of a network of words ? No fear is seen at all. See Śiva stationed in the body. Why do you wander amongst the network of scriptural texts, that is but darkness ?

56. After understanding this perfectly through the help of scholars after splitting the asamarasa (i.e. the state where things exist in unequalled proportions) into five[102] one shall resort to fearlessness in the Ātman. This has been mentioned by Śiva unto the sages.

CHAPTER TEN

The greatness of the consort of Umā

Sanatkumāra said:

1. O lord Nandikeśvara, O devotee of Bhava of great intelligence, recount to me once again, the greatness of the consort of Umā.

Śailādi said:

2. O Sanakumāra, I shall briefly mention to you the greatness of Maheśa, Bhava, Parameṣṭhin.

3-6. He has no binding attachment with Prakṛti, cosmic intellect, cosmic ego, mind, will, ears, skin, eyes, tongue, nose,

102. pañcadhā kṛtvā—*ST*. disjoins as pañcadhā akṛtvā and explains as 'pañcakośarūpam akṛtvā, not dividing it into five sheaths.

foot, hand, speech, the organ of generation or the five subtle elements. As he is eternally pure by nature he is eternally enlightened.

7-12a. He is mentioned as eternally liberated, by the sages who know the principles. At the behest of Śiva Parameṣṭhin who has no beginning, middle or end as well as that of Puruṣa, Prakṛti gives birth to cosmic Intellect.

At the behest of the self-born lord who is well known in all bodies as the Antaryāmin (the immanent soul), its intellect gives birth to cosmic ego. At the behest of lord Śiva, ego gives birth to the eleven sense-organs and the subtle elements. At the behest of the intelligent lord the subtle elements give birth to the gross elements entirely. At the behest of Śiva all the elements bring about the contact with the bodies in the case of the embodied beings from Brahmā to the blades of grass. At the behest of that lord, intellect ponders upon all objects.

13b-20. Prosperity, power and riches are achieved by the lord naturally. It is at his behest that the ego takes pride in all objects; the mind becomes conscious of the objects and thinks. It is on account of his power that the ear perceives sound, the body feels touch. Thanks to the power of command of Siva, Bhava, Parameṣṭhin that the organ of speech utters words and does not take up things from the physical body. The hand does the work of taking up and never that of motion, etc. in respect to all creatures, at the control of the creator. It is due to the behest of Śiva that the foot does the work of movement and not that of excretion. At the behest of supreme lord, the rectum does the work of excretion and not that of speech. The organ of generation generates at the instance of of the lord. It is due to the behest of the lord that it causes pleasure to all living beings.

21. It is due to the bidding of great lord that the ether yields sufficient space always.

22. It is due to the directive from Śiva that the wind sustains the bodies of all living beings through its divisions such as Prāṇa, etc.

23. At the directive from the lord of Devas, the atmospheric wind having seven skandhas[103] carries out worldly activi-

103. **sapta-skandha—seven branches or seven divisions.**

ties by means of its subdivisions, viz. Āvaha,[104] etc.

24. Due to the advice of the great lord the wind functions within our bodies by means of its five-fold divisions Nāga,[104a] etc.

25-27. At the behest of the lord, the fire carries Havya to Devas, and Kavya[104b] to the pitṛs. Moreover, it carries out cooking also. The fire that is within the belly digests the food taken in by the embodied beings. This it does at the behest of the lord of the universe. At his behest the waters enliven the living beings. His behest which is very weighty cannot be transgressed.

28. At the behest of that lord of Devas Indra sustains all living beings consisting of the mobile and immobile.

29. Lord Viṣṇu sustains the worlds by warding off the pain of those alive and of the dead from hundreds of tortures (in hell). His order cannot be transgressed.

30. At the bidding of the lord, Viṣṇu protects Devas and destroys Asuras. He is stationed in all the three worlds and he destroys all unrighteous persons.

31. At his behest, Varuṇa sustains the worlds through water. At his behest, he submerges them. He binds Asuras by means of his bonds.

32. At his bidding Kubera, the lord of riches, offers wealth to the living beings in accordance with their merit.

33. At the behest of the eternal, truthful great Ātman, the sun marks time by causing sunrise and sunset.

34. At the behest of the lord the destroyer of Death, the moon that has nectarine rays and holds all digits delights people and makes the flowers and herbs flourish.

35. The Ādityas, Vasus, Rudras Aśvins, Maruts and all other Devas have been created at his bidding.

36. The Gandharvas, Devas, Siddhas, Sādhyas, Cāraṇas, Yakṣas, Rākṣasas and Piśācas, all abide by the behests of the lord.

104. āvaha, etc. seven courses of wind one above the other : They are (i) āvaha, (ii) pravaha, (iii) saṁvaha, (iv) udvaha, (v) vivaha, (vi) parivaha and (vii) parāvaha.

104a. nāga—five vital airs, of which five kinds are enumerated.

104b. havya-kavya —oblations to the gods and to the manes or spirits of deceased ancestors—MS. 1. 94; 3. 97, 128; *et seq.*

37. The planets, stars, constellations, sacrifices, Vedas, austerities and sages abide by his bidding.

38. The manes pitṛs, seven oceans, seven mountains, seven rivers, forests and lakes abide by his bidding.

39. The various units of time, such as Kalās, Kāṣṭhās, Nimeṣas, Muhūrtas, days, nights, seasons years, fortnights and months are stabilised at his behest.

40-41. Yugas and manvantaras abide by his behest. The Para, Parārdha and the other units of time, eight species of Devas, five species of the lower animals and human beings, all function because of the intelligent lord of Devas (i. e. Śiva).

42. The living beings born of the fourteen wombs and living in all the worlds abide by his bidding alone.

43-45. The subjects born and stationed in the fourteen worlds abide by the bidding of the lord. The nether and the upper worlds with their coverings and the rest of the current worlds surrounded by all living beings abide by his bidding.

46-47. The innumerable past universes functioned at his behest along with all their beings. The future universe too will carry out his behest along with all their entourage.

CHAPTER ELEVEN

The superhuman magnificence of Śiva

Santakumāra said:

1. O lord of the Gaṇas, O most excellent among those who know the greater and the inferior, O lord sanctified by the supreme lord Śiva, recount to me the superhuman excellences of Śiva and Śivā (Umā).

Nandikeśvara said:

2. O Sanatkumāra, O leading yogin, O most excellent among the sons of Brahmā, I shall recount the excellences of Śiva and Śivā, listen.

3. The supreme soul is spoken of as Śiva as well as Śivā.[105] These are the masculine and feminine forms of the one supreme Ātman. Learned men call Śiva as Īśvara and Śivā as Māyā.

4. The brahmins call Puruṣa as Śiva and Prakṛti as Śivā. Śiva is the meaning and Śivā is the word denotative of the meaning. The eternal lord is the day and Śivā is the night.

5. The lord is the deity of sacrifice [106] and his consort is Dakṣiṇā (gift of sacrifice). The lord is the firmament and his beloved is the earth.

6. Lord Śiva is the ocean and Umā, the daughter of the chief of the mountains, is the sea-shore. The trident-armed lord is the tree and his beloved is the creeper.

7. The lord is Brahmā and the goddess having half the body of the lord is Sāvitrī. The lord is Viṣṇu and the great goddess is Lakṣmī.

8. The lord is the thunderbolt-armed Indra and the daughter of the leading mountain is Śacī. The lord is the fire and the goddess having half the body of the lord is Svāhā (wife of fire).

9. The lord is Yama and the daughter of the mountain is Yamī. The lord is Varuṇa and his consort is Varuṇānī the bestower of all objects.

10. The lord is Vāyu and the mistress of Vāyu is Śivā. The lord with the semicircular moon for his crest is the king of Yakṣas. Śivā herself is Ṛddhi.

11. The crescent-crested lord is the moon and the beloved of the lord is Rohiṇī. The lord is the sun and the goddess Umā is Suvarcalā.

12. The destroyer of the three cities (puras) is the six-faced deity (Kārttikeya) and his beloved is Devasenā. Umā is prasūti while the lord is Dakṣa.

13. The lord is Manu called Puruṣa. His beloved is Śatarūpā. They know Bhavānī as Ākūti and the lord as Ruci.

14. The lord who plucked out the eyes of Bhaga is Bhṛgu and the beloved of the three-eyed lord is Khyāti. Lord Rudra is Marīci and the beloved of the lord is Sambhūti.

105. sā ca, i.e. Śraddhā, the first wife of Śiva.
106. saptatantu—yajñaḥ, *ST.* a kind of sacrifice.

15. They know Bhavānī as Rucirā and the lord as Kavi.[107] The lord is Aṅgiras and Umā is Smṛti.

16. The lord with the crescent moon at his crest is Pulastya and the beloved of the Pināka-bearing lord is Prīti. The lord, the destroyer of the three cities (puras) is pulaha and the beloved of the slayer of Kāla (i. e. Śiva) is Dayā.

17. The destroyer of Dakṣa's sacrifice is Kratu and the beloved of the lord is Sannati. The three-eyed lord is Atri and Umā herself as his consort Anasūyā.

18. They call Umā as the elderly lady Ūrjā and the lord as Vasiṣṭha. All men are Śiva and all women are Śivā.

19. All those who are expressed by words in the masculine gender are forms of the lord. All those that are expressed by words in the feminine gender are the magnificences of Śivā.

20. All the women and men are their [Śiva's and Umā's] own excellences. Learned men know that all the Śaktis of the objects are Gaurī.

21. She is the goddess of the universe and he is the overlord of all. All objects that are possessed of Śakti are parts of Maheśvara.

22. The eight Prakṛtis are the physical forms of the goddess. The vikṛtis are her Vibhūtis in embodied forms.

23-24. Just as sparks come out of the fire so also the Jīvas (individual souls) come out of the lord. Hence, the lord attains dual existence. The physical bodies of the embodied beings are the form of the goddess. All the embodied beings are stabilised as parts of the lord.

25. Everything audible is of the form of Umā and the hearer is the lord himself. The lord is the inherer of objects while Umā is the object herself.

26. The beloved wife of the lord holds all the objects to be created while the lord with the crescent moon on his crest, the soul of the universe is the creator.

27. The goddess of the world sustains the forms of subjects and objects while the seer is the moon-crescented lord.

28. All tastes and smells are the forms of Umā, while the lord of the worlds is the feeler of the taste and smell.

107. Kavim—śukram *ST*. Venus.

29. The great goddess Śivā assumes the form of every object worthy of being thought of, while the thinker is the lord, the soul of the universe and the great Īśvara.

30. The beloved of the lord sustains the form of objects worthy of being understood and the deity that understands is the same lord with the crescent moon for his crest jewel.

31. Goddess Umā has the form of the pedestal. Śiva has the form of Liṅga. After installing them assiduously Devas and Asuras worship them.

32. All the objects marked with the phallic symbol are the superhuman magnificences of the lord. All the objects marked by the symbol of the vaginal passage are the superhuman excellences of the goddess Umā.

33. The eight coverings of the Cosmic Egg ending with the upper and lower regions and all that is knowable are the forms of Umā while lord Maheśvara is the knower.

34. The goddess, the beloved of the slayer of the three cities (puras) is the field[108] while the lord the slayer of Andhaka is the knower of the field.[109]

35. If people forsake Liṅga and begin to worship other deities they will go to the Raurava hell along with the king,[110] their ruler.

36. If a king ceases to be a devotee of Śiva and becomes attached to other Devas, it is like the behaviour of a young woman who discarding her husband revels among her paramours.

37. Brahmā and other Devas, the kings of great prosperity, the subjects as well as sages worship the Liṅga.

38. After killing Rāvaṇa[111] the son of Brahmā along with his army, the Liṅga was duly installed on the shore of the ocean by Viṣṇu.

39. Even after committing thousands of sins and even after killing a hundred brahmins, if one resorts to lord Śiva with full devotion he is undoubtedly liberated.

108-109. The goddess is kṣetra in the form of subtle body (liṅga-śarīra) while the god is kṣetrajña in the form of jīva.

110. Mark the sectarian character of this Purāṇa.

111. Rāvaṇaṁ hatvā—according to Vālmīki's Rāmāyaṇa, this Liṅga known as Rāmeśvara was installed by Rāma at the time of constructing the bridge (setu-bandha-kāle), and not after slaying Rāvaṇa as mentioned here.

40. All the worlds are full of Liṅgas. They are founded on the Liṅga. Hence, one should worship the Liṅga if one wishes for eternal region.

41. Śiva and Śivā are stationed in the shapes of all beings. They should be worshipped by men for their own welfare. They should always be bowed to and contemplated upon.

CHAPTER TWELVE

The cosmic form of Śiva

Sanatkumāra said:

1. O leader of the Gaṇas, of great intellect, recount to me the eight cosmic forms of Śaṅkara the great Ātman, the lord of universal forms.

Nandikeśvara said:

2. O son of the lotus-born deity, verily will I recount the greatness of the consort of Umā, the lord of universal forms.

3. The following too viz.—the earth, waters, fire, wind firmament, sun, moon and the sacrificer are the physical forms of the lord Śiva.

4. The following too, viz:—the firmament, Ātman, moon, fire, sun, waters, earth and wind are the eight[112] physical forms of the intelligent lord of Devas.

5. Hence, when Agnihotra is dedicated unto the great lord of the nature of the sun, his emànations Devas, pitṛs, etc. become satiated.

6. Just as the branches and twigs of a tree are also propitiated when the root is watered so also Devas and the emanations of the lord are all propitiated through his worship.

7. Leading sages worship the solar form of the lord that has twelve[113] aspects and is worthy of worship and is identical with Devas.

112. The eight forms of the lord are constituted by ether, fire, water, earth, air, sun, moon and jīva.

113. Śiva has twelve bodies in the form of twelve suns, who preside severally over the twelve months of the year.

8. The digit named Amṛta belonging to the lord in the form of the sun is beneficial to this world as one enlivening the living beings. They drink it always.

9. The rays named Candras belonging to Dhūrjaṭi of the form of the sun, create shower of snow for the growth of the medicinal herbs.

10. The rays named Śuklas belonging to the lord in the form of the sun create heat which is the cause of maturity and ripeness of plants as well as grains.

11. The ray named Harikeśa, belonging to the lord in the form of the sun is the cause of development and nourishment of the stars.

12. The ray named Viśvakarman belonging to the lord in the form of the sun nourishes Budha (Mercury).

13. The ray of the trident-bearing lord in the form of the sun, that is known as Viśvavyaca is the nourisher of Śukra (Venus).

14. The ray that is known as Samyadvasu, belonging to the trident-bearing lord in the form of the thousand-rayed sun is the nourisher of Mars.

15. The ray that is known as Arvāvasu, belonging to the Pināka-bearing lord in the form of the sun, develops Bṛhaspati (Jupiter) always.

16. The ray known as Svarāṭ, belonging to Śiva of the form of the sun nourishes Śanaiścara (Saturn) by day and night.

17. The ray known as Suṣumnā belonging to the lord, the consort of Umā, the source of origin of the universe and solar in form, develops the moon always.

18. The form named Soma belonging to Śaṅkara the preceptor of the universe is the material cause of the universe.

19. The lunar form of the lord the slayer of Death is stationed in all embodied beings in the form of the semen.

20. The body in the nature of the moon belonging to the lord, the preceptor of the universe is stationed in the minds of all embodied beings.

21. The physical form of the lord named Soma is the most excellent among the bodies in all living beings. It is stationed in the form of the nectarine digit in sixteen parts.[114]

114. The sixteen digits of the moon are said to be the sixteen bodies of Śiva.

22. The form named Soma, belonging to the divine ruler, the lord of Devas, nourishes Devas and Pitṛs always by means of the immortal nectar.

23. The physical form of the lord named Soma nourishes clusters of medicinal herbs for the purity of the souls of all embodied beings. This form is called Bhavānī.

24. The form of the consort of Umā in the nature of the Moon is known as the lord of the individual souls, sacrifices and austerities.

25. The physical form of lunar nature belonging to the lord is known as the lord of waters and medicinal herbs.

26-27. The nectarine lord is beyond the grasp of the senses or even of their presiding deities or of those who are expert in discriminating between the sentient and the insentient. When lord Śiva of the lunar form is stationed as the individual soul, the sweet Māyā (prakṛti)[115] which is the sole protector of all the worlds withdraws herself.

28-29. The physical form Yajamāna (the sacrificial priest) belonging to Śiva nourishes by day and night all the deities by means of Havyas and all the Pitṛs by means of Kavyas. Then this physical form Yajamāna, propitiates the mobile and immobile beings by means of the shower of waters[116] caused by the sacrificial offering.

30. The water that is within and without the universe and the water that is within the physical body of all living beings constitutes the great physical (watery) form of the lord Śiva.

31. The nectar-like water of the rivers and the streams and the ubiquitous water of the oceans constitute the physical form of the consort of Umā.

32. This body enlivens and sanctifies all living beings. It is stationed in the vital airs. It is of the form of the moon.[117]

33. The fire that is situated within and without the

115. Madhurā—Māyā *ST.* lord's power of illusion.

116. A body of Śiva is represented by yajamāna (a sacrificer) who by sacrificing oblations into the fire becomes the indirect cause of rain that nourishes creepers and plants. Cf. "yajñād bhavati parjanyaḥ."

117. ambikā—the moon that is only a watery substance in the sky is in fact stationed in the heart of lord Śiva.

आकाशाम्भोनिधिर्योऽसौ सोम इत्यभिधीयते।"

universe, the fire that is stationed in the body of the sacrifice constitutes his physical form.

34. The physical form of the lord, the form that is excessively honoured and worshipped is stationed in the bodies of living beings for their welfare.

35-36. The physical form of the lord in the nature of fire and identical with all Devas is the most excellent one. Its forty-nine[118] subdivisions are cited by those who know the Vedas. The lord's physical body in the form of the sacrificial fire carries Havya to Devas. The fire used by the twice-born for Homas carries Kavya to the pitṛs.

37-38. Those who are conversant with the Vedas and the ancillary texts speak about these and worship them.

The wind that is within and without the universe, and the wind that is stationed in the bodies of living beings constitute the powerful body of Śiva. There are different types of winds such as Prāṇa[119] etc., Nāga,[120] Kūrma etc., Āvaha[121] etc. These are the different forms of the sole lord Īśāna.

39-43. The ether, that is within and without the universe as well as that stationed in the bodies of living beings constitutes the powerful body of lord Śiva.

The earthly form of Śiva has the entire Brahman for it presiding deity. It is considered competent to sustain all living beings—mobile and immobile. Learned men say they are physical bodies of living beings—mobile and immobile. O leading sages, the five elements are evolved out of the five physical forms of Īśa. These together with the moon, sun and Ātman are

118. Forty-nine forms of Agni. For the pedigree of Agni, see MP.—A Study, pp. 169-170.

Agni is the primeval heat (Liṅga I. 7. 105) that permeating the Cosmic Egg creates universes upon universes (Ibid. II. 12. 33). Agnis are the different forms of Rudras (Ibid. 1. 6. 4) and in spite of elasticity in their names and numbers, are finally settled to fortynine.

119. Prāṇa etc. five vital airs. The wind with its quality of touch (sparśa-guṇaḥ) is born of the ether. Cf.
आकाशात्तु विकुर्वाणात्सर्वगन्धवहः शुचिः । बलवाञ्जायते वायुः स वै स्पर्शगुणो मतः ॥—cited in *ST*.

120. According to some authority, Nāga, Kurma, Kukara, Devadatta, Dhanañjaya are identical with prāṇa, apāna, samāna, vyāna and udāna respectively.

121. See p. 207 verses 36-39.

called the eight cosmic forms of Śiva, the intelligent lord of Devas. The Ātman is his eighth physical body. It has another name that of yajamāna.

44-46. This form (i.e. ātman) is stationed in the bodies of all mobile and immobile beings. The leading sages call the Ātman as Dīkṣita (one initiated). It is the body of Śiva, the bestower of auspiciousness; it is called Yajamāna as well. All these eight bodies of Śiva should always be worshipped assiduously by men who seek welfare. They are the sole causes of welfare.

CHAPTER THIRTEEN

The Eight Bodies of Śiva

Sanatkumāra said :

1. O Nandin, recount to me further about the greatness of the consort of Umā, the great lord having eight cosmic forms, of Śiva, Parameṣṭhin.

Nandikeśvara said :

2. I shall recount to you the greatness of the lord the consort of Umā, Parameṣṭhin, having eight cosmic forms, pervading the universe.

3. The lord and creator of all living beings mobile and immobile is of the nature of the sustainer of the Universe and is called Śarva by the masters of scriptural texts and their meanings.

4. Vikeśī is the wife of Śarva, Parameṣṭhin, in the form of Viśvambhara. Aṅgāraka (Mars) is their son.

5-9. The lord is called Bhava by the expounders of the Vedas. Umā is known as the consort of Bhava, the great Ātman, who enlivens the worlds. Venus is their son. In the form of the fire the great Paśupati is remembered by the learned as the lord who pervades the universe consisting of seven worlds, of which he is the sole protector. The beloved wife of Paśupati in the form of the fire is Svāhā. The six-faced lord is cited as their son by the learned.

The lord in the form of the wind pervadas the worlds. He is the sustainer of all embodied beings. He is glorified as Īśāna by the learned men. The goddess of Īśāna, the lord in the form of the wind, the creator of the universe, is mentioned as Śivā and their son is Manojava.

10-17. The lord in the form of the firmament, is the bestower of all desires on all living beings. He is called Bhīma by the learned. The ten quarters are the goddess of lord Bhīma in the form of the firmament, having great magnanimity. Creation is their son. The lord in the form of the sun is called Rudra by Devas. He bestows prosperity on all, and yields all worldly pleasures and salvation. Suvarcalā is the goddess of Rudra when the latter is in the form of the sun, the bestower of devotion on his devotees. Śanaiścara (Saturn), is their son. The lord in the form of the moon is Mahādeva and he is known as the source of origin of all gentle objects. Rohiṇī is the beloved of lord Mahādeva in the form of the moon. Budha (mercury) is their son.

Lord Mahādeva in the form of yajamāna who apportions Havya and Kavya to Devas and Pitṛs is called Ugra. He is also called Īśāna by others.

18. Dīkṣā is the wife of the lord Ugra when the latter is in the form of yajamāna and their son is named Santāna.

19. The hard part in the bodies of the embodied souls like Koṅkaṇa[122] etc. is known as the earthly body by the principle of lord Śiva.

20-26. The lord of Devas is present in every body. The unchanging thing in the embodied souls in the form of solid matter pertains to Bhava the great Ātman and it is known as such by those who know reality and have mastered the Vedas.

The fiery principle that is seen in the bodies of the embodied beings is known as the physical form Paśupati by those who understand reality. The body which is a gaseous transformation in the bodies of the embodied beings is known by the learned as Īśa. The crevisse that is in the body of all the

122. Koṅkaṇa—tatsaṁjñaka-deśaḥ *ST*. Contextually not clear, though it refers to the strip of land lying between the Sahya mountain and the Indian ocean.

embodied beings is known as the physical form of Bhīma by those who seek to know facts. The glowing element in the eyes etc. of the bodies of the embodied beings is known as the physical form of Rudra by those who know precise facts. The mind that is lunar in form and stationed in the bodies of all living beings is known as the physical form of Mahādeva by those who ponder over facts. The Ātman that is named Yajamāna and is present in the bodies of all living beings is known as the physical body of Ugra by those who know the greatest Ātman.

27-29. Great sages aver that all the living beings born of the fourteen different species are not different from Śiva possessed of the eight cosmic bodies. They say that the bodies of embodied beings are identical with the seven bodies of Īśa. The Ātman is his eighth physical body and is present in the bodies of all living beings. If you wish to attain welfare resort by all means to the eight-formed lord Aṣṭamūrti, the lord identical with all the worlds.

30-37. If one is able to do some thing that is beneficent to any living being it is as good as propitiating Maheśa with eight cosmic bodies. If one suppresses or obstructs any embodied being it amounts to perpetrating the same to Maheśa with eight cosmic forms. If protection from fear and danger is accorded to any embodied being, undoubtedly, it is the propitiation of the eight-formed lord. Helping all the people and affording shelter in times of fear is undoubtedly the propitiation of Aṣṭamūrti. Leading sages say that the help rendered to everyone and the blessings offered to all is the great worship of the eight-formed lord. Blessings to other embodied beings and offerings of freedom from fear should be pursued by you if you wish to propitiate Śiva.

CHAPTER FOURTEEN

The five Brahmans

Sanatkumāra said:

1. O Nandin, the most excellent among the Gaṇas, recount to me the five Brahmans, that cause welfare and that sanctify all the embodied beings.

Nandikeśvara said :

2. O most excellent one among the sons of the lotus-born deity, I shall precisely recount to you the five forms of Śiva himself, called the "Pañca Brahmans."[123]

3. Śiva identical with the Pañca-Brahmans, is the sole creator, the sole protector and the sole annihilator of all the worlds.

4. They say that Śiva is both the material as well as the efficient cause of all the worlds. That Śiva is said to be of five forms.

5. The great forms of Śiva the greatest Ātman, worthy of being the refuge of all the worlds are five. They are known by the name Pañca Brahmans.

6. The first form of Śiva Parameṣṭhin is termed Īśāna. He is Kṣetrajña the knower of the field and the enjoyer of Prakṛti that is worthy of being enjoyed.

7. What is called Tatpuruṣa is said to be the second physical form of the lord. That is identical with Prakṛti as the residence of the supreme soul.

8. What is called Aghora is the third important physical form of the lord. It is the physical form pertaining to the cosmic intellect and it has eight ancillary parts beginning with Dharma.

9. What is called Vāmadeva is the fourth important physical form of the lord. It pervades everything in the form of ego.

123. The five forms of Śiva are called Īśānā, Tatpuruṣa, Aghora, Vāmadeva and Sadyojāta. In fact, they represent the pañca mahābhūtas (five gross elements), the source of the entire universe.

10. What is called Sadyojāta is the fifth physical form of the lord. It is stationed in all embodied beings in the form of the mind.

11. The greatest lord Īśāna is the eternal Parameṣṭhin. He is stationed in all living beings in the form of the sense-organ ear.

12. Lord Tatpuruṣa is stationed in the bodies of the embodied beings in the form of the sense-organs of touch.

13. The great lord Aghora is glorified by the learned as stationed in the eyes in the bodies of all living beings.

14. Vāmadeva is known as firmly established in the sense-organ tongue in the parts of the embodied beings.

15. It is mentioned that Sadyojāta is stationed in the bodies of all living beings in the form of the sense-organ of smell.

16. It is said that Īśāna is stationed in all the bodies of living beings in the form of the organ of speech.

17. Learned men say that Tatpuruṣa is stationed in the bodies of all embodied persons in the form of the organ of action, the hands.

18. Those who know the truth say that Aghora is stationed in the bodies of all living beings in the form of the organ of action, the feet.

19. Sages say that Vāmadeva is stationed in the bodies of all living beings in the form of the organ of action, the rectum.

20. Lord Sadyojāta is stationed in the bodies of all living beings in the form of the organ of generation. It is said by those who are conversant with the Vedic and scriptural texts.

21. The sages and Devas mention that lord Īśāna is the lord of living beings, that he is of the subtle form of sound and is the cause of the firmament.

22. Leading sages say that lord Tatpuruṣa is in the subtle form of touch and is the cause of the wind.

23. Persons conversant with the Vedas say that the terrible lord Aghora in the subtle form of Rūpa is the cause of the fiery element.

24. Those who know the real principles say that the well-known lord Vāmadeva being in the subtle form of Rasa is the cause of the waters.

25. All those who know the real principles praise the great lord Sadyojāta as the cause of the earth element in the subtle form of smell.

26. Leading sages say that the primordial lord Īśāna is the wonderful entity in the form of the firmament.

27. The wise know that lord Tatpuruṣa is the Wind, in view of his pervading all the worlds.

28. Those who know the meanings of the Vedic texts speak of the noble-souled Aghora as having the form of the fire worshipped by all.

29. In view of his enlivening nature in regard to the Universe, the sages know the great lord Vāmadeva as having the form of water. They mention him to be pleasing to the mind

30-33. Wise men know that lord Sadyojāta is in the form of the earth. He is the preceptor of the world. He is the sole great sustainer of the universe consisting of the mobile and immobile beings.

The entire unit of the universe both the mobile and immobile is in the form of the five brahmans. The sages who have realised the truth call that the Bliss of Śiva.

He who is seen in the universe in the form of the twentyfive principles is Śiva and none else, who reveals himself in the form of the five Brahmans.[124]

Hence, by all those who seek welfare, Śiva the soul of the twentyfive principles, identical with the five Brahmans, shall be assiduously thought of.

124. nānyatāṁ gataḥ—abhedam prāptaḥ—has become the constituent of the universe.

CHAPTER FIFTEEN

The form of the Supreme Lord

Sanatkumāra said :

1. O chieftain of the goblins, O highly intellgent, of great qualities, thou art omniscient, recount once more the grandeur of Śiva.

Sailādi said :

2. O sage, listen to the greatness of Śiva which I shall tell you now. It has already been mentioned by many excellent sages in different words.

3. The wise speak of Śiva of the form of "Sat" and "Asat"[125] as also the lord of "Śat" and "Asat" and the sages say also the same.

4. With the effect of the living beings for its second, the manifest[126] is called existent and the unmanifest[127] is called non-existent because it has no second.

5. Both the existent and the non-existent are the forms of Śiva. There is nothing else other than Śiva. Since he is the lord of both of them, Śiva is called Sadasatpati.

6. Some sages who ponder over realities speak of Śiva Maheśvara as kṣarākṣarātmaka[128] identical with the perishable and the imperishable as well as that which is beyond.

7. The unmanifest is called imperishable and the manifest is cited as perishable. These are the two forms of Śaṅkara

125. sad-asad-rupam. According to *ST*. this refers to the doctrine of Nyāya philosophy. The all-pervading Lord is eternal (nitya) as well as non-eternal (anitya). This latter quality he derives from his functions as Jīva.

126.-127. *ST*. offers another interpretation of 'sad-asad'. 'sad' is manifest (vyakata) while 'asad' is unmanifest (avyakta). In fact, manifest (vyakta) and, unmanifest (avyakata) are the attributes of prakṛti-pradhāna while the lord is the cognizer (Jña) of both—prakṛti as well as pradhāna.

128. The lord is kṣara—perishable as well as imperishable. Since he is all-pervasive, he identifies himself with the perishable beings, Jīva etc. he is therefore called kṣara. He is also called imperishable (akṣara) because he is ever existent.

alone; and there is nothing greater[129] than himself.

8. Śiva is greater than both the perishable and the imperishable. So he i.e. Mahādeva Maheśvara, is verily called kṣarākṣarapara by the learned.

9. On pondering over all forms of the manifest, it is found that they exist collectively and individually. Therefore, He (Śiva) is said to be the cause for Samaṣṭi and Vyaṣṭi.

10. Others[130] speak of him as the greatest cause. The leading sages know Samaṣṭi as the unmanifest and Vyaṣṭi as the manifest.

11. These two are said to be the forms of Śiva. Their origin from another source is not possible. It is, indeed, by virtue of being the cause of both the collective and the individual that Śiva is known as Parameśvara.

12. Śiva is mentioned as the cause of both Samaṣṭi and Vyaṣṭi by those who are conversant with the yoga philosophy. By some Śiva is cited as existing in the form of body as well as soul.[131]

13-14. Śiva, lord Parameśvara is the greatest Ātman, the greatest brilliance. The learned say that the twentyfour principles constitute the body and they speak of Puruṣa the enjoyer by the word Kṣetrajña. These two, viz., the Kṣetra and Kṣetrajña are the forms of that self-born deity.

15-18. The learned say that there is nothing else other than Śiva. They call the worldly matter consisting of elements, sense-organs, the inner organ, (will, etc.) [132] Pradhāna etc. as the Aparabrahma[133] form. Some say that Śiva is in the form of the supreme Brahman and the lord has neither beginning nor end. The paramabrahman is of the form of consciousness. In fact, the form of Maheśa, Śiva the self-born deity is Brahman.

129. The lord is characterized by both forms—*kṣara* and *akṣara* (ubhe te Śivarūpe). He is rightly called *na paraḥ* (=aparaḥ), i.e. not any other. According to *ST*. this is Sāṅkhya doctrine.

130. ācāryāḥ. According to *ST*. this refers to the yogins Matsyendra and others, but this purāṇa cannot be posterior to Matsyendra

131. kṣetra-kṣetrajñarūpin—this refers to the doctrine of Vedāntins.

132. apara-brahma-rūpam—śābda-brahmādirūpam *ST*. of the form of brahma as sound.

133. According to some ācāryas, the lord is identical with the subtle elements.

It is that of Śaṅkara the great being. There is nothing other than Śiva. By some, Śaṅkara is said to be of the form of Vidyā and Avidyā.

19. The primordial lord Śiva is the creator and ordainer of worlds. The leading sages call him alone as Vidyā and Avidyā.

20-26. The entire universe consists of these two forms of the self-born lord. The excellent forms of Śiva are Bhrānti, Vidyā and Param. Some sages[134] who are conversant with the scriptural texts have attained the excellent form of Śiva by means of yoga. The perception of objects of multifarious forms is called Bhrānti. The cognition in the form of the Ātman is known as Vidyā. The principle devoid of alternatives or doubts is called Param which is the third form of Īśa. There is nothing else other than these three. By some he is said to be of the form of Vyakta, Avyakta and Jña. Parameśvara is the ordainer and the creator of all the worlds. Poets mean by the word Vyakta the twentythree principles[135] and by the word Avyakta the unmanifest Prakṛti. They denote Puruṣa, the enjoyer of the Guṇas. by the word Jña. These three are the forms of Śaṅkara. There is nothing else which is "not Śaṅkara."

CHAPTER SIXTEEN

The principle of Śiva

Sanatkumāra said:

1. Once again, O extremely intelligent one, I wish to hear the truth, viz., the forms of Śiva mentioned by the leading sages in different words.

Śailādi said:

2. Again and again, O sage, I shall recount to you the forms of Śiva mentioned by the leading sages in different words.

134. According to *ST*. this refers to yoga-vedāntins.

135. The twentythree tattvas constitute Prakṛti—the manifest form of pradhāna.

3. By certain leading sages and preceptors who have crossed the ocean of Āgamas (scriptures), Śiva is called Kṣetrajña, Prakṛti, Vyakta and Kālātman (soul of time).

4-5. They call Puruṣa by the word Kṣetrajña and they call Pradhāna by the word Prakṛti. The evolutes of Prakṛti are called Vyakta (the manifest). Kāla[136] (time) is the sole cause of the transformation of Pradhāna into the manifest Prakṛti. This set of four constitutes the four[137] forms of Īśa.

6. Some preceptors speak of Śiva Parameśvara as having the forms of Hiraṇyagarbha, Puruṣa, Pradhāna and Vyakta.

7. Hiraṇyagarbha is the maker of this universe; Puruṣa is the enjoyer; the evolutes of Pradhāna are named Vyakta and Pradhāna is the greatest cause.

8. Know that this set of four constitutes the four forms of Śiva. There is no other object different from the lord.

9-10. Some mention Īśvara as having the forms of Piṇḍa and Jāti.[138] The physical bodies of the mobile and immobile beings are Piṇḍas, while the ordinary generalities as well as specific generality sattā is called jāti. These are also the forms of the intelligent lord.

11-13. Some others mention Īśa as the form of Virāj and Hiraṇyagarbha. Hiraṇyagarbha is the cause of the worlds and Virāj is identical with the world.

Some recount Śiva in the forms of Sūtra and Avyākṛta.[139] Indeed, the Avyākṛta is the Pradhāna and that is a form of Parameṣṭhin. Just as the collection of jewels is held together in a thread so also the worlds are held together by the lord. That form of wonderful exploit is known as Sūtra.

14. Śiva the great lord, Śambhu, Maheśvara is glorified by some as the immanent soul; by others as the great Īśa, by yet others as self-luminous and self-known.

136. Kāla (Time) is the single factor in the modification of the unmanifest in the process of transformation into the manifest (Prakṛti).

137. The group of four—Pradhāna, Prakṛti, Puruṣa and Kāla-constitutes the lord.

138. piṇḍa-jāti svarūpī—vyakti-jāti-rūpaḥ.

139. sūtrāvyākṛtarūpam—in the form of Sūtrātman and Pradhāna.

15-16. Śiva is known as one present within and as one who controls all living beings. Since he is greater than all living Beings he is called Para (the great Being). Śiva, Śambhu, Śaṅkara, Parameśvara is the greatest Ātman.

They know his threefold[140] form named Prājña, Taijasa and Viśva.

17-19. Suṣupti (slumber) Svapna (dream) and Jāgrat (wakefulness) are the three[141] states wherein Prājña, etc. constitute the presiding deities. The two forms called Virāj and Hiraṇyagarbha are meant by the word Avyākṛta. They constitute the fourth state of Śiva passing through the three states. Hiraṇyagarbha, Puruṣa is mentioned as Kāla. The three states are the causes of creation, sustenance and annihilation of the universe. The three states of the lord are termed Bhava, Viṣṇu and Viriñca. The embodied beings devoutly propitiate them and attain salvation.

20b-21a. The following four forms of Parameṣṭhin, Śambhu are mentioned by the learned, viz:—Kartṛ (doer), Kriyā (action), Kārya (effect) and Karaṇa (instrument).

21b-22a. Undoubtedly the following four forms pertain only to Śiva, viz. Pramātṛ (cognizer), Pramāṇa (valid means of knowledge), Prameya (the object of cognition) and Pramiti (the act of cognition).

22b-25. The following are also the forms of Śiva alone, like the billows of the ocean, viz:—Iśvara, Avyākṛta, Prāṇa, Virāj, Bhūtas and Indriyas (sense-organs). They call the efficient cause of the worlds by the name Iśvara. Pradhāna itself is mentioned as Avyākṛta by the expounders of the Vedas. Hiraṇyagarbha is called by the name Prāṇa. Virāj is identical with the worlds. The word Bhūta connotes Mahābhūtas (elements). The Indriyas (sense-organs) are their effects. Excellent sages glorify these as Śiva's forms.

26-31. The wise know that the supreme soul is no other

140. The lord has three forms: (i) prājña, soul of the gross body i.e. the animal soul; (ii) taijasa, soul of the subtle body i.e intellectual soul and (iii) viśva, soul of the universe, i.e. universal soul.

141. Three stages of consciousness are known as jāgrat (a waking state), svapna (a dreaming state) and suṣupti (a state of profound sleep). The individual soul has to pass through all these stages before he merges into the supreme soul.

than Śiva. The twenty-five principles[142] are recounted by the learned as originating from Śiva. They are also not different from him, like the series of waves that are not different from waters. They know that the principle of Śiva is greater than the twenty five categories. Hence, those principles are not different from him in the same way as the bangle is not different from the gold.

The principles Sadāśiva, Īśvara, etc. are born of the principle Śiva and hence not different from it like the variety of jar that is not different from the material mud.

Māyā, Avidyā, Kriyāśakti, Jñānaśakti and Kriyāmayī—these five[143] are undoubtedly born of Śiva like the rays originating from the sun.

If you wish to acquire welfare with all emotional attachments you shall resort to lord Śiva who is the soul of all and who arranges support unto all.

CHAPTER SEVENTEEN

The greatness of Śiva

Sanatkumāra said:

1-3. Once again, O most excellent one among Devas, let me hear the greatness of Śiva. I am not satiated by listening to the excellent greatness of Śiva. I am not satisfied fully with your present nectarine speech.

How did the lord become an embodied soul? Wherefore is Rudra powerful and strong? How is he considered the Ātman of all? How is the holy rite Pāśupata to be performed. How was Śaṅkara listened to by the chiefs of Devas? How was he delighted?

142. Śiva-tattva is beyond twentyfive tattvas, still he is related to the tattvas as the gold is related to the ornaments or as the ocean to the waves.

143. The five entities māyā, vidyā, kriyā, śakti and jñāna emanate from the lord as rays from the sun.

Śailādi said:

Sthāṇu, Śiva, the great cause originated from the unmanifest.

4-5. He was a lordly sage superior to the universe. He was the sage equipped with all causes. At the outset, he saw Brahmā, the first[144] Deva born out of his lotus-face. He glanced at him by way of command.[145] On being seen by Rudra, he, the lord of Devas, created everything.

6-7. The Virāj (immense Being) established the order of the castes and stages of life. For the sake of sacrifice, he created the soma juice. All these originated from the soma juice: the sacrificial offering, fire, sacrifice, lord Indra the consort of Śacī armed with the thunderbolt, Viṣṇu, Nārāyaṇa the glorious being and the entire earth identical with soma.

8-9. Devas eulogised lord Rudra by reciting the Rudrādhyāya. The lord stood in the midst of Devas with his face beaming with pleasure. It was as though the great lord took away their wisdom.

Devas then asked lord Śaṅkara, "Sir, who are you ?"[146]

10. Lord Rudra said:—"O excellent Devas, I was the sole ancient Being. I continue to be the first among all beings.

11. I will be so in this world. There is nothing other than myself. There is nothing separate from me.[147] O excellent Devas, there is nothing else.

12. I am both eternal and non-eternal. I am the sinless Brahmā as also the lord of Brahmā. I am the quarters as well as the intermediary direction. I am Prakṛti as well as Puruṣa.

13. I am Triṣṭup, Jagatī and Anuṣṭup metres of prosody. I am the omnipresent Truth, the tranquil one. I am the threefold sacrificial fire. I am the preceptor as well as preceptorhood.

14. I am the cow. I am the cavity. I am always perceptible in the impenetrable depth. I am the eldest and best of all the principles. I am the lord of the waters.

144. davānām prathamaṁ devam. TA. 10. 10. 3. Mahān. U. 10. 3.

145. ājñayā—pāramaiśvaryā *ST*. Cf. tasyājñā pārameśvarī—cited in *ST*.

146. ko bhavān. Cf. devā ha vai svargaṁ lokamagamaṁs te devā rudram apṛcchan ko bhavān—Atharvopaniṣad—cited in *ST*.

147. Read matto for bhakto.

15. I am the waters; lord Īśa; fiery brilliance, the sacrificial altar; I am the *Ṛgveda*, the *Yajurveda*, the *Sāmaveda*. I am the self-born deity.[148]

16. I am the *Atharvaveda*, the mantra, the most excellent among the Aṅgiras. I am the Itihāsa, the Purāṇa; the Kalpa[149] (science of Rituals) as well as the Kalpanā (imagination).

17. I am the imperishable and perishable; I am forgiveness, calmness, forbearance, the secret of all the Vedas, the most excellent and the unborn one.

18. I am the holy Puṣkara. I am the middle and beyond it. I am the exterior and interior. I am the unchanging one in front.

19. I am the brilliant light as well as darkness. I am Brahmā, Viṣṇu and Maheśvara. I am the cosmic intellect, ego, subtle elements and the sense-organs.

20. O excellent Devas, he who knows everything to be myself, is alone omniscient,[150] Parameśvara, the soul of all.

21-22. O excellent Devas, by means of my brilliance, I propitiate the cow by means of the cows; the brahmins by means of the brahminical power; longevity and offerings by means of longevity; truth by means of truth[151] and Dharma by means of Dharma. I propitiate all by my own brilliance.

After saying this at the outset, the lord vanished there itself.

23-24. Thereupon, Devas did not see lord Rudra. Including Nārāyaṇa and Indra, Devas and sages meditated upon him who was the greatest Ātman and the greatest cause. With their arms raised up, they praised and propitiated him.

148. ātmabhūḥ—in the form of ether. Cf. 'tasmād vā etasmād ātmanaḥ ākāśaḥ sambhūtaḥ—cited in *ST*.

149. kalpāḥ—karma-prayogaracanāḥ *ST*.—treatises dealing with the ritual. Cf. siddha-rūpaḥ prayogo yaiḥ karmaṇām avagamyate te kalpāḥ—cited in *ST*.

150.. sa eva sarvavid Cf. brahmavid bramaiva bhavati—cited in *ST*.

151. Cf. gāṁ gobhir brāhmaṇān brāhmaṇyena havīṁṣi haviṣā āyuḥ āyuṣā satyaṁ satyena dharmaṁ dharmeṇa tarpayāmi svena tejasā—*Atharvopaniṣad*—cited in ST.

CHAPTER EIGHTEEN

The holy Pāśupata rite

Devas said :—

1-3. Lord Rudra alone is identical with Brahmā, Viṣṇu and Maheśvara. He is Skanda; he is Indra; he is the fourteen worlds, Aśvins, planets, constellations, stars, firmament, quarters, elements, sun, moon and the eight planets. He is Prāṇa, Kāla, Yama, Mṛtyu and Amṛta.[152] He constitutes things of the past, present and future; he is the universe as well as truth. Obeisance to him.

4. At the outset you had been the universe, you are Bhūḥ, Bhuvaḥ and Svaḥ. At the end also you are of the form of the universe. You are always at the head of the universe.

5-6. You are the sole[153] Brahman. You are dual[154] in form, triple[155] in form. You are beneath.[156] You are the lord of Devas. You are peace, nourishment, and contentment. You are what is offered and what is not offered in Homa. You are the universe and non-universe. You are what is given and what is not given. You are Īśvara. You are what is done and what is not done. You are certainly the great Deva and the lesser Deva. You are the greatest goal of the good as well as of the bad. You are Śaṅkara.

7-8. May we drink soma juice and become immortal. May we approach light and not go to Devas. Indeed, what will the enemy do to us ? Is death synonymous with immortality ?[156] This form of Śiva is beneficent to the universe. It is divine, imperishable, subtle and unchanging.

9-10. It is holy. It pertains to Prajāpati. It is gentle. It cannot be comprehended. It is unchanging. It can be grasped by the mind[157] just as the wind is grasped by a gaseous thing.

152. amṛtaḥ—mokṣarūpaḥ *ST*. in the form of salvation.

153. Cf. the oft-quoted formula "ekam eva brahma na dvitīyam".

154. dvau i.e Prakṛti and Puruṣa.

155. tridhā—threefold in the form of Brahmā, Viṣṇu and Rudra.

156. apāma somam. RV. VIII. 8. 48. TS. 3. 2. 5. 4.

157. agrāhyeṇāpi grāhyam, yathā sparṣaguṇena vāyuḥ *ST*. just as air is perceived through its quality 'touch', similarly the ungraspable lord is grasped by mental realization.

It swallows the gentle by means of the gentle refulgence of its own sportively. Obeisance to the trident-bearing lord who puts a stop to everything and grabs everything.

11-12. The deities are stationed in the heart, in the vital breath. You are one always present in the heart in the form of the three Mātrās. You are beyond them. Your head is to the north; your feet are to the south. You are directly attached to the north; you are the eternal Oṁkāra.

13-14. What is Oṁkāra is Praṇava itself pervading everything. The Infinite being (Tāra), the subtle being (Sūkṣma) and the refulgence called Vaidyuta (pertaining to the lightning), the great Brahman—all these are Īśāna, Rudra, Maheśvara, the great Deva.

15. That which uplifts is Oṁkāra. Praṇava is Oṁkāra because it protects the vital breaths.

16-17. The eternal lord pervades everything. Hence, he is all-pervasive. Rudra the greatest cause is infinite because neither Brahmā nor Viṣṇu nor others could trace out his beginning or end. He who redeems from the ocean of worldly existence is called Tāra.

18. Lord Nīlalohita is subtle and stays always in the heart in the bodies, Hence, he is called Sūkṣma (subtle).

19. He is both blue and red since both Pradhāna and Puruṣa merge in him. Since the semen flows out from him he is termed Śukla.

20-21. Since he is refulgent, he is mentioned as Vaidyuta. He is Parabrahma because he is huge [Bṛhattvāt] or because he swells up [Bṛṁhaṇatvāt]. The lord without a second is the fourth Being; he is Parameśvara.

22-24. They call him Īśāna the heavenly and lordly eye of the universe. The wise such as Indra and others worship Īśāna on all occasions. He who is the lord of all lores[158] is Īśāna. What the lord sees and causes others to see[159] with the behest what should be seen is the knowledge of the Ātman. The great

158. Īśānaḥ sarva-vidyānām. TA. 10. 47. 1; Mahān. U. 17.5.

159. yad īkṣate ca bhagavān. Cf. atha kasmād ucyate bhagavān? yaḥ sarvān bhāvān īkṣate, ātmānaṁ nirīkṣayati, yogaṁ gamayati—*Atharvaśiras*—cited in *ST*.

lord himself makes people attain yoga.[160] Lord Maheśvara the lord of Devas is, therefore, called "Bhagavān."

25. It is the great lord (Maheśvara) who grasps the worlds duly. He, the lord of Devas, creates everything and resides in them sportively.

26. It is this lord who is present in all quarters. He is the one born at the outset and also one who enters into the foetus. He is one who is born or one who will be born. O men of inferior sight, he stands with his faces all round.

27. He should be assiduously worshipped, this unchanging lord from whom the words recede after not reaching him along with the mind.[161]

28. What the organ of speech utters strenuously is without grasping him. He is the greatest refuge whether Apara or Para.

29. The organs of speech call him omniscient, Nīlalohita. This tawny coloured Śiva is the Puruṣa. Obeisance to him.

30. He is the great Rudra, he is the whole universe[162] in the past, present and future, in many ways, here and there.

31. The lord is gold-armed.[163] He is the lord of gold. He is the consort of Umā; the bull-bannered lord is gold-semened.

32-34. The lord is odd-eyed. He is the creator of the universe, his vehicle is the universe. It is he who, at the outset, created Brahmā[164] as his eternal son and gave him perfect knowledge revealing the Ātman. Those who perceive Rudra the sole Puruṣa, oft-invoked and oft-eulogised, having the form of fire, the excellent Deva in the middle of the heart, the lord stationed in the Ātman and having the size of the tip of hair are self-possessed and courageous. Theirs is the perennial tranquillity, not of the others.

35. He is the lord greater than the greatest, one who

160. yogaṁ gamayati—yogam prāpayati. It is the lord who sets his devotees on meditation.

161. "yato" vāco nivartante TA. 8.4.1; 9.1; TU. 2.4.1; 9.1.

162. Cf. "Viśvam bhūtam bhuvanaṁ citram bahudhā jātam jāyamānaṁ ca yat" *TA*. 10.16.1; Mahān. U. 13.2.

163. hiraṇya-bāhu—one with golden arms. Cf. "namo hiraṇyabāhave" VS. 16.17; TS. 4.5.2.1.

164. brahmāṇam vidadhe. Cf. "yo brahmāṇam vidadhāti pūrvam"—cited in *ST*.

never changes, minuter than the minutest[165] atom, and concealed in the cavity of the heart of living beings.

36. He is the abode of this universe, he is stationed in the lotus of the heart; the cavity is deep within[166]; the lord is stationed deep within as well as above.[167]

37. Oṁkāra, Parameśvara, is of the size of the tip of the hair. It is in the middle of the subtle cavity of the heart. He is Ṛta the eternal law, the greatest cause.

38. He is the truthful Brahman. He is the Puruṣa dark and tawny-coloured. He is Virūpākṣa of sublimated sexuality. He is Īśāna the source of origin of Brahmā.

39. He is the ancient Īśāna who presides over the fivefold physical body. He is the sole Īśvara who occupies the Yonī (the phallus that is put in the symbol of the pudendum muliebre).

40. He is within the vital breaths. They call him the Liṅga (symbol) of the mind wherein the qualities of anger, desire and forbearance persist. By dispelling desire that is at the root of the series of causes of worldly existence and by stabilising it in Rudra, he should be meditated upon by means of the intellect.

41. They call him Rudra, the perpetual Parameśvara and the most fixed and greater than the greatest Being.

42-44. One shall meditate upon him who is the procreator of Brahmā, Viṣṇu, Vahni (Fire god) and Vāyu (Wind god). A sādhaka should purify himself by means of fire. He shall separately sanctify his limbs. Then the five elemens shall be compressed in the order of their origin and qualities. At the outset, the five Mātrās shall be contemplated upon, then four, three, two and one in due order. Then the deity shall be meditated upon without any Mātrā stabilising him at the cerebrum. Becoming immortal thus, one shall perform the Pāśupata rite.

165. aṇo api aṇu. Cf. aṇor aṇīyān mahato mahīyān TA. 10.10. 1. Mahān. U. 8.3. K.U. 2.20; Śvet. U. 3. 20.

166. gahvaraṁ gahanam. ST. explains gahvaram as ākāśam—ether or empty space.

167. ST. supplies vahni-śikhā and construes it with antaśca ūrdhvataḥ. The flame of fire is stationed in the lotus-heart. Cf. "tasya madhye vahniśikhā aṇīyordhvā vyavasthitā"—cited in *ST*.

45. Now, I shall mention this Pāśupata rite in brief. One shall duly consecrate the sacred fire repeating the mantras from Ṛk, Yajus and Sāman.

46. He shall observe fast, remain pure after taking bath, and wear white clothes, white sacred thread and white garlands. He shall smear himself with white unguents.

47-52. Free from Rajoguṇa, he shall perform Homa. He shall become free from sins. The devotee then repeats the following mantras—"May the five vital airs[168] be sanctified. May the organ of speech, mind, feet etc. be sanctified. May all these be sanctified, viz—the ears, tongue, breath, intellect, head, hands, sides, back, belly, calves, penis, vagina, rectum, scrotum, skin, flesh, blood, fat, bones, sound, touch, colour, taste, smell etc. May these elements be sanctified. So also the fat. May, by the grace of Śiva's will, the cooked rice, the vital airs, mind and perfect knowledge be purified." He shall then perform the sacrifice with ghee, sacrificial twigs and Caru offerings in due order. Thereafter, he shall extinguish the Rudra fire and take the bhasman assiduously. Repeating the mantra "Agni"[169] etc. the intelligent devotee shall wipe off his limbs and touch them.

53. This Pāśupata rite is divine and conducive to liberation from bondage. It is beneficial to the brahmins as well as to Kṣatriyas.

54. It is beneficial to deserving Vaiśyas and particularly to the ascetics. It is beneficial to those who are in the stage of life of a forest dweller and also to the good householders.

55-57. Salvation of Brahmacārins (religious students), due to this holy rite, has been noticed. One can take ashes from the fire of the Agnihotra sacrifice, repeating the mantra "Agni" etc. and wipe off the limbs and touch them. That brahmin is also a devotee of Paśupati. A learned brahmin who smears himself with ashes is undoubtedly liberated from all sins, even those

168. virajāś ca bhaviṣyati—by performing virajā homa the devotee becomes devoid of rajoguṇa. According to ST. this homa purifies the internal winds—prāṇa, apāna, vyāna, udāna and samāna. Cf. "Prāṇāpānavyānodānasamānā me śuddhyantām" TA. 10.51.1; Mahān. U. 4.20.15.

169. Agniḥ TS. 3.1.9.1. There are several mantras addressed to agni. Which mantra is meant is not clear.

that are called "mahāpātakas" (great sins). The ashes is the virile essence of Fire and a person who uses Bhasman becomes a virile person.

58. A brahmin engaged in the ablution of Bhasman or a person lying down on the ashes or a person who has conquered his sense-organs will be liberated from all sins and shall attain identity with Śiva.

59. Hence, by all means, the learned man shall sanctify his body by means of Bhasman. The words "re re" shall not be uttered Nor shall one say "tum tum" [i.e. one shall not be rude or impolite in speech].

60-62. The lord of Devas does not brook it even if he be Brahmā or Viṣṇu.

The lord said thus:—"O excellent-faced lady, a person who applies Bhasman is on a par with my son Gaṇeśa. What is repugnant to them[170] should be eschewed. A householder who is devoid of Brahman (Vedic knowledge)[170] and who does not wear the caste mark Tripuṇḍra falls into the depths of hell. All his holy rites of worship, charitable gifts and holy ablutions are in vain like the Homa performed in the ashes.

63-67. Hence, in the course of all holy rites, the learned men shall wear the caste mark Tripuṇḍra.

After saying this and after eulogising the lord in the company of Devas who had smeared themselves with Bhasman, lord Brahmā who too applied himself with Bhasman stopped his speech, O king (?).

Thereupon, in order to bless them the lord of the individual souls, graced the place with his presence along with his consort and the Gaṇas.

Thereafter, Devas eulogised the leading Deva Rudra who was present there, the lord of all, the lord of Devas by means of Rudrādhyāya. The bull-bannered lord glanced at Devas with merciful glances in order to grant them boons. The lord, the slayer of the enemies of Devas, said to Devas—"I am pleased."

170. The Purāṇa in this respect shows a compromising nature but the following *pādas* of this verse impose strictness in the observance of Śaivite rites.

CHAPTER NINETEEN

The mode of Śiva's worship

Śailādi said :

1. After bowing down to the bull-bannered lord who had been pleased, the sages and Devas who felt the sense of horripilation due to pleasure said.

Devas said :

2. O lord Śaṅkara, it behoves you to relate this. By what means are you to be worshipped by the twice-born? where? in what form?

3. Who is authorized in thy worship? O lord, how is a brahmin authorized? O lord, how are the Kṣatriyas authorized? O bull-bannered one, how are the Vaiśyas authorized?

4. How are the women and the Śūdras authorized? How are the bastards and illegitimate sons of widows authorized? For the welfare of the worlds, it behoves you to mention everything to us.

Sūta said :

5. On seeing the fervent emotion of the sages, Nīlalohita, Sadāśiva stationed in the mystic diagram said in a majestic tone.

6-8. Devas and sages saw the lord of Devas in the company of Umā in the Maṇḍala[171] in front of them. His lustre was like that of ten million streaks of lightning. He had eight arms, four faces and twelve eyes. He had big mighty arms. Half of his body was female in form. He wore the coronet of matted hairs. He was bedecked in all ornaments. He wore red garlands and had smeared red unguent over his body. He who was the cause of creation, sustenance and annihilation was clad in red garments.

9. His face to the east[172] was pleasing in appearance and yellow in colour. That is in the form of Tatpuruṣa. His face to the right (i.e. to the south) in the Aghora form was comparable to a mass of blue collyrium.

171. maṇḍalasthaḥ—sūryamaṇḍalasthaḥ *ST*. stationed in the solar orb.
172. purāmukham—the eastern face, viz. Tatpuruṣa.

10-11. His face to the north, named Vāmadeva, was very fierce and terrible with curbed fangs and red moustache. It was enveloped by clusters of flames and matted hairs. It had the lustre of coral. It was pleasing with the universe for its form. It was the bestower of boons.

His western face was splendid and white as the cow's milk.

12. The divine face Sadyojāta that destroyed Kāma was shining with the splendour of the sun as the caste mark on the forehead. It was bedecked in garlands consisting of pearls.

13-14. In the maṇḍala they saw Āditya in the east, Bhāskara in the west, Bhānu in the south and Ravi in the north; all with four faces as before (?) (all these are the different forms of the sun-god).

15-16. In the Maṇḍala they saw in the east the Śakti Vistārā, in the south Uttarā, Bodhanī in the west and Āpyāyanī in the north. All these Śaktis had one face and four arms, were bedecked with all ornaments and were approved by all Devas.

17. On the right side they saw Brahmā and on the left they saw Viṣṇu. They saw Śiva identical with the three Mūrtis by way of Ṛk, Yajus and Sāman.

18. They saw lord Īśāna the bestower of boons, Īśāna Parameśvara, seated on the dais of Brahmā. The bestower of boons was on the seat of virtue and perfect knowledge.

19. They saw the lord Sarveśvara on a seat equipped with detachment and prosperity which was very pure and worthy of being propitiated, which was highly pleasing and which contained all essence (?).

20-22. The lord was seated in the middle of a white lotus and surrounded by Dīptā[173] and other lustres. Dīptā (Refulgent) had the form of a bright and brilliant flame. Sūkṣmā (subtle) was splendid with the lustre of lightning. Jayā (victorious) had the shape of fiery flame. Prabhā (lustre) had golden lustre. Vibhūti (magnificence) had the refulgence of coral. Vimalā (spotless) resembled the lotus. Amoghā (invincible) had the

173. dīptādyaiḥ—the nine Śaktis beginning with Dīptā are described in the following verses.

shape of Karṇikāra flower. Vidyut (lightning) had universal colour. Sarvatomukhī had four faces and four colours.

23-24. They saw the planets all round the lord:—viz., the lord Soma (Moon), Aṅgāraka (Mars), Budha (Mercury) the most excellent among the intelligent, Bṛhaspati (Jupiter) of enormous intellect, Bhārgava (Venus) the storehouse of refulgence and Manda (Saturn) slow in gait. Sūrya (Sun) was Śiva, the lord of the universe and Soma (Moon) was Umā herself.

25-26. The five elements[174] were the rest. The universe of the mobile and immobile beings was seen as identical with them. On seeing Śiva the consort of Umā, the lord of Devas, the sages and Devas joined their palms in reverence and eulogised him who was the bestower of boons, by means of pleasing and delightful words.

The sages said:

27-30. Obeisance to Śiva, to Rudra, to Kadrudra, to Pracetas, to Mīḍhuṣṭama (the bountiful one), to Śarva, to Śipiviṣṭa, to Raṁhas. I bow down to lord Bhāskara (refulgent like the sun) seated in the lotus and surrounded by the nine Śaktis on a pedestal which was highly pleasing, large, spotless and essentially powerful. I bow to Āditya, Bhāskara, Bhānu, Ravi and lord Divākara. I bow down to Umā, Prabhā, Prajñā, Sandhyā, Sāvitrī, Vistārā, Uttarā, and Bodhanī as well as Āpyāyanī the bestower of boons. I bow to Brahmā, Viṣṇu and Śiva.

31. After worshipping the group beginning with Soma in due order by means of the mantras in accordance with the prescribed injunctions I remember lord Sadāśiva, Śaṅkara the primordial deity stationed in the Solar disc.

32. I remember Indra and other Devas as well as Īśvara, Nārāyaṇa, and the lotus-born first Deva in due order from the east, etc., beneath and above. I remember the thunder-bolt and the lotus.

33. Obeisance unto you of the colour of saffron. Obeisance unto you with golden ornaments and diamonds. Obeisance unto

174. śeṣāṇi pañca bhūtāni—the rest of the five grahas (following the sun and the moon), beginning with Bhauma are represented by the five gross elements, viz. ether etc.

one having eyes resembling the lotus, to one holding the lotus, to the cause of Brahmā, Indra and Nārāyaṇa.

34. I remember the chariot fitted with seven horses and having Anūru as a charioteer. I remember the gaṇas of seven[175] kinds in due order by way of the continuous flow of the seasons. I remember the Vālakhilyas.[176] I remember the lord who destroyed the group of Mandeha giants.

35. O lord of Devas, after performing Homa in the fire by means of gingelly seeds, etc. of various kinds and after dedicating everything once again, I remember your disc stationed in the middle of the lotus of the heart after duly discharging it ritualistically.

36. I remember the disc in the due order. I remember the pure lotus-like eyes red in colour. I remember the lotus in the right hand and the gesture of granting boons in the left. I remember the ornaments that adorn the lord.

37. I remember your divine face that is terrible due to the curved fangs, that has the lustre of lightning, that frightens the Daityas, that is engaged in protecting the brahmins and that threatens the groups of Rākṣasas.

38-43. I remember Soma [Moon] white in colour, Bhūmija (Mars) who has the colour of fire, Budha (Mercury) the son of Moon who has golden lustre, Bṛhaspati [Jupiter] who resembles gold, Śukra [Venus] who is white in colour, and Manda [Saturn] who is very dark. I remember the right hand with the gesture of granting fearlessness, and the left-hand that rests on the thighs. I remember all those planets ending with Saturn. I remember Mahādeva and Bhāskara. O lord, be pleased. I shall offer Arghya unto you in a strong vessel made of copper and filled with splendid water resembling the full moon in colour and having a prastha of flowers and sweet scents.

Obeisance to lord Śiva, Īśvara, Kapardin, Rudra, Viṣṇu. Obeisance to you Brahman of the form of the sun.

175. gaṇaṁ saptavidham. According to ST. the sevenfold group comprises ādityas, ṛṣis, nāgas, gandharvas, gramaṇīs and rakṣas.

176. Vālakhilyas—a class of ṛṣis, sixty thousand in number, are said to be Brahmā's sons. A number of eleven hymns of the *Ṛgveda* (inserted after vi.ii 48) are attributed to these sages.

Sūta said :

He who worships thus, with concentration and mental purity, lord Śiva in the mystic diagram, he who reads this excellent hymn in the morning, mid-day and evening, acquires no doubt, identity with Śiva.

CHAPTER TWENTY

The means of worshipping Śiva

Sūta said :

1. Rudra, Mahādeva, the grandfather stationed in the mystic diagram is worthy of being worshipped by the Brahmins, Kṣatriyas and Vaiśyas as well.

2. For the Śūdras[177] the service rendered to a worshipper is enough. Undoubtedly women are not authorised to perform worship.

3. If the worship is conducted through leading brahmins, women and Śūdras shall derive the same benefit. In order to help kings special worship shall be conducted by brahmins and others.

4. May the brahmins and others worship Sadāśiva thus.

After saying thus, lord Rudra vanished there itself.

5. All those noble-souled sages and Devas bowed down to the lord. They were excited due to meditation on Rudra.

6-11. Devas and sages whose assets are austerities went away in the direction from which they had come.

Hence, one shall continuously worship the solar deity who has the form of Śiva, for the sake of virtue, love, wealth and salvation. He shall worship him mentally, verbally and physically.

The sages said :

O Romaharṣaṇa, the most excellent one among those who cherish all the scriptures, O omniscient one, O highly blessed

177. Persons of Śūdra class and female sex are excluded from worship. However, they are allowed to worship the devotees of Śiva.

disciple of Vyāsa, now mention the sacred doctrine of Agni and the sacred scripture thereof recounted by Śiva for the achievement of virtue, love, wealth and salvation. It was mentioned by Śiva the lord of Devas, with a desire for the welfare of devotees. After performing an elaborate penance difficult to be practised by Devas and Dānavas he extracted this doctrine from the Vedas, the six ancillary treatises as well as from the systems of philosophy, Sāṁkhya and Yoga. It extends to a hundred crores of verses. It is full of meaning. It contains behests. It is a great hidden secret. It decries ignorance. In some respects it agrees with the orthodox religion based on the four castes and stages of life. In some respects it is antagonistic to it.

There, in that doctrine, how is the worship of the lord ? How is the sacred ablution, yoga etc ? We are eager to hear about it.

Sūta said :

12-14. Formerly, Nandīśvara the son of Śilāda, the lord of the Gaṇas and a favourite of Śiva, was asked thus by Sanatkumāra on the peak of the splendid Meru. After bowing down to him the chiefs of all sages put the same question to him. O leading sages, may ye now listen to that doctrine of perfect knowledge narrated to Sanatkumāra by the delighter of his race.

15-17. This doctrine pertaining to Śiva is the gist of what is mentioned in the Vedas or is defined by Śiva. It is devoid of eulogies and rebukes and is capable of giving immediate conviction. Resulting from the grace of elders and preceptors it is a divine doctrine that yields salvation without strain.

Sanatkumāra said:

"O Śailādi, how is the worship of Śiva to be performed for the realisation of virtue, love, wealth and salvation. It behoves you to recount this to me who have approached you in all humility.

Sūta said:

18. On hearing these words, lord Nandin the most excel-

lent among eloquent ones, mentioned the opportune moments, occasions, necessary qualifications for practising this.

Śailādi said:

19-20. I shall mention the necessary qualifications as revealed by preceptors and the scriptural texts. The nomenclature of Śaiva preceptor (the propounder of Śaiva doctrines) is based on his gravity and not otherwise. Ācārya[178] (preceptor) is so called because he practises the doctrines himself, stabilises others in the practice of those doctrines and gathers together the topics mentioned in the sacriptural texts.

21-23. A true devotee shall search for an Ācārya with the following qualifications:—He must be conversant with the principles expounded in the Vedic passages. He must be one lying down in Bhasman. He must be graceful and pleasing in appearance. He must feel the necessity of acquiescing in the delight of the general public. He must be a follower of the path of Śrutis and Smṛtis. He must be one who accords fearlessness by means of his learning. He must be devoid of covetousness and ficklemindedness. He shall be one who scrupulously fosters proper conduct and adherence to customs and conventions. He must be bold and self-possessed. He must, cling to accepted usages and conventions. After finding out such a preceptor the devotee shall worship him like Śiva with every sort of emotional attachment.

24. The disciple must propitiate him in accordance with his faith and financial capacity. He must serve him physically and by monetary gifts. He shall continue serving him till he becomes pleased.

25. If that highly blessed personage is delighted the bonds of the disciple shall snap instantaneously. The preceptor shall be honoured and worshipped. The preceptor is Sadāśiva himself.

26. The preceptor shall test the brahmin disciples for three years by sending them on errands here and there and by giving them only such articles as will sustain their life.

27-32. The excellent person shall be engaged in the meanest of jobs and the base person shall be engaged in the loftiest

178. ācārya. Cf.
आचार्य : आचारं ग्राहयति, आचिनोत्यर्थान्, आचिनोति बुद्धिम् N. I. 4.

ones. If they do not resent being scolded or beaten they are the most deserving disciples. The following types of Brahmins become deserving disciples: Those who are learned in Śaiva doctrines, who are devoted to the holy rites pertaining to Śiva; who are righteous and self-restrained; who follow the path of Śrutis and Smṛtis; who endure all Dvandvas (mutually clashing opposites); who are self-possessed and perpetually persevering mentally; who are engaged in rendering help to others; who are devoted to the service of the preceptors; who are tender-hearted, healthy and straightforward; who are loyal and faithful; who speak pleasing words and are not arrogant; who are intelligent and without rivalry and covetousness; who are endowed with the qualities of cleanliness and adherence to the conventions; who are free from haughtiness and maliciousness and who are engaged in devotion to Śiva. Persons like this, who are endowed with disciplined conduct thus should be further sanctified for the purity of principles.

33. A disciple who is pure, who is richly endowed with the quality of humility, who eschews false pretensions and harsh words and who obeys the behests of preceptor deserves blessings.

34. The preceptor who is conversant with the scriptural texts, who is intelligent, who is favourably disposed towards common people, who performs penance, who is engaged in following accepted worldly conventions and who knows the principles is known as one who bestows salvation.

35. He may be endowed with all characteristic qualities; he may be an expert in all sacred texts, and he may be conversant with all means and modes, but if he is devoid of the real truth, all the other qualities shall be futile to him.

36. If he has no decisive knowledge of the Ātman which is self-evident great principle, he is not blessed himself. How can he bless others?

37. The brahmin who is enlightened is pure and is capable of accomplishing things. But whence can there be enlightenment in one who is devoid of principles? Whence can there be comprehension of self?

38. All those who are devoid of comprehension are said to

be Paśus. All those who are incited by Paśus are also spoken as Paśus.

39. Hence, those liberated souls who are conversant with the principles (realities) can redeem others. The principle that produces perfect cognition originates from his greatest bliss.

40. Only he who has understood the truth can be a guide unto bliss and not one who is a preceptor only in name but who is devoid of cognition.

41. Such people cannot redeem one another. Can a rock redeem another rock? Those who have perfect cognition only in name can have salvation only in name.

42. Command that causes the destruction of bonds is instantaneously born by the sight and touch of the yogins or even by conversing with them.

43. Or, the preceptor may enter the physical body of the disciple by the yogic path and enlighten him by means of the yogic power after understanding all the entities.

44-47. The three-fold[179] purity mental, verbal and physical is ordained by the path of knowledge. The preceptor shall test the disciple, ascertain his piety and virtue as well as his knowledge. He must test him to find out if he is devoid of faults whether he is a Brahmin, a Kṣatriya or a Vaiśya. The preceptor shall whisper from ear to ear and from the knowledge shown perceive what he has known. The preceptor's line shall thus be perpetuated duly as in the case of lamps where one lamp is lighted from another. O highly blessed one, what are called tattvas consist of the following:– Bhauvanam,[180] Padam, Varṇākhyan Mātram, and Kālādhvaram. Only he who cuts across these tattvas can realise Siddhi and salvation by means of his own ājña śakti (will power) through the mercy of the preceptor.

48-52. The elements beginning with the earth are included in Bhauvanam; sound, touch, colour, taste and smell are Padam

179. ṣaḍardha-śuddhiḥ—guṇatraya-śuddhi ST. purification of the three guṇas, viz. sattva, rajas and tamas.

180. Along with the purification of the threefold set of the guṇas, the Purāṇa enjoins the purification of tattvas, viz. bhauvana (five gross elements), pada (five subtle elements), varṇa (five organs of knowledge), mātra (five organs of action) and kālādhvara (the fourfold group consisting of intellect, ego, consciousness and mind).

due to their common characteristics. O Brahmin, Varṇākhyam connotes the different varieties of the sense-organs. The Mātram connotes the organs of action. The mind, intellect, ego and the unmanifest are known as Kālādhvaram. By Unmanatva is meant the principles beginning with Puruṣa and ending with Brahmā. Īśatva is greater than the greatest. This is the meaning of all tattvas. One who is not a yogin cannot know the real nature of the tattvas which is the nature of Śiva himself.

CHAPTER TWENTYONE

The mode of Initiation

Sūta said:

1-4. The ground intended for the mystic diagram should be duly tested in regard to smell, colour, taste, etc. It should be rendered befitting the invocation of the lord by decorating it with canopies, etc. The maṇḍala of the magnitude of a Hasta (hand) shall be made. In the middle the diagram of a lotus set with five diamonds shall be marked by means of powder. It shall be circular with eight petals. It shall be white or red in colour. It shall be bright and splendid. In the pericarp Śiva the cause of the universe shall be invoked along with the attendants. Then the devotee shall worship it assiduously in accordance with the extent of his wealth.

5. O great sage, the Siddhis are to be invoked in the petals, detachment in the pericarp, knowledge in the stalk and virtue in the bulbous root pleasing to the mind.

6-8. The Śaktis are in the filaments as follows:—Vāmā, Jyeṣṭhā, Raudrī, Kālī, Vikaraṇī, Balavikaraṇī, Balapramathinī and Sarvabhūtadamanī in due order. Manonmanī the great māyā shall be in the pericarp in the seat of Śiva. The Śaktis shall be fixed along with Vāmadeva and others in pairs. Mahādeva who is Manonmana shall be placed in the middle along with Manonmanī.

9. In the eastern petal (leaf) shall be fixed the Puruṣa

who has solar lustre, in a curved manner [transversely]. This Puruṣa is identical with Śiva. He is called Pranava in view of his contact with the sun, moon and fire.

10. In the southern petal, Aghora who resembles a mass of blue collyrium shall be fixed. The deity called Vāmadeva having the lustre of the Japā flower shall be placed in the northern petal.

11-15. In the western petal the devotee shall fix Sadya who is as white as the cow's milk. In the pericarp he shall fix Īśāna who resembles pure crystal. He shall fix the deity repeating the mantra beginning with "Hṛdayāya" in the south-east quarter. He shall fix the deity of smoky lustre in the north-east quarter repeating "Śirase". In the south-west petal he shall fix the deity with red lustre repeating—"Śikhāyai". He shall fix the deity having the lustre of the collyrium in the north-west petal repeating—"Kavacāya". He shall fix the deity having the lustre of the fiery flame in all the quarters repeating—obeisance to Astra (miraculous weapon). In the north-east quarter he shall fix repeating "Obeisance to the tawny-coloured eyes".

He shall then remember lord Śiva, Sadāśiva and Maheśvara. Thereafter, he shall meditate on Rudra, Viṣṇu and Viriñci in the order of creation.

16. Obeisance to Śiva in the form of Rudra, to Śambhu who is beyond peace. Obeisance to Candramas (moon) the tranquil one, to one who has quietened the Daityas.

17. Obeisance to Vidyā, to the support of Vidyā; obeisance to Vahni (fire), to one who has the lustre of fire. Obeisance to Kalā, to Pratiṣṭhā (establishment); obeisance to the redeemer, to the annihilator.

18-20. Obeisance to Nivṛtti, to the lord of wealth. Obeisance to Dhārā (current), to Dhāraṇa (the act of holding). By means of these mantras the devotee shall remember the following deities, viz:—Sadāśiva having elements for his physical form, the ancient lord called Puruṣa having Īśāna for his crown, the delighted lord having Aghora for his heart, Maheśvara having Vāmadeva for his private parts, the lord who is the cause of the manifestation of the "Sat" and "Asat" and who has the form of Sadya and the lord who consists of thirtyeight digits and who has five faces and ten arms.

21-30. The devotee then splits Sadya full of Kalās, into eight ways. He splits Vāma the great lord into thirteen; Aghora stationed in the form of Kalās into eight; Puruṣa full of Kalās into four and Īśāna of five forms into five. Repeating the mantra "Haṁsa Haṁsa[181] etc. with great devotion to Śiva he makes the "O" a mātrā of Om, similar in form with "A". Repeating the letters "A" "I" "U", "E"and Ambā in due order, he shall remember the lord in the form of the Ātman. The lord is remembered as follows:—He is accompanied by Pradhāna and is devoid of dissolution and origin. He is unborn; minuter than the minutest atom; greater than the greatest Being; He is Īśāna who has sublimated the sexual urge. He is Virūpākṣa the consort of Umā. The eternal lord has a thousand heads, a thousand eyes, a thousand hands and feet. He is the ultimate Nāda (sound) with Nāda for his physical form. His form is like that of a glowworm—or that which illuminates the firmament. The lord has the shape of the lunar line (contour). The lord is stationed at the end of the twelfth[182] nerve (i.e. the crest), between the eyebrows in the middle of the palate, in the throat and in the region of the heart in due order. He is self-bliss; nectar; Śiva (the auspicious one). He resembles the circular lightning streak. He has a lustre similar to that of ten million lightning streaks. He is dark as well as red. He has the form of the Kalās. He is seated along with the three Śaktis. He is Sadāśiva. He is accompanied by the three tattvas. The devotee then gradually worships the lord identical with the deity of learning.

31. He shall then severally worship the guardians of the quarters along with their weapons beginning with the one in the east. After duly preparing the Caru (the cooked rice offering) he shall dedicate it to Śiva.

32. After offering half[183] of it to Śiva he shall perform Homa with the remaining half repeating the Aghora mantra. He shall then give that excellent thing to the disciple to eat.

181. haṁsa-mantra:
"हसहंसाय विद्महे परमहंसाय धीमहि । तन्नो हंसः प्रचोदयात्" —cited in ST.

182. dvādaśānte—i.e. on the forehead. Cf. "dvādaśānte pare tattve parānandaṁa-lakṣaṇaḥ"—*Agnipurāṇa*—cited in *ST*.

183. ardham—caruardham, half of oblation.

33-34. He shall then perform the rite of Ācamana and become pure. Then he shall duly worship Puruṣa[184] and take in Pañcagavya that is inspired with the mantra of Īśāna. Applying Bhasman over the limbs repeating the mantra of Vāmadeva he shall gradually dust them with Bhasman. He shall then repeat the Gāyatrī mantra into the ears of the disciple, the mantra whose deity is Rudra.

35-36. He shall then place five golden pots covered with lids. Threads should be wound around them. They shall be covered with a pair of cloths. Gold pieces and gems should be put into them before-hand. Then Homa should be performed with Caru according to one's affluence through five brahmins.

37. He shall engage the disciple in the meditation on Śiva and stay him in a place to the south of the Maṇḍala. He shall be his devotee and be occupying a bed of Darbha grass.

38. In the morning Homa should be duly performed with ghee one hundred and eight times, repeating the Aghora mantra and thereby the devotee can dispel the dirt of his evil dreams.[185]

39-42. When the disciple has taken his bath after observing the rite of fasting he shall be adorned and made to wear a fresh cloth and an upper garment. He shall be made to wear a turban as a mark of auspiciousness. With a silken cloth or any other material his eyes shall be bound and he shall be taken in. In accordance with one's monetary capacity a handful of flowers mixed with golden flower or gold in lieu of flower shall be offered to the lord, repeating the mantra of Īśāna. After performing three circumambulations repeating Rudra adhyāya he shall be engaged in the meditation on Śiva repeating the Praṇava alone. After meditating on the lord, he shall put the flowers himself over Īśāna.

43-45. The mantra with which he places the flower on the lord shall be repeated by him. The preceptor then touches the disciple with the sacred water of Śiva, applies Bhasman over

184. puruṣam—tatpuruṣam.

185. With the aghora mantra. he shall wipe off the evil effects of bad dreams. Cf.

गजाश्वारोहणं स्वप्ने शुभं शुक्लाशुंकादिकम् । तैलाभ्यङ्गादिकं हीनं होमोऽघोरेण शान्तये ।। *Agnipurāṇa*—cited in *ST*.

his head[186] repeating the Aghora mantra and then worships him with scents and other things. The door for entering on the western side is the most excellent one for pupils of all castes. It is remembered as excellent particularly for the Kṣatriyas. Then the cloth with which the disciple has been blind-folded is untied and the Maṇḍala is shown to him.

46. He is then made to sit on a seat of Darbha grass with his face turned to the south. Thereafter, the rite of consecration of the principles shall be performed severally for the five tattvas.

47-48. O son of Brahmā, the consecration of the Cosmic Egg ending with Rudra shall be done by means of recession; beyond that until the ambit of Avyakta (shall be done) by means of Pratiṣṭhā (Establishment). O sage of good holy rites, up to the end of Viśveśvara the tattvavidyā shall be consecrated by means of Kalās (the digit of the lores) alone. After consecrating the path beyond by means of Śivabhakti (devotion to Śiva) (the preceptor) shall lead the disciple to the tattva Śiva (i.e. Śānti).

49. He shall then be taken for the worship of the tattva of the Īśvara in his bhoga form (enjoyment) by cutting across the previous three tattvas or four (i.e. by excluding Śānti or including it).

50-51. He shall perform Homa for Sadāśiva who is the Śāntyatīta Kalā by means of Aṅga mantras and by separately invoking the previous four tattvas ending with Śānti, with the mantras Sadya, etc. O excellent sage, beyond Śāntyatīta, Kalā shall be consecrated by means of Īśāna mantra. In regard to each, one hundred and eight 'Homas' shall be performed in the directions indicated.

52-53. In the north-east the Pradhāna is sung in the Pañcama note. Thereafter, seven articles are to be consigned to fire by way of Homa—viz.:—the sacrificial twigs, ghee, caru, fried grains, mustard, barley and gingelly seeds, repeating Om at the outset and Svāhā in the end. O brahmin, their concluding Homa is performed by means of Īśāna mantra.

186. **śiṣya-mūrdhani. Cf.**

पूर्वाननस्य शिष्यस्य मूलमन्त्रेण मस्तके । शिवहस्तः प्रदातव्यो रुद्रेशपददायकः ।
Agnipurāṇa—cited in *ST*.

54. O sage of good holy rites, expiatory rite shall then be performed by means of Aghora mantra beginning with "Om Haṁsa".

55. Then the rites in the sacred fire beginning with "Jayā" (Homa) and ending with "Sviṣṭa" Homa, are gradually performed. They shall be combined with Pradhāna three times.[187]

56-58. (?) The elements shall be combined with Pradhāna by means of Brahmanirvāpi, Maunibīja, etc. Then by means of Pradhāna Mātrā (the chief of organs of action) the Prāṇa and Apāna shall be controlled. By means of the sixth[188] Bīja, the Kulākula ending with the Ātman and Praṇava shall be pierced. Brahmā, Keśava and Hara shall be assimilated in Rudra. Rudra is assimilated in Īśāna and lord Maheśvara (i.e. Īśāna) in Śiva. Then he shall meditate on the destroyer of worldly existence in the order of creation (Sṛṣṭiprakāra).

59-66. After stabilising the Ātman, the individual soul, the following rites shall be performed in accordance with the injunctions—Tāḍanam, Dvāradarśanam, Dīpanam, Grahaṇam, Bandhanam along with the worship and Amṛtīkaraṇa. The sixth one shall be along with Sadya and accompanied by the third (i.e. Dīpanam). The Saṁhṛti Prakāra (i.e. the order of destruction) shall be in the order of the five elements and ending with the sixth. With Sadya at the beginning and accompanied by the sixth (Bīja ?), ending with Śikhā along with "phaṭ"—this rite is called Tāḍanam.

The rite of Dvāradarśanam consists of indicating the tattvas to the yogin.

The rite of Dīpanam is by means of Sampuṭīkaraṇa (ritualistic covering up) of the Pradhāna by the third Bīja. (?)

The rite of Grahaṇam is by means of Sampuṭīkaraṇa of the Pradhāna by the first Bīja.

The rite of Bandhanam is also by means of Sampuṭīkaraṇa of the Pradhāna by the first Bīja which is full (because Pūjā is performed).

187. guṇa-saṁkhyā-prakāreṇa—in threefold manner, as described in the *Pāśupatatantra* : वैदिकं कल्पमेवं हि मिश्रं चैवानुकल्पकम् । शैव कल्पानुकल्पञ्च अग्निकार्यं त्रिधा भवेत् ॥

188. ṣaṣṭhena—with the sixth mantra, i.e. namo hiraṇya-bāhave—cited in *ST*.

The rite of Amṛtīkaraṇa is flooding with nectar.

The combination of Kalās (in the order of destruction) is as follows—Śāntyatītā, Śānti, Vidyā, Amalā, Pratiṣṭhā and Nivṛtti. This combination of the Kalās is to be accompanied by tattva, varṇa, kalā and bhuvana.

The hymn should be duly sanctified by mantras and Pādas (metrical feet) and used for prayer after evolving it as before by means of the first yonibīja.

67-70. Know that the rites of worship, Samprokṣaṇa (sprinkling with holy water), Tāḍana, Haraṇa, the Saṁyoga (joining) of the Saṁhata (what is combined and collected) and Vikṣepa (throwing off) shall be performed in due order. Arcanā (worship), Garbhadhāraṇa (conceiving), Janana (nativity) (are the rites thereafter ?). Then the rite of Bhānu knowledge and its dissolution in particular shall be performed. O sage of good holy rites, the first one i.e. the mantra Īśāna has been mentioned along with the yonibīja.[189] Undoubtedly, O great sage, the conclusion of the rites in Uddhāra (uplifting) Prokṣaṇa (sprinkling with the holy water), and Tāḍana is performed by the Aghora mantra ending with Phaṭ. O sage of good holy rites, this is the orderly procedure by means of the Yogic path in regard to every tattva.

71-72. All through the rite the preceptor shall lead the disciple by holding his fist; when there is combination with equinotical transit[190] the Kalās beginning with Nivṛtti and ending with Śivā combine in one place. Otherwise, they remain separate. O leading brahmin, at the tip of the nose and at the crest of the head along with the back part, the yogins should forbear [?]. This is the behest of the lord of Devas.

73-78. With the sacred water taken in gold, silver, copper or other vessels the preceptor shall sprinkle the righteous disciple who is a devotee of Śiva. Darbha grass shall be put inside

189. yonibījena—i.e. with "hrīm."

190. The process is elaborated in the *Agnipurāṇa*. Cf.

प्रथम प्राणसंयोगः स्वरूपमपरं ततः । हृदयादिक्रमोच्चारविसृष्टं मन्त्रसंज्ञितम् । सुषुम्नानुगतं नादं स्वरूपं तु तृतीयकम् । चतुर्थं कारणत्यागात्प्रशान्तविषुवं नभः । शक्तिनादोर्ध्वसंरावस्तच्छक्तिविषुवं मतम् ।। प्राणस्य निखिलस्यापि शक्तिप्रमेयवर्जितम् । तत्कालविषुवं षष्ठं शक्त्यत्यतीतं च सप्तमम् ।। तदेतद्योजनस्थानं विषुवं तत्त्वसंज्ञितम् ।।—Cited in ST.

the pot. It should be covered with a cloth and a string should be tied round it. O sage of holy rites, gems should be put inside the vessel. The holy water should be inspired with the holy passages of Vedic Saṁhitā and Rudrādhyāya hymns. The disciple shall take initiation in the presence of Śiva, the fire and his preceptor. After initiation he shall practise in accordance with the behest of the preceptor. It is better to abandon life, or cut off one's head rather than take food without worshipping lord Sadāśiva. The rite of initiation shall be performed thus. The worship shall be performed in due order. One shall perform the worship of Parameśvara three times or at least once a day.

79. The rite of Agnihotra, the recital of the Vedic mantras and the sacrifices consisting of many monetary gifts are not on a par with even the sixteenth part of the worship of the Liṅga of Śiva.

80. He who worships Śiva even once is like that person who always performs sacrifices, who always gives charitable gifts and who always performs penance taking in only air.

81. Those who worship Mahādeva once, twice, thrice or continuously are Rudras. There is no doubt about this.

A non-Rudra shall neither touch Rudra nor worship nor glorify him. A non-Rudra shall not attain Rudra.[191]

Thus, succinctly the procedure and injunction regarding the persons who are qualified for the worship of Śiva, have been mentioned to you. Listening to it yields the benefit of virtue, wealth, love and salvation.

CHAPTER TWENTYTWO

The consecration of the Tattvas

Śailādi said :

1. After performing the rite of ablution and sacrifice and other sacred rites of the sun, the devotee shall observe the rites of Śivasnāna (the ablution pertaining to Śiva), Bhasmasnāna (ablution with Bhasman) and the worship of Śiva.

191. Mark the sectarian character of the Purāna.

2. Repeating the sixth Bīja mantra he shall take some earth and devoutly place it on the ground. Repeating the second Bīja mantra he shall sprinkle it with water and by repeating the third Bīja mantra he shall sanctify it.

3-6. Repeating the fourth Bīja mantra he shall divide the earth into two parts. With one part he shall dispel dirt. He shall then bathe. Repeating the sixth Bīja mantra he shall divide the remaining part of the earth kept in the hand, into three parts; he shall apply the middle one all over the body repeating the fourth Bīja mantra. Repeating the sixth Bīja mantra he shall smear the earth over the middle part of the body seven times. Repeating the Mūla mantra he shall stroke the left side. The ritualistic binding of the quarters (Diśābandha) shall be performed repeating the sixth Bīja mantra ten times. The holy water shall be smeared with the left side portion of the mud and the body with the right portion. Repeating all the Bīja mantras he shall take bath remembering the sun. He shall then perform the rite of ablution by means of a horn, leaf-cups or the petal of the Palāśa flower repeating these splendid mantras pertaining to the sun. They are conducive to the achievement of all Siddhis.

7-12. O sage of good holy rites, I shall mention the mantras pertaining to the sun. They are Bāṣkala and others, which constitute the essential parts of all the Vedas. The following mantra of nine syllables is glorified as Bāṣkala viz:—Om bhūḥ. Om Bhuvaḥ. Om Svaḥ. Om Mahaḥ. Om Janaḥ. Om Tapaḥ. Om Satyam. Om Ṛtam. Om Brahma. The word Ṛta means Akṣara i.e. imperishable which means truth. Each syllable is used with praṇava in the beginning and namaḥ (obeisance) in the end. The following is the Mūla mantra of the sun the great Ātman: Om bhūrbhuvaḥ svaḥ tat savitur vareṇyaṁ bhargo devasya dhīmahi dhiyo yo naḥ pracodayāt:

"We meditate upon the excellent refulgence of the lord sun, the refulgence that urges and guides our intellect. Om obeisance to the sun; obeisance to the great comet in the firmament.

The devotee shall worship the sun of bright face by means of the nine-syllabled Mūla mantra. I shall mention the ancillary mantras, Om bhūḥ, obeisance to Brahman's heart. Om Bhuvaḥ, obeisance to the head of Viṣṇu. Om svaḥ, obeisance to the tuft of Rudra. Om Bhūrbhuvaḥ svaḥ, obeisance to one whose tuft has clusters of fiery lustre. Om Mahaḥ, obeisance to Maheśvara in coat of mail. Om Janaḥ obeisance to Śiva in the eyes. Om Tapaḥ Phaṭ unto the scorcher, unto Astra the miraculous missile. Thus, the different kinds of mantras pertaining to the sun have been mentioned to you. The devotee shall pour water over himself by the tip of horn or other vessels repeating these mantras.

13. A brahmin or a kṣatriya or a vaiśya shall pour water with a copper vessel also with flowers and Kuśa grass all the while repeating the mantras with great concentration.

14-15. O excellent brahmin, he shall then wear a red cloth and perform the rite of Ācamana. During day time he shall repeat the Ācamana mantra beginning with "Sūryaśca." During the night he shall repeat the mantra beginning with "Agniśca". During the midday he shall repeat the mantra "Āpaḥ Punantu". This is called mantrācamana. After performing the purificatory rite repeating the sixth Bīja mantra he shall repeat the first excellent Bīja mantra.

16. Then he shall repeat the excellent nine-syllabed Mūla mantra ending with Vauṣaṭ. He shall perform the Nyāsa rite on the fingers, viz.—the thumb, middle and ring fingers.

17-21. Then he shall perform Nyāsa in the palm, index finger, thumb and the parts of the fist. He shall then make the lord ritualistically fettered by the nine-syllabled as well as Aṅga mantras. He shall then think thus, "I am the sun". Holding water in the palm of his left hand shaped like a cup he shall sprinkle it over his body by means of a bundle of kuśa grass repeating the mantras in order.[192] Scents and white mustard shall be mixed in the water. While sprinkling with water, the mantra "āpo hi ṣṭhā" etc. split into eight sentences shall be repeated. The water that remains shall be smelt through the left nostril. He shall then conceive that Śiva pervades his body. He shall then take up the vessel, keep it over his body and smell through the right nostril. He shall imagine that the lord is outside, seated on the rock and is dark in colour. He shall then perform the rite of Tarpaṇa unto all Devas and sages in particular.

192. etair mantraiḥ—such as, "āpo hi ṣṭhā mayo-bhuvaḥ" *TS.* 4.1.5.1.

22. He shall then offer Arghya unto the Bhūtas (goblins) and the Pitṛs (manes). He shall worship Sandhyā (junction) and the full moonlight.

23-28. He shall offer Arghya in the morning, midday and evening with water and red sandal paste taking a handful of it and throwing it up in a circle. O excellent brahmins, he shall draw a perfect circle on the ground and pray facing the east. He shall fill a copper vessel with a Prastha of scented water mixed with red sandal paste, red flowers, gingelly seeds, kuśa grass and raw rice grains. It shall be filled with cow's urine along with Dūrvā grass and Apāmārga or with ghee alone. The devotee shall kneel on the ground and bow down to the lord of Devas. Holding the vessel over his head he shall offer the Arghya repeating the Mūla mantra. By giving Arghya unto the sun he will attain that benefit which is reputed to accrue after performing ten thousand horse-sacrifices. After offering the Arghya he shall worship the three-eyed lord of Devas.

29. Or, after worshipping the sun he shall perform the fiery bath i.e. applying Bhasman over the body. The Śivasnāna shall be as before, only the mantra is different.

30. The ablution pertaining to the sun and Śiva is preceded by the washing of teeth. Then he shall worship Gaṇeśa, Varuṇa and the preceptor in the holy river.

31-32. He shall sit in the lotus pose (padmāsana) inside the holy river and worship the same. He shall take the holy water in a pot and enter the place of worship. He shall walk over the path with sandals in his feet and sanctify the path with the Arghya water. As before, he shall perform the rites of Nyāsa on the fingers and the limbs of his body.

33. Thus, the material of Arghya has been succinctly mentioned. Then the yogin shall sit in the lotus pose and practise Prāṇāyāma.

34-37. He shall collect lotus and other red flowers and put them to his right. He shall place the water-pot towards his left. Copper vessels are sacred to the sun and they are conducive to the achievement of all desired objects. The Arghya vessels shall then be taken and washed duly with the water as stated before. The water shall also be collected in the bigger vessel. The Arghya water shall contain all the articles meant for Arghya. It shall be kept there together with the water consecrated with the Astra mantra. It shall be inspired with the Saṁhitā mantras and worshipped by repeating the first Bīja mantra. Repeating the fourth Bīja mantra he shall cover the mouth of the vessel and place it over its pedestal.

38-39. As before, he shall place the Pādya (the water for washing the feet) and Acamanīya (the water for sipping) separately in vessels washed with water. The water shall contain scented flowers. After performing the Nyāsa rite with the Saṁhitā mantras and covering it up with Kavaca mantras he shall sprinkle the materials of worship with the Arghya water. He shall perform the japa of the sun bowed to by all Devas.

40. After bowing down to the lord repeating the mantra "Indeed, Āditya increases him, his energy, his strength and his fame," he shall offer a seat unto the lord.

41. The seat offered shall be ample, free from dirt, strong, very comfortable and worthy of being commended. In the corners beginning with the south-east the rite of Hṛdayanyāsa (fixation in the heart) shall be performed ending with the middle finger.

42-43. The parts of the lotus shall also be fixed, viz:—the seed, the sprout, the stalk containing pores, the fibre containing thorns, the petal, the tip of the petal very white in colour or golden or red. It shall have the pericarp and the filaments too. It shall be surrounded by Dīptā and other Śaktis.

44. There are eight Śaktis beginning with Dīptā, viz. Dīptā, Sūkṣmā, Jayā, Bhadrā, Vibhūti, Vimalā, Aghorā and Vikṛtā.

45. All of them face the sun. They are splendid and they keep their palms joined in reverence or they hold lotuses in their hands. All of them are bedecked in all ornaments.

46. He shall instal goddess Sarvatomukhī[193] the bestower of boons, in the middle. Then he shall invoke the goddess, the sun and the lord.

47. He shall invoke the sun by repeating the nine-syllabled mantra mentioned as Bāṣkala. The rites of invocation and presence shall be performed only by this mantra.

193. **sarvatomukhīm—gāyatrīm** *ST*. **Of course, Rudra-gāyatrī is meant.**

48. The Mudrā (ritualistic show of hand) of the sun, the great Ātman, is called Padmamudrā (the gesture of the lotus). Thereafter, Arghya, Pādya and Ācamana shall be offered separately repeating the Mūla mantra.

49-50. Arghya shall be offered once again in accordance with the injunctions, repeating the Bāṣkala mantra. Red lotuses, flowers and red sandal shall also be offered. Light shall be shown, incense offered and Naivedya dedicated. Smelling scents etc. to render the mouth fragrant, betel leaves, wicks, lights shall be offered repeating Bāṣkala mantra.

51. They are offered in six ways (?) in the quarters south-east, north-east, south-west, north-west, east and west.

52. After worshipping duly and performing the Nyāsa rite of all limbs upto the eyes in the pericarp, repeating the mantras beginning with Praṇava and ending with Namaḥ, the devotee shall perform meditation on the form of the lord.

53. All the Mūrtis have the lustre of lightning and are calm. But the Aṣṭamūrti is terrible. This form has the terrible face due to the curved fangs.

54-56. The right hand shows the symbol of bestowing boons; the left hand is adorned with lotus. All Mūrtis are richly bedecked in ornaments; they wear red garlands and clothes and have red unguents smeared over their bodies. Mahādeva is accompanied by his multitude of attendants. His physical form is pink in colour like saffron. He holds the lotus in his hand. Nectar exudes from his face. The lord has two hands and two eyes. He possesses red ornaments, wears red garlands and smears red unguents.

57-61. The devotee shall meditate on the sun, the lord of the worlds who has the form thus—

Outside the lotus all round in the mystic diagram he is accompanied by the splendid Moon, Mars, Mercury Jupiter, Venus, Saturn, Rāhu and Ketu. All these have a pair of eyes and hands but Rāhu has only the upper part of the body. His face is circular. He has joined his palms together. Saturn has curved fangs in his mouth. His hands show the gestures of granting boons and freedom from fear. For realising virtue, love and wealth they shall be worshipped assiduously by their respective names prefixed with Praṇava and suffixed with namaḥ. They shall be worshipped with their respective emotions.

62-63. The devotee shall worship outside the mystic diagram the seven groups of Gaṇas: sages, Devas, Gandharvas, serpents, Apsarases, Grāmaṇīs, Yātudhānas and prominent Yajñas. He shall worship the seven horses of the lord constituted by the seven Vedic metres.

64. The groups of Vālakhilyas shall be worshipped then. The remnants of worship of the lord shall then be taken out. He shall worship the pedestal of the Mūrti and the deity as well.

65. At the time of invocation, at the conclusion of the worship and at the time of the ritualistic dismissal of the deities Arghya shall be severally offered in accordance with the injunctions.

66. Thereafter, he shall repeat the Bāṣkala mantras a thousand times, five hundred times or one hundred and eight times. He shall then do Homa up to a tenth part of the japa number.

67. To the west the sacrificial pit shall be dug in a circle. There shall be a circular guiding ring too. The depth and the width of the pit shall be four Aṅgulas.

68. In the obligatory and optional rites the external diameter of the pit shall be a Hasta (hand) in extent. The navel of the pit shall be of the shape of the leaf of the Aśvattha and extend to ten Aṅgulas.

69. The Gala (throat) shall be one Aṅgula in width and five Aṅgulas in length. It shall resemble the lip of an elephant. The remaining part shall be two Aṅgulas in width.

70. The Mekhalā (outer ring) of the pit shall be made after leaving a margin of the same width (i. e. two aṅgulas). After making all these assiduously, the devotee shall perform the Homa.

71. He shall perform the rite of Ullekhana (scraping) and sprinkle it with water, repeating the sixth Bīja mantra. He shall offer seat in the middle repeating the first Bīja mantra with great concentration.

72-73. Thereafter, he shall perform the Nyāsa rite of the Śakti named Prabhāvatī, repeating the first Bīja mantra. After worshipping by means of scents and fragrant flowers, repeating the Bāṣkala mantra in due order he shall once again perform the rite of Kriyāyajña with the Bāṣkala mantra itself. Thereafter the rite of Pūrṇāhuti shall be performed by the Mūla mantra alone.

74-75. After performing thus, in due order, the solar fire shall be produced. He shall then perform the Nyāsa rite of the lotus mentioned before in accordance with the injunctions laid down before. After worshipping lord sun as before over the face ten Āhutis shall be offered by the Bāṣkala mantra.

76-79. In all the Homas beginning with "Jayā" Homa and ending with "Sviṣṭa" Homa, each of the Aṅga (ancillary) rites shall be separately performed with the Saṁhitā mantras. The offering of Arghya is common to all schools of worshippers in the traditional style. He shall then offer food offering to the sun, the lord of Devas of unmeasured Ātman. After performing these rites, viz:—the Pūjā, Homa, Arghya, circumambulation, worship of the Aṅgas, the Udvāsana (the ritualistic dismissal) and Namaskāra (obeisance) the devotee shall perform the worship of Śiva for the realization of virtue, love and wealth.

Thus has been succinctly recounted the worship of the solar deity.

80. He who even for once worships the sun, the lord of Devas, the preceptor of the universe the great Ātman attains the greatest goal.

81. He shall be liberated from all sins. He shall be devoid of all sins. He shall be endowed with all prosperity. He shall be unequalled.

82. Surrounded by his sons, grandsons and great grandsons as well as kinsmen he shall enjoy extensive pleasures here in this world itself. He shall possess in abundance riches and food-grains.

83. He will be richly endowed with vehicles and carriages as well as different kinds of ornaments. Even after passing away he shall rejoice along with the sun for indefinite period.

84-85. Thereafter, he comes back here and becomes a righteous king. Or he may be born as a brahmin endowed with the knowledge of the Vedas and the Vedāṅgas.

In view of the impressions of his previous existence he will be righteous and master of the Vedas. By worshipping the sun he shall attain identity with the sun-god.

CHAPTER TWENTYTHREE

The mode of worship of Śiva

Śailādi said:

1. Henceforth, I shall recount to you the excellent worship of Śiva. One shall worship Īśa during the three Sandhyās (morning, midday and evening) and perform the sacred rites in the fire in accordance with one's capacity.

2-3. The devotee shall at the outset perform Śivasnāna (ablution pertaining to Śiva) and the purification of the Tattvas as before. With flowers in the hand he shall enter the place of worship with great concentration and mental purity. He shall then perform Prāṇāyāma three times and the rites of Dahana and Āplāvana. With the hands rendered fragrant with scents, he shall perform the rite of the Nyāsa of the Mahāmudrā (the great gesture).

4-8. With great effort he shall make his body sanctified by the nectar of Śiva as well as by the perfect knowledge of Śiva and the fire of Brahman. He shall make his body originating from Avyakta (the unmanifest), Ahaṁkāra (ego) and the Tanmātrās (subtle elements) sanctified by this perfect knowledge. The Hṛdaya (heart) stands above, the umbilicus about a Vitasti (twelve Aṅgulas) away from it. It stands about the same distance below the cerebrum. The devotee shall recognize it as the great abode of the universe. He shall meditate on the lord Sadāśiva in the pericarp of the lotus of the heart in the following form. He has five faces, ten arms and three eyes in every face. He is bedecked in all ornaments. The moon adorns his crest. He is seated in the lotus pose. He resembles pure crystal. His upward face is white and the eastern face resembles saffron.

9. The southern face has blue colour. The northern face is very red. His western face is as white as cow's milk.

10-12. In his hands on the right side he holds the javelin, axe, sword, thunderbolt and Śakti. In the hands to the left he holds the noose, goad, bell, serpent and the excellent dart or his hands show the gestures of granting boons and freedom from fear.[194] The rest is as mentioned before. He wears all kinds of ornaments and garments of diverse colours. He shall worship lord Śiva whose form is the Vedāṅga, who is the most excellent of all excellent Devas and who is the lord of Brahman. He shall worship him with all fervour.

13. The five Brahmans have already been mentioned. Now listen to the Śivāṅgas (the ancillaries of Śiva). O sages of good holy rites, listen also about heart etc., that are the Śaktis.

14-20. Om the lord is Īśāna of all lores. Obeisance to Hṛdaya the Bīja of Śakti. Om the lord is Īśvara of all living beings. Obeisance to the head, containing Amṛta. Om obeisance to the tuft, to the overlord of Brahmā, to one in the form of black fire. Om obeisance to the Kavaca (coat of mail), to the overlord of Brahman, to the black and fierce gust of wind. Om obeisance to the eye, to Brahman, to one who swells, to the Mūrti of perfect knowledge. Om Phaṭ Phaṭ to Śiva, to Sadāśiva, to the miraculous weapon Pāśupata, to one who is not thwarted. Om obeisance to Sadyojāta. Protect me when there is an attack from worldly existence. Obeisance to that form of Śiva which is the source of origin of all worldly existences.

Om Obeisance to Śiva the most auspicious one, to one who has Haṁsa in the tuft, to one whose physical body is learning, to one whose form is Ātman and to one who is greatest with none greater. The Aṅgas of Śiva have been mentioned. His Mūrtividyā (the lore of the deity) is accompanied by the ancillaries of the Mūrtividyā which is an Aṅga of Brahman (the Vedas) also in the Śivaśāsana (the order laid down by Śiva).

194. Varadābhaya-hastām—anena caturbāhudhyānaṁ sūcitam *ST*. The devotee shall meditate on the four-armed lord.

O sage of good holy rites, I shall mention the mantras pertaining to the sun, viz., Bāṣkala and others. O sage of good holy rites, the Aṅgas are the gist of all the Vedas.

"Om Bhūḥ, Om Bhuvaḥ, Om Svaḥ, Om Mahaḥ, Om Janaḥ, Om Tapaḥ, Om Satyam, Om Ṛtam, Om Brahman.

This nine-syllabled mantra is glorified as Bāṣkala. It is called Akṣara because is does not perish in this world. Śatyam (truth) is called Akṣara. It is prefixed with Praṇava (i. e. Om) and suffixed with Namaḥ (obeisance).[194a]

21. Om Bhūrbhuvaḥ Svaḥ. We meditate on that excellent refulgence of the lord, the refulgence that urges and guides our intellect. Obeisance to the sun the greatest planet in the firmament.

22-24 Thus the Mūla mantra of the great Ātman has been mentioned. He shall worship Dīptā and other Śaktīs with the nine-syllabled mantra and the sun with the Mūla mantra. I shall succinctly mention the Aṅga mantras. The first one is mostly covered with Vedic mantras and the middle one with Praṇava.

Om Bhūḥ obeisance to the heart, to Brahman. Om Bhuvaḥ obeisance to the head, to Viṣṇu. Om Svaḥ obeisance to the tuft, to Rudra. Om Bhūrbhuvaḥ svaḥ obeisance to the lord having clusters of flames. Om Mahaḥ obeisance to the Kavaca (coat of mail), to Maheśvara. Om Janaḥ obeisance to the eyes, to Śiva. Om Tapaḥ obeisance to the Astra (miraculous missile), to one who scorches. Thus incidentally the mantras pertaining to the sun have been mentioned. O sage of good holy rites, the mantras pertaining to Śiva also have been succinctly mentioned along with the mode of Nyāsa (fixation).

25-31. Thus, he shall worship the lord identical with the mantras, in the lotus of the heart. The Homa is to be performed after duly generating the Śiva fire in the umbilicus by means of the mind. All the holy rites are to be performed in the Śiva fire. He shall meditate on lord Īśvara originating from the Aṅgas of the five Brahmans. The Mūrti of Śiva is seated on the seat of red lotus. He is turned into the Sakala form assiduously. O sage of good holy rites, the Mūrti is medi-

194a. The six lines beginning with oṁ bhūḥ and ending with astrāya phaṭ (N.S. Ed. p. 284) are repetitions of the same (N.S. Ed. p. 281).

tated upon with Mūla mantra and the mantras of the Vedāṅgas, etc. The Homa with the sacrificial twigs and ghee is performed mentally. He shall then remember the complete Dhārā (current of nectar) originating from the abode of the moon in the lunar sphere. In accordance with the injunction regarding the Purnāhuti in the Śivaśāsana (the treatise on Śiva) he shall meditate on Śiva Śaṅkara in the form of refulgence in the face. He shall again remember the lord of the chiefs of Devas in the forehead or in the middle of the eyebrows. This detailed worship shall be concluded in the lotus of the heart. He shall meditate on the destroyer of worldly existence in the shape of the pure flame of the lamp. He shall worship the lord in the Liṅga also or worship Sadāśiva on the bare ground.

CHAPTER TWENTYFOUR

The mode of worship of Śiva

Śailādi said :

1. Succinctly I shall comment upon the mode of worship of Śiva according to the manner in which it has been mentioned in the Śaiva treatises and which has been formerly recounted by Śiva.

2. Both the hands shall be smeared with sandal paste. The devotee shall perform the rite of offering handful of flowers by the mantra ending with Vauṣaṭ. He shall repeat the japa of the mantras of Mūrtividyā and Śiva. In the fingers beginning with the thumb and ending with the little finger, Īśāna and other deities shall be installed; by the fingers beginning with the little finger and ending with the middle finger, Hṛdaya[195] etc. shall be installed. The fourth[196] one shall be fixed by means of the thumb and the fifth one by means of the ring finger. The sixth one shall be installed by both the palms. The rite of Nārācāstra Prayoga (hurling of the missile, dart) by means of

195. It refers to the mantra of Aghora.
196. turīyam—the fourth, i.e. tatpuruṣa mantra

the index finger and thumb shall be performed. He shall again perform the japa of the Mūla[197] mantra and everything shall be veiled by repeating the fourth Bīja-mantra. This is called Śivahasta (Śiva's hand).

3-10. The worship of Śiva should be performed by means of this hand. The devotee shall stabilise the Ātman present in the Tattvas and perform the consecration of the Tattvas as before. After stabilising the five[198] elements—the earth, water, fire, wind, and firmament—within the ambit of the four[199] pure ones along with the current[200] he shall perform the consecratory rite of the Tattvas as before. The consecration of the Tattvas is by means of the sixth[201] Bīja mantra. The consecration of the earth is by means of Sadya and the third Bīja-mantra ending with Phaṭ. The consecration of the Vāritattva, the principle of water, shall be made by means of Sadya and the third Bīja mantra accompanied by the sixth Bīja mantra and ending with Phaṭ. The consecration of Agni Tattva shall be made by means of the third Bīja mantra pertaining to Agni and ending with Phaṭ. The consecration of Vāyu shall be made by means of the fourth Bīja mantra pertaining to Vāyu, accompanied by the sixth Bīja mantra and endīng with Phaṭ. The consecration of the firmament shall be made by means of the sixth Bīja mantra accompanied by Sadya and the third Bīja mantra ending with Phaṭ.

11. After concluding this the rite of Tāḍana (beating) shall be performed by means of the sixth Bīja mantra along with the Sadya mantra, the third Bīja mantra and the Mūla mantra ending with Phaṭ. The rite of Grahaṇa (grasping) shall be performed by means of the third Bīja mantra after the rite of Sampuṭīkaraṇa (covering up). The rite of Bandhana

197. The five-syllabled mantra of Śiva: "namaś śivāya"

198. The number five 'pañca' refers to the preceding tattvas, viz. earth, water, fire, wind and ether.

199. Among the four, viz. ego, intellect, Prakṛti and Brahma only the latter is Śuddha—pure.

200. dhārāsahitena—amṛtadhārayā yuktena *ST*. accompanied by the stream of nectar. It qualifies 'suṣumnānāḍīmārgeṇa' which is supplied by *ST*.

201. ṣaṣṭhena—with the sixth mantra beginning with 'namo hiraṇyabāhave'.

(binding) shall be performed by means of Yonibīja[202] after the covering up of the Mūla mantra. Thus is the rite of Bandha.

12. The following rites are performed one after the other. The Kalās beginning with Śāntyatīta and ending with Nivṛtti shall be meditated upon as before. Three[203] Tattvas shall be meditated upon by means of Praṇava. The Ātman along with the eight Puris[204] and having the shape of the flame of a lamp shall be meditated upon as situated beyond the three[205] Tattvas. The nectarine current flows into the Suṣumnā vessel due to the agitation[206] of Śakti.

13. Within the Kalās beginning with Śāntyatīta and ending with Nivṛtti, the Nāda, Bindu, the syllables A, U, and M, Śiva, Sadāśiva and three Mūrtis Rudra, Viṣṇu and Brahmā shall be meditated upon in the order of the creation, etc. This rite is called Brahmanyāsa (fixation of the Brahman) which consists of Amṛtīkaraṇa (transforming into nectar or eternal bliss) in order of creation. Then after fixing the five faces with the fifteen eyes and repeating the Mūla[207] mantra, the form of the deity beginning with the feet and ending with the tresses shall be meditated upon and the Mahāmudrā (great gesticulation) shall be shown. The devotee then contemplates—"I am Śiva." Śaktis and others shall be fixed in the heart. Along with the Śaktis the following shall be meditated upon viz.—the Bīja (seeds), sprouts, lotus with the stalk containing pores, thorns, leaves, filaments, virtue, knowledge, detachment, prosperity, sun, moon and fire; the Śaktis, viz.—Vāmā, Jyeṣṭhā, Raudrī, Kālī, Kālavikaraṇī, Balapramathanī and Sarvabhūtadamanī shall be meditated upon in the filaments and Manonmanī in the pericarp.

14. Then the rites of Ātmaśuddhi, Sthānaśuddhi and Dravyaśuddhi shall be performed as follows:—

202. yoni-bīja i.e. "hrīm".

203. tattva-trayam—Brahma-Viṣṇu-Rudra rūpam *ST*.

204. puryaṣṭaka-sahitam—a set of eight beginning with mūlādhāra as explained in the yoga-śāstra.

205. trayātītam—beyond the categories of Viśva, Taijasa and prājña.

206. śaktikṣobheṇa—kuṇḍalinīprabodhena *ST*. by awakening the Serpent Power.

207. mūlena—see note 197 above.

Ātmaśuddhi. The seat shall be offered alongwith all homages. The inner organs of will shall be thought of as an exterior thing by means of yogic Upacāra. The seat of the lord then shall be conceived as before in the fire-pit in the umbilicus. Sadāśiva shall be meditated upon with the nectarine current falling on the mystic diagram of Śiva. Maheśvara shall be meditated upon in the forehead in the form of the flame of a lamp. This is Ātmaśuddhi (consecration of the Ātman).

Sthānaśuddhi. The consecration of the spot is as follows:—

The devotee controls the Prāṇa and Apāna. Wind shall be stabilised by means of the Suṣumnā. Then Tālumudrā[208] (gesture of the palate) and the rite of Digbandha (binding of the quarters) shall be performed, repeating the sixth Bīja mantra.

Dravyaśuddhi. The consecration of the materials of worship is as follows:—

The three Tattvas are fixed by means of Praṇava in the Arghya vessel, the inner part of which is wiped with cloth, etc. The Bindu is meditated upon above them. They are filled with water. The materials are then arranged and flooded with nectar. In the vessels intended for Pādya (water for washing the feet) etc. the seat is offered unto them as in the case of Arghya. It is inspired with the Saṁhitā mantras and is worshipped by means of the first Bīja mantra. It is turned into Amṛta (nectar) by means of the second Bīja mantra. It is purified by means of the third Bīja mantra. It is covered up by means of the fourth Bīja mantra. It is looked at by means of the fifth Bīja mantra. Protection is accorded by means of the sixth Bīja mantra. The materials shall be sprinkled with the Arghya water by means of a bundle of Kuśa grass repeating the fourth Bīja mantra. The self and the materials shall again be sprinkled with the Arghya water along with flowers. The several materials are thus separately purified.

15-18. Then the devotee shall inspire with the mantras the following things thus:—The scent with the Sadya mantra, the cloth with the Vāma mantra; the ornament with the Aghora mantra, the Naivedya with the Tatpuruṣa mantra, and

208. tālu-mudrām—Khecarī-mudrām *ST*. one of the twenty-four *mudrās* (positions of the fingers) practised in religious worship.

the flowers with the Īśāna mantra. He shall sprinkle the remaining things repeating Śiva Gāyatrī. He shall inspire the Pañcāmṛta, pañcagavya and other things by means of the Vedāṅgas, Mūla[209] mantras and other mantras. He shall consecrate the materials by offering Arghya, Dhūpa (incense) and Ācamanīya severally, repeating the Mūla mantra. He shall show the Dhenumudrā (the gesture of cow) to them, cover them up by means of Kavaca mantra and accord protection by means of Astramantra.

19. *Mantraśuddhi* (the consecration of the mantras) is as follows:—

Arghya water is offered at the outset. The scent is taken up by means of the chest (?); it is consecrated by means of the Astra mantra; the performance of the worship, etc., upto the end of protection is pursued; the consecration of the materials till the dedication of the worship is performed silently; then a handful of flowers is offered; all the mantras are repeated with the Praṇava at the beginning and Namaḥ at the end; and then the handful of flowers shall be offered.

20. *Liṅgaśuddhi* (the consecration of the Liṅga) is as follows:—

At the outset the common Arghya vessel is filled with water. Offering scents and fragrant flowers, etc. it is inspired with the Saṁhitā mantras; then the Dhenumudrā is shown; it is covered up by means of the Kavaca mantra; it is then protected by the Astra mantra. The pūjā that has already been performed shall again be done by means of the Gāyatrī mantra, the usual Arghya shall be offered; scents, fragrant flowers, incense and Ācamanīya shall be offered with mantras ending with Svadhā or Namaḥ; flowers are offered severally by means of Vedic mantras; the Nirmālya (remnants of the worship) is removed by means of the Astra mantra ending with Phaṭ; Caṇḍa is worshipped in the north-east; Caṇḍa the deity of the pedestal is consecrated by means of the common Astra mantra; the pedestal of the Liṅga and Śiva are consecrated by means of the Pāśupata missile; keeping a flower on the head, the deity is worshipped.

209. **mūlādyaiḥ—pañcākṣara bījaiḥ** *ST.* **with the pañcākṣara bīja mantras.**

21. The devotee meditates on Sadāśiva who is full of Kalās beginning with Nivṛtti, who is accompanied by the six varieties (? of Kalās) and whose physical body is an ancillary of the Kalās of Karman.[210] The seat is conceived on the rocky back of the tortoise [incarnation of Viṣṇu], the seeds and sprouts above it, on the rock of Brahmā; in the pores of the stalk of the endless being the following shall be conceived—the fibres, the leaves the thorn, the pericarp, the filaments, Dharma (virtue), Jñāna (perfect knowledge), Vairāgya (detachment), Aiśvarya (prosperity), the sun, moon, fire, filaments and Śakti; Manonmanī is conceived in the pericarp along with Manonmana; briefly the seat is conceived by saying "for the seat of the endless being." Then, above it, Sadāśiva is meditated upon in the manner as stated before.

22. Flowers shall be taken in both the hands; they shall be pressed with the thumbs. By means of the gesture of invocation, they are gradually taken from the heart upto the head, uttering the Mūla mantra along with the Hṛdaya mantra in the Pluta (prolated) note; the deity who has the form of the flame of a lamp and who has faces and hands all round is invoked very much from the spot of the Bindu and is installed as the pervader of everything showing the gesture of pervading.

23. The rite of Paramīkaraṇam (rendering the deity as the greatest one) is performed at the outset by means of the Hṛdaya mantra and the inseparable union of Śiva and Śakti; the rite of Amṛtīkaraṇa (rendering everything nectarine) is performed by means of the Mūla mantra beginning with Hṛdaya; the rite of Āvāhana (invocation) is by means of the mantra of Sadya; the rite of Sthāpana (founding) is on the top of the Mūla mantra by means of the Hṛdaya mantra (?) as well as Vāma mantra; the rite of Sannirodha (obstruction of the existent one) by means of Aghora mantra on the top of Mūla mantra; the rite of Sānnidhya (proximity) is performed by means of Tatpuruṣa mantra, over the Mūla mantra and the Hṛdaya mantra. He shall worship the deity by means of the Hṛdaya mantra, the Mūla mantra and Īśāna mantra. This is the directive.

210. Karma-kalāṅga-deha—Karma-kalāṅgo Vedaḥ sa deho yasya *ST*. Cf. yasya niśśvasitaṁ Vedāḥ.

24. Then he performs the rite of Dehanirmāṇa (creation of a body) for oneself, as before, as well as for lord Fire by means of the Bīja mantra along with the five mantras.

25. After meditating on the Rūpaka (the diminutive form of the lord) by means of the Mūla mantra he performs the rite ending with obeisance, and offers Ācamanīya ending with Svadhā. He then offers Arghya and all other things, ending with obeisance or utterance of Svāhā. The offering of flowers is performed by means of the Mūla mantra ending with Vauṣaṭ. Every rite ending with obeisance may be performed by means of Hṛdaya mantra, or Īśāna mantra or Rudragāyatrī. Or he shall worship by means of the Mūla mantra "Om Namaḥ Śivāya" (Om obeisance to Śiva).

26-27. The devotee offers again flowers, incense and the Ācamanīya. The rites of Puṣpāpasāraṇa (removal of the flowers) and Visarjana (casting off) shall be performed by means of the sixth Bīja mantra. The devotee bathes all the materials of worship by means of the water inspired with the mantras and repeating the Mūla mantra. The rite of Abhiṣeka ablution is performed by means of the Īśāna mantra. Eight flowers are offered for every article. Arghya is also similarly offered. The scents, the fragrant flowers, the incense and the Ācamanīya are offered by means of the Astra mantra ending with Phaṭ. The rite of concluding the Pūjā shall also be similarly performed. The Liṅga-Mūrti along with its pedestal is bathed by means of pure water at first after repeating the Mūla mantra. Pounded grains, embylic myrobalan are put in the water. Or the Liṅga Mūrti can be bathed and consecrated by means of hot water with turmeric etc. put therein. The devotee then recites Rudrādhyāya and bathes the Liṅga by means of scented water in which gold has been placed and Mantrodaka (water inspired with mantras). He repeats Nīlarudra, Tvaritarudra, Pañcabrahman and other mantras together with Namaḥśivāya (obeisance to Śiva).

28-29. While bathing the Liṅga, a flower should be placed on its head. The head of the Liṅga should not be kept bare. In this respect there is a verse—If, in the realm of a king the head of the Liṅga is left bare, he shall have to face misfortune, great ailment, famine and destruction of vehicles.

30. Hence, the king shall avoid this and strive for virtue, love, wealth and salvation. If the Liṅga is bare-headed the king and the realm too shall perish.

31. After bathing, the devotee shall offer Arghya and wipe off the Liṅga with a cloth. Repeating the Mūla mantra he shall offer scents, fragrant flowers, garments, ornaments, etc.

32. The devotee shall offer incense, Ācamanīya, lamp, Naivedya (food offering) etc. by repeating the Mūla mantra. The worship over and above this with the Mūla mantra is called the rite of Pavitrīkaraṇa (sanctifying).

33. The devotee shall show Āratidipa [waving of the lamps] above the Liṅga, on the Liṅga, beneath the Liṅga and in a general way all round. The lamps shall be inspired with the Dhenumudrā, covered up by the Kavaca mantra and protected by the sixth Bīja mantra.

34. After bowing down the devotee shall worship with the Mūla mantra in the manner of Brahmāṅgabhoga[211] (partial enjoyment of the Brahman) with all these items of service, viz.—invocation, installation, obstruction, presence, Pādya (water for washing), water for ritualistic sipping, homage of holy articles, scents, fragrant flowers, incense and food offering, the second ritualistic sipping and wiping of the hands and chewing the scented nuts for rendering the mouth fragrant.

35. The following rites shall be duly performed, viz.—meditation on the lord in Sakala and then Niṣkala form; meditation on the major as well as minor Devas, the Japa of the Mūla mantra and of the Brahmāṅga mantras extending to a tenth of the previous dedication, self-surrender, eulogy, prostrations, etc. The preceptor shall be worshipped in the east and Vināyaka in the south.

36. For the achievement of all desired objects, Gaṇeṣa, the lord of the universe, shall be worshipped at the outset and in the end by brahmins and Devas.

37. He who worships lord Śiva in the Liṅga or on the ground attains identity with him by continuing the holy rites for a year in full.

211. brahmāṅga-bhoga-mārgeṇa—in the manner prescribed for the worship of Brahmā.

38. He who worships the Liṅga attains identity, no doubt, within six months. The devotee shall make seven circumambulations and prostrate like a straight pole.

39-41. He will attain the fruit of a hundred horse-sacrifices for every step made in the course of circumambulation. Hence, one shall worship the lord every day for achieving all desired objects. He who seeks enjoyment shall attain enjoyment; he who seeks a realm shall attain realm; he who seeks sons shall attain sons; the ailing patient shall be liberated from sickness. Any devoted man will attain his all desires.

CHAPTER TWENTYFIVE

The holy rites of fire pertaining to Śiva

Śailādi said:

1-2. I shall mention the holy rites of fire pertaining to Śiva as defined by Śiva. In a well-polished, scrubbed and splendid spot in the form of a square the devotee shall dig the pits assiduously. He shall then make three straight lines pointing to the east and three pointing to the north.

3-4. The perpetual pit in the altar for the sacred fire of sacrifice shall have three girdles round it. The outer girdle is four Aṅgulas in width, the middle one three Aṅgulas, the inner one two. The width of the Kuṇḍa shall be one cubit. The central portion where the sacrificial offerings are poured shall be about nine inches. The Yoni shall be like the leaf of Aśvattha in shape and formed higher than the girdle.

5. O son of Brahmā, in the middle of the Kuṇḍa the umbilicus shall be duly made in the form of a lotus. It shall have eight petals and a pericarp, a Prādeśa in width.

6. The rite of scratching shall be performed by means of the sixth[212] Bīja mantra. The rite of sprinkling shall be made with the coat of mail.[213] Viewing the Kuṇḍa with the eye the devotee shall draw six lines.

212. ṣaṣṭhena—with the sixth, i.e. the astra mantra.

213. Varmaṇā—with the Kavaca mantra.

7. O leading brahmin, the three lines extending towards the east represent Brahmā, Viṣṇu and Maheśa. The devotee shall sprinkle water over the lines extending to the north, by means of the Varman mantra.

8-10. The wood for generating fire by attrition shall be from Śamī or Pippala tree. It shall be sixteen Aṅgulas long. It shall be churned and fire shall be produced as prescribed repeating the Vahnibīja mantra and performing the Śaktinyāsa rite by the Hṛdaya mantra. The splendid sacrificial twigs shall be a Prādeśa in length. They shall put in the fire silently. The rite of Samūhana shall be performed as prescribed, by sprinkling water in the eight quarters beginning with the east in order.

11. The sacrificial Kuśa grass with its tip to the north shall be placed in the east. The same with its tip towards the east shall be placed to the south. The same with the tip to the north is placed to the west and the same with the tip towards the east shall be placed in the north.

12. In the vessel belonging to Indra the two deities Indra and the fire-god shall be invoked. In the vessel belonging to Yama the deities Yama and Agni shall be invoked. In the vessel belonging to Soma (moon), the two deities the moon and the fire shall be invoked. Beneath it the two deities Varuṇa and Agni shall be invoked.

13. O sage of good holy rites, the vessels are placed in two on Kuśa grass with faces downwards, to the north of the Kuṇḍa.

14. Darbhas are spread over them. The vessel of Śiva shall be placed to the south. The devotee shall worship them by the Mūla-mantra. Afterwards, he shall perform Homa.

15. He shall take the Prokṣaṇī vessel and fill it with water. He shall place two Darbha grasses, a Prādeśa in length over the water.

16-18. He shall put in the water tips of the Kuśa grass repeating the mantra "vasoḥ sūryasya raśmibhiḥ." He then turns with face upwards all the vessels and sprinkles them with water in accordance with the injunctions. He shall take the Praṇītā vessel and fill it with water. O sage of good holy rites, he covers the other water perfectly with the tips of Kuśa grass. He lifts the vessel level with the nose, with both the hands and places it in the north-east. Thereafter, he shall perform the splendid rite of warming the ghee in the north-west corner.

19-20. He shall take a small quantity of burning coal mixed with ashes. Taking the vessel from the west to the north he shall warm the ghee. He shall burn the tips of Kuśa grass and whirl it round the fire three times. After putting Kuśa grass into the fire he shall place the ghee vessel above the fire.

21-22. He shall then take two bits of Kuśa grass, wash them duly and perform the rite of burning the tips and whirling them round the fire. He shall perform the rite of Paryagni with nine bits of Kuśa grass. Then he shall take the vessel off the fire taking it from north to west.

23-26. He shall set fire to a twig, wash it and put it to the west. He shall perform the rite of Utpavana over the ghee. With Darbha grass twisted into a ring-like loop in the fingers, he takes the ghee vessels with both the hands. He dips the grass-loop into the ghee and then places them over the fire.

O sage of good holy rites, the ladles shall be about a cubit in length. They shall be made of gold or silver and they shall have all characteristi cmarks. Or the ladles shall be made of a wood worthy of sacrifice.

27. The length of ladles shall be one cubit. In its snout there shall be a hole. O great sage, the root of the handle shall be six aṅgulas in girth.

28-32. The neck shall be half of that (i. e. three aṅgulas). The tongue shall be like the root. The stick shall be similar in shape to a cow's tail.[214] The tip of the ladle shall be like a nose with two round holes filled with pearls. If the length is thirty-six aṅgulas, the width shall be eight aṅgulas. The height shall be half of it rendered level by means of a thread. The mouth shall be seven aṅgulas in length and width. After making the tip one-third of the whole in length the remaining part shall be left off. The neck shall be two aṅgulas in length and its expanse shall be four aṅgulas. The altar shall be eight aṅgulas in length as well as expanse. In its middle a hole shall be dug four aṅgulas in width.

33-34. The hole shall be perfectly circular with eight petals and a good pericarp. All round the hole there shall be a

214. gobāla-sadṛśam—in the shape of the cow's tail.

fringe on the outside half an aṅgula in width. Outside, it shall open out like a full blown lotus embellished with petals. Outside it, there shall be a fringe two barley grains in width.

35. Through the middle of the altar shall be dug a long groove of the girth of the little finger extending upto the mouth. The hole shall be sloping downwards.

36. The stick shall be six aṅgulas in length and hollow. At the tip of the Daṇḍa, three Daṇḍikās i.e. three long lines in a series, shall be made, the latter ones half an aṅgula more than the former and the last shall be four aṅgulas in length.

37. At the root of the Daṇḍa, there shall be a jar[215] thirteen aṅgulas in length. The pot-like dome shall be two aṅgulas in height. The umbilicus shall be ten aṅgulas.

38-39. After making the umbilicus in the middle of the altar the devotee shall make its foot two aṅgulas in extent. The foot shall be shaped like the back of the lotus and the leg shall be like the pericarp in shape. The shape of its back shall be like that of the lips of an elephant. In the rites concerning black magic, it shall be made with an iron rod.

40-43. The devotee shall wipe the ladle with a bundle of Kuśa grass twentyfive in number. O sage of good holy rites, the tip shall be wiped off with the tip, the middle with the middle, and the root with the root. It shall be warmed in the fire repeating the Hṛdaya mantra.

The three vessels, viz. the vessel of ghee, Praṇītā and Prokṣaṇī may be made of gold, silver, copper or mud. They shall not be made otherwise in the splendid rites conducive to peace and prosperity. In the Abhicāra rites they shall be made of iron. In the rites of peace they shall be of mud. The mouths of the vessels shall be six aṅgulas in width.

44. The Prokṣaṇī vessel shall be two aṅgulas in height; the height of Praṇītā shall be two aṅgulas more. The vessel for ghee shall be two aṅgulas more in height.

45-46. The twigs with which the border is strewn shall be by means of the same twigs as in Homa. They shall be equal to the middle finger in girth. They shall not be bent. There shall be no cracks in them. They shall be of equal

215. ghaṭam—śiraḥ *ST*. the upper part. Cf. *Viśva*: 'ghaṭaḥ samādhi bhede nā śiraḥ kūṭakuṭeṣu ca.'

length. There are three Paridhis each thirtytwo aṅgulas in length. Darbha grass thirty in number, each measuring thirty-two aṅgulas shall be strewn all round.

47. Darbha grass shall be tied round in the middle by means of Kuśa grass four aṅgulas in length. In the rites of Abhicāra etc. the consecration of Agni pertaining to Śiva shall be avoided.

48-49. O brahmin, in the Abhicāra rite the sacrificial twigs shall be firm. They shall not be tender, whole, stout. Twigs of equal length having the girth of the little finger should be collected. O sage of good holy rites, in all other rites, glossy twigs measuring twelve aṅgulas shall be taken. They shall not be curved. They shall be free from cracks.

50. The ghee derived from the cow's milk is excellent; that derived from the milk of a tawny cow is more excellent. The measure of ghee for each offering is as much as fills the ladle.

51. Cooked rice shall be as big as the fruit of Terminalia Belerica; gingelly seeds as much as they contain an oyster shell; barley grains shall be half that in quantity. The fruits shall be of their own respective sizes.

52. The quantity of milk, honey and curds shall be like that of ghee. The final offering shall be made with the sruk ladle which is equal to four śruva measures.

53. Half of that is called Sviṣṭakṛt or all that remains after the offerings have been made which shall be poured together in the sacrificial fire. Homas intended for peace and prosperity shall always be performed in the Agni pertaining to Śiva.

54-56. O highly blessed one, enchanting, exorcising and other rites shall be performed in the secular fire. O sage of good holy rites, in every rite Śiva-fire shall be generated. After making seven flames all holy rites shall be performed. Or all rites can be accomplished by means of one flame only.

O leading brahmins, Śiva-fire can be achieved by means of the tongue alone.

57. Om Svāhā (offering) unto the middle tongue of the flame, to one that has many forms, to one that has many colours, to one that goes to the south, to the north and to the

middle, to one that bestows the benefit that is conducive to peace, prosperity, salvation, etc.

58-65. Oṁ Śvāhā unto the tongue of Īśāna, that bestows perfect knowledge, to the golden one, to one that has the lustre of gold.

Oṁ Svāhā unto the tongue of Indra, to the golden one, to one resembling gold, to the beautiful one.

Oṁ Svāhā unto the tongue of the fire that is red, that has the red colour, that has many colours, that incites hatred and that fascinates.

Oṁ Svāhā unto the tongue of Nirṛta that is black and destructive.

Oṁ Svāhā unto the western tongue that has good lustre, that has pearly appearance, that brings about peace and that is conducive to nourishment.

Oṁ Svāhā unto the tongue of wind that is fully manifest, and that dispels enemies.

Oṁ Svāhā unto fire that is refulgent.

So far the consecration of fire has been mentioned. Or in the rites of fire the devotee shall generate Śiva-fire again by means of the mode prescribed for naimittika rites.

66. The rites of surveying (sprinkling) and beating shall be performed by means of the sixth Bīja mantra ending with Phaṭ; the rite of sprinkling by means of the fourth Bīja mantra, the rites of digging and scattering upwards by means of the sixth Bīja mantra; the rites of filling and levelling by means of the first Bīja mantra; the rite of watering by means of the mantra ending with Vauṣaṭ; the rite of thrashing by means of the sixth Bīja mantra, the rite of sweeping by means of the fourth Bīja mantra; the rite of conceiving the sacrificial pit by means of the three Kalās beginning with Nivṛtti; the rite of covering up the sacrificial pit by means of the fourth Bīja mantra; the rite of worshipping the sacrificial pit by means of the first Bīja mantra; the rite of accomplishing the four lines by means of the sixth Bīja mantra ending with Phaṭ and the rites of rendering it adamantine and endowed with four feet by means of the first Bīja mantra. Thus the consecration of the sacrificial pit is of eighteen varieties.

67. After the rite of the consecration of the sacrificial pit

the rite of tearing of the Akṣa (?) the fruit of Terenelia Belerica by means of the sixth Bīja mantra and the rite of placing of the seat by means of the first Bīja mantra shall be performed. Then the goddess of speech is invoked in the adamantine seat.

68. Oṁ Hrīm I invoke Vāgīśvarī the Śakti of Vāgīśvara, whose colour is black, whose eyes are large, whose body is fully agitated due to youth and who is in her menses.[216]

69-72. I worship Vāgīśvarī. Then the rite of invocation of Vāgīśvara is performed. I invoke Vāgīśvara who has a single face, and four arms, who has the lustre of pure crystal, whose hands show the gesture of offering boons and freedom from fear, who holds the axe and the deer, who is bedecked in matted hairs serving the purpose of a coronet and who is adorned by all ornaments.

Oṁ Īm obeisance unto Vāgīśvara. After meditating on Vāgīśvarī till all these rites, viz. invocation, installation, presence, obstruction and worship are performed the rites of impregnation and consecration of the fire shall be performed.

73. The fire originating from wood or magnet or Agnihotra shall be brought in a copper vessel or in a mud platter. The rite of viewing, beating, sprinkling and washing shall be performed by the first Bīja mantra. The rite of scaring demons and avoidance of inauspicious things shall be performed by the first Bīja mantra. The fire shall be divided into three parts. The fire-god is invoked from the stomach and the middle of the eyebrows. The rite of kindling in the liṅga, the cause of the universe, shall be performed by the first Bīja mantra pertaining to the fire. The rites of Dhāraṇā and Dhenumudrā shall be performed by the Puruṣa mantra and Saṁhitā mantras. The vessel shall be covered by the fourth Bīja mantra. The devotee shall kneel on the ground and lift up the platter and place it on the sacrificial pit. It is then whirled around the fire by the fourth Bīja mantra. He shall meditate on Vāgīśvarī face to face with himself. The rite of impregnation is performed in the vessel of the womb. The rite of offering the lotus is performed by the first Bīja mantra ending with Vauṣaṭ. He shall offer Arghya by

216. ṛtumatīm=ṛtusnātām (meditating upon Vāgīśvarī) as one who has taken bath after the menses. Cf. ṛtusnātām tato dhyātvā—cited in *ST*.

means of the Kuśa grass. The rite of feeding the fuel by the first Bīja mantra shall be performed; the rite of kindling and impregnation by Sadya mantra; the rite of worship by the first Bīja mantra; the rite of Puṁsavana by the Vāma mantra; the rite of worship by the second Bīja mantra; the rite of sīmantonnayana by the Aghora mantra and the rite of worship by the third Bīja mantra.

74. The rites of pervading of the limbs, opening of the mouth and removal of the face shall be performed by the third Bīja mantra.

The post-natal rite is performed with the Puruṣa mantra. The rite of worship is performed with the fourth Bīja mantra. For the purification of the post-natal pollution the rite of prokṣaṇa is performed with the sixth Bīja mantra. The rite of according protection is performed by spreading the Kuśa grass with the Vaktra mantra (?). The Kuśa grass is spread thus: The tip of one Kuśa is towards the north-east and its root is towards south-east. The root of one Kuśa is towards the south-west and its tip is towards the north-west. The root of one Kuśa is towards the north-west and its tip is towards the north-east. Thus the rite of Kuśāstaraṇa is performed. Homa shall be performed with the sacrificial turf mentioned before for dispelling spittle. It shall be consigned to fire with the sixth Bīja mantra after soaking its tip and the root in ghee.

75. The rite of fixing the Paridhi and Viṣṭara shall be performed with the mantras succeeding the five previous ones with the first Bīja mantra. Then the devotee shall worship Brahmā, Śiva and Viṣṇu over the Viṣṭara (seat).

76-80. He shall worship the guardians of the quarters beginning with Indra and the circular diamond jewels at the borders. (?) The worship of Vāgīśvara and Vāgīśvarī shall be performed thus. After ritualistically dismissing them the sacrifice shall be completed.

Henceforth, the rite of consecration of the ladles shall be performed. The rites of Nirīkṣaṇa, Prokṣaṇa, Tāḍana, Abhyukṣaṇa etc. shall be performed in the manner described before. The ladles shall be held in the hands. The rites of installing and striking shall be performed with the first Bīja mantra. The ladles are scraped with the Darbha grass three times with its root, middle and tip. The ladles are then placed on the Kuśa grass on the right side of Śiva saying—obeisance to Śakti, obeisance to Śiva.

Thereafter, the devotee shall bind the ladles with the thread near at hand with the fourth Bīja mantra and worship them.

81. The devotee then shows the Dhenumudrā. He covers them with the fourth Bīja mantra, and performs the rite of according protection with the sixth Bīja mantra. The rite of consecration has already been described to you.

82. Thereafter, the rite of consecration of the ghee is performed. It too has already been mentioned. The rites of Nirīkṣaṇa, Prokṣaṇa, Tāḍana, Abhyukṣaṇa, etc. shall be performed as before.

83. The rite of sanctifying

The rite of warming the ghee is in the north-east with the sixth Bīja mantra. The vessel of ghee shall be placed on the altar. Darbha grass shall be made into a loop a Vitasti long. The devotee holds its tip with the thumb and the ring finger of the left hand and its root with the thumb and the ring finger of the right hand. The rite of blowing of the air over the flame shall be performed with the fourth Bīja mantra ending with Svāhā. Again he shall take six Darbhas and as before perform the rite of flooding the self with the first Bīja Mantra ending with Svāhā. The rite of tying the loop with two blades to Kuśa grass shall be performed with the first Bīja mantra. The loop shall be placed in the ghee. This is the rite of sanctifying it.

84. The devotee shall take two blades of Darbha grass and burn them. Then, he shall whirl them round the ghee three times. After sprinkling with water the devotee shall consign them to the fire. This is the rite of waving of light.

85. The devotee then takes the Darbha grass and scrutinises them to find out whether worms are there. He shall then sprinkle them with the Arghya water and place them on the fire. This is the rite of illuminating.

86-90. The devotee then takes two blades of Darbha grass, lights them and scrutinizes the ghee by means of the flame.

He takes some ghee with the tips of two blades of Darbha grass and remembers two halves one bright and one dark half of the month. He shall divide the ghee into three parts. He takes one part of the ghee with the ladle and consigns it into fire repeating "Svāhā unto Agni." The second part of ghee is offered repeating "Svāhā unto Soma". Repeating "Om Svāhā unto Agni and Soma", "Svāhā unto Agni who brings about the realization of the desired things" he pours the third part of ghee into the fire.

He shall take the ghee again by the blades of Kuśa grass and inspire it with the Saṁhitā mantras ending with namaḥ. After inspiring it with the mantra the rites of showing Dhenumudrā with Kavaca mantra, Avaguṇṭhana with Astra mantra and Rakṣā (according protection) are performed. It shall then be placed on the consecrated ghee. This is the rite of the consecration of the ghee.

Then the rite of opening the mouth is performed as follows:—With the ghee in the ladle he whirls it in the form of a circle repeating the Śaktibīja[217] mantra "Svāhā unto Īśānamūrti" as before: "Svāhā unto the mouth (face) of Puruṣa", "Svāhā unto the heart of Aghora", Svāhā unto Vāmadeva, to the private parts", "Svāhā unto Sadyojātamūrti". Ghee is poured into fire after each Svāhā mantra. Thus is the rite of Vaktrodghāṭana.

91-92. Svāhā unto Īśānamūrti, unto the face of Tatpuruṣa, Svāhā unto the face of Tatpuruṣa, unto the heart of Aghora, Svāhā unto the heart of Aghora, unto the private parts of Vāma, unto Sadyojātamūrti.

This is the rite of joining or closing of the mouth.

Svāhā unto Īśānamūrti, unto Tatpuruṣa, unto the face, unto the heart of Aghora, unto Vāmadeva, unto the private parts, unto Sadyojāta.—This is the rite of unifying all the faces.

93. The devotee shall perform all holy rites after generating Śivāgni or he shall always perform the rites of Śāntika conducive to peace, etc. by means of tongue alone.

94-95. O unchanging one, in the rites of Garbhādhāna, etc. ten offerings shall be made in the fire for each. In the Śivāgni the great divine seat shall be conceived in five ways with

217. śaktibīja—the same as yonibīja.

the Yonibīja[218] mantra. The rites of Āvāhana and Nyāsa in regard to the lord are in the same way as in the worship.

96-97. The devotee shall repeat the Mūla mantra once and bow down to the lord of Devas. Then he shall perform three Prāṇāyāmas of the Sagarbha type (i. e. with the repetition of Om) as approved of by all yogins. After sprinkling water he shall pour ghee on to the sacrificial twig. O great sage, then he shall consign it into the kindled fire.

98-99. Along with the vessels he shall take the ghee, the two parts together, and pour into the fire in accordance with the injunctions in all the six faces. (?) O excellent brahmins, the two parts of ghee in the south-east and north are the two eyes. They are offered unto the fire and unto the moon towards the rite of oneself (?)

100-101. O son of Brahmā, O highly-blessed one, the ghee part on the right and left are the eyes on the left and right of Śiva fire since the lord sits facing west. It is undoubtedly so. Ten offerings are made there with ghee repeating the Mula mantra.

102. The offerings can be duly performed with Caru and the sacrificial twigs also. O sage of good holy rites he shall then offer the Pūrṇāhuti with the Mūla mantra.

103-108. To all the deities surrounding the lord, five offerings are made individually in the order of Īśāna, etc. or Śaktibīja, etc. The atonement is done with Aghora mantra. The rites ending with Sviṣṭakṛt are performed as before. Thus, the splendid rite in the fire of three types has been mentioned by me. O great sage, as opportunity offers, these shall be performed daily. At the end of his life the devotee attains heaven. He attains the power of igniting the gastric fire. He never falls into the hell whatever be his actions. The aspirant who seeks salvation shall perform the non-violent sacrifice. One shall meditate on the fire stationed in the heart and perform sacrifice Dhyānayajña (meditation). After realizing Śiva stationed in the body of all living beings, the lord of universe, he shall devoutly perform the sacrifice by Prāṇāyāma perpetually. He who performs the external Homa becomes a frog in the rock.

218. yonibīja—see note 202 above.

CHAPTER TWENTYSIX

The mode of worshipping Aghora

Śailādi said :

1. Or the devotee shall worship lord Śiva, Īśāna in the Liṅga, the devotee who is a brahmin, has faith on Śiva and is engrossed in the meditation on Śiva.

2. He shall take Bhasman originating from the Agnihotra fire repeating the mantra beginning with "Agni" etc. and dust it all over his body from head to foot.

3. He shall wear the sacred thread, sit facing the north and perform the rite of Ācamana with the sacred water of the Brahman. Repeating "Oṁ namaḥ Śivāya" he shall then inspire his own body.

4. He shall worship the lord with that mantra as well as the Praṇava. The greatest of all the worship is that of the trident-bearing lord Aghora.

5. O sage of good holy rites, the actual worship and all the holy rites in the fire are common. But the difference is in the mantras for that lord and in the meditation on Aghora.

6-8. This is the mantra:—"Obeisance to you. Obeisance to Aghoras who are terrible, very very terrible. Obeisance to all Śarvas. Obeisance to those in the forms of Rudras". (aṅg-nyāsa is done as follows using the above mantra). "Obeisance to Aghoras." Obeisance to the tranquil heart; "and then to the terrible ones." Svāhā in the head of all Ātmans and Brahmans "unto those very very terrible ones." Vaṣaṭ in the tuft with clusters of flames, "unto all and all Śarvas. Hum unto the tawny-coloured coat of mail"; "Obeisance be to you, to those of the forms of Rudra", Vauṣat unto the deity in the three eyes; "Obeisance unto the thousand-eyed one, to one difficult to be pierced," Hum phat to the missile pertaining to Paśupati.

The rite of Aghamarṣaṇa after bathing, performing the Ācamana and sprinkling water all over the body, the Tarpaṇa rite, Arghya unto the sun and worship of the sun, (all these as explained in chapter 24) are common to the worship of Aghora. The only difference is in the mantras to be uttered. The rites of Mārga Śuddhi (purification of the path) and the worship of Vāstvadhipa (the lord of the site of dwelling place) at the portals are performed first.

9-12. After performing this worship he shall wash his hand, sit on a splendid seat, place the Bhasman over the lotus-like nose and allow it to be blown by the wind that wafts[219] the fire from his eyes.[220] He shall sanctify it by the holy water. He shall conceive of the Kalā of the Brahman in the nectarine juice by means of the Śakti. He shall split Aghora mantra into five parts and perform aṅganyāsa (as mentioned above) accompanied by the five aṅgas. Thus the Nyāsa rite is performed in accordance with the injunctions by fixing the Jñānakriyā (the process of knowledge). The deity is meditated upon in the heart as seated in an excellent seat in the umbilicus as seated on fire; and in between the eyebrows as shining like a lamp. This is called Trinetra Nyāsa.

13-21. He shall then meditate on the lord as follows—he is seated in the Śivāsana which contains Śānti, Bīja, Aṅkura, Ananta, Dharma and others, where Soma (moon), the sun and the fire are present, where the three mūrtis of the trinity are present, which holds Vāmadeva and others and where Manonmanī is also present. The lord is stationed as the Ātma Mūrti; his form is Akṣaya (imperishable). Thirtyeight Kalās constitute his physical body. Lord Śiva is accompanied by the three Tattvas. He has eighteen arms; elephant's hide forms his upper garment. He wears the garment of the lion's hide. Aghora, Parameśvara is surrounded by the thirtytwo Śaktis in the form of thirtytwo syllables. He is bedecked in all ornaments. He is bowed to by all Devas. A garland of skulls forms his ornament. Even serpent and scorpions adorn him. His face is gentle and resembles the full moon. He has the lustre of ten million moons. He holds the crescent moon on his crest. He is blue in form and accompanied by Śakti. In his right side hands he holds a sword, a club,[221] a noose, a goad studded with jewels and a Nāga kakṣā (a kind of noose), a bow, a Pāśupata missile, a staff and a club. In his left side hands he holds a Vīṇā, a bell, a trident, a drum, a thunderbolt, an iron club, a deer, a bright axe and an iron rod. His hand shows the gesture

219. dagdhākṣaḥ—having burnt (given up) all ceremonials.
220. kṣubhikāgninā viraktyanalena *ST*. by the fire of detachment.
221. kheṭakam = carma *ST*. shield.

of granting boons and freedom from fear. The devotee shall meditate on the excellent Parameśvara in the above manner and worship him. He shall then perform Homa in the fire.

22-25. The entire Homa is to be performed as before, with difference in the mantras as has already been mentioned. The worship shall be made with eight flowers, scents, etc. The rites of eulogy dedication and inner oblation shall be performed as before. The sacrificial altar and pit are prepared as before in accordance with the injunctions pertaining to fire (Vāhneya).[222] The oblations are then offered by means of these mantras after duly drawing the maṇḍala (mystic diagrams) in it. "Unto the Rudras, unto the Mothers, unto the Yakṣas, unto the Asuras, unto the planets, unto the Rākṣasas, unto the stars, unto the Viśvas and unto the Kṣetrapālas (guardians of frontiers)." Thereafter, he shall offer oblations unto the Kṣetrapālas in the quarters of the north-west and west.

26-31. Arghya, scents, flowers, incense, lamps, food offerings and articles to render the mouth fragrant shall be offered duly, O sage of good holy rites. Thereafter, the devotee shall submit his requests, ritualistically dismiss the deity and worship with eight flowers. O leading sage, all these rites are common to all worships. O sage of good holy rites, thus has succinctly been mentioned the worship etc. of Aghora. The worship of Aghora is in the Liṅga or on the bare ground. The excellent worship on the Liṅga has ten million times the benefit of the worship on the bare ground. A brahmin who is engaged in the worship on the Liṅga is not affected by the sins called Mahāpātakas like the leaf of the lotus that is not affected by water. The viewing of the Liṅga is holy. Touching it is holier than viewing it. Undoubtedly, O son of Brahmā, there is nothing that excels the worship. It cannot be recounted in detail even in the course of a hundred crores of years.

222. Vāhneyena i.e. as prescribed in the Agnipurāṇa *ST*.

CHAPTER TWENTYSEVEN

The description of the Jaya ablution

The sages said :

1-3. It is due to the grace and power of Nandin that the benefit of the worship of the Liṅga has been heard. O Romaharṣaṇa of good holy rites, everything that we heard is on a par with the Vedas. The rite of "Jayābhiṣeka" had been recounted formerly on the top of the Meru by the trident-bearing lord Īśa to Manu for the welfare of the Kṣatriyas. How is that? How is the splendid Mahādāna (great gift) of sixteen varieties? O Sūta, the most excellent among the intellectuals, it behoves you to recount it to us.

Sūta said :

4. At the outset the self-born lord Manu performed the rite of Jīvacchrāddha (the Śrāddha unto the living). After going to the Meru, then, he eulogised Nīlalohita, the lord of Devas.

5. Delighted at his penance, Bhava, Īśāna granted unto that humble devotee his divine vision. Thereby he saw the unchanging lord.

6. After bowing to and worshipping him duly he stood there with his palms joined in reverence. With his voice choked due to excess of delight he spoke thus.

7-9. O lord of Devas, O lord of the Universe, O lord of the worlds, obeisance unto you. Thanks to the grace of the great lord, Jīvacchrāddha has been offered by me and the lord has been worshipped. Therefore, the lord has been seen by me now. O lord, O lord of Devas, it behoves you to recount to me the rite of Jayābhiṣeka that yields virtue, love, wealth and salvation and that has been previously related to Indra by you.

Sūta said :

Lord Mahādeva, Nīlalohita, Parameśvara recounted to him the rite of Jayābhiṣeka in all details.

The glorious lord said :

10-13. With a desire for the welfare of kings I shall recount the Jayābhiṣeka rite that is conducive to the victory over enemies and premature death. When the time to go to war has arrived the king shall perform this ablution rite, sprinkle water over the lord and then go to the battlefield. After duly making a raised platform, a water shed[223] or a prominent abode[224] the brahmin who is a master of the Vedas shall deposit fire in nine places. Thereafter, for the purpose of ablution, he shall make lines with threads.

14-18. The first thread from the east and the first thread from the south shall be coloured. Altogether there shall be two thousand four hundred threads. With these as boundaries a square shall be made. Outside, all round, a marginal pathway a foot in width shall be made. The subsidiary threads shall be separately taken. For each line thirtysix threads shall be twisted together. There shall be thirtysix squares formed by seven rows running east to west and seven rows running from south to north. Therefore, there shall be fortynine rows (i.e. boundary lines for the squares ?). He shall clean nine rows in the middle with water mixed with cow-dung.

19. There, he shall draw the diagram of a splendid lotus of a hand's width. It shall be circular and white in colour with eight petals. It shall have the pericarp and the filaments.

20. The pericarp resembling gold in lustre shall be eight aṅgulas long. The filaments shall be four aṅgulas long.

21. In the corners beginning with the south-east he shall instal Dharma (virtue) Jñāna (knowledge), Vairāgya (Detachment) and Aiśvarya (prosperity) in due order repeating the Praṇava.

22. He shall fix Avyakta, etc. in the quarters beginning with east in the form of their bodies. The four are Avyakta (the unmanifest) Niyata (the regular) Kāla (time) and Kālī.

23. Dharma, etc. have these colours in order—white, red, golden and black. O sages of good holy rites, the body is in the shape of a swan and has the refulgence of gold.

24. The lotus that is the cause of creation is in the middle of the supporting Śakti. In the middle of the Kalā, there is only the Bindu and beyond that is the shape of Nāda (sound).

223. prapām pānīyaśālām *ST*. a place where water is distributed to travellers.

224. kuṭam—a resting place.

25. Above the Nāda he shall meditate on Śiva the preceptor of the universe, called Oṁkara. He shall meditate on Manonmanī and Mahādeva having the lustre of the lotus.

26-27. The filaments, Vāmā, etc., shall be meditated upon, beginning with the east and in order. They are—Vāmā, Jyeṣṭhā, Raudrī, Kālī, Vikarṇī, Balā, Pramathinī and goddess Damanī. They are to be fixed along with Vāmadeva and others by means of the Praṇava.

28-30. With these mantras he shall duly worship the circular assembly:—"Obeisance to Vāmadeva; obeisance to trident-bearing Jyeṣṭha; obeisance to Rudra; obeisance to the lord having the form of Kāla; obeisance to Kalavikaraṇa; obeisance to Bala; obeisance to the suppressor of all living beings; obeisance to bold Manonmana; obeisance, obeisance to Manonmanī".

31. The first Āvaraṇa (covering) has been recounted. Now listen to the second Āvaraṇa. In the second Āvaraṇa there are sixteen Śaktis.

32-35. In the third Āvaraṇa there are twenty-four Śaktis in order. The Piśācavīthi (the pathway of ghosts) is in the middle. The Nābhivīthi is all round. It is laid down that the worship of the Piśācas should be duly performed by means of these mantras. The Padas (words, steps) are one thousand and eight and each Pada has eight corners. The devotee shall conceive a lotus in each of these Padas separately by means of Śāli rice grains, Nīvāra rice grains, wheat grains, barley grains, rice grains or gingelly seeds mixed with white mustard. Or he shall formulate these in accordance with the injunctions as and when the time comes.

36-37. In them he shall draw an eight-petalled lotus equipped with pericarp and filaments. An Āḍhaka measure of Śāli rice grains shall be used severally for each of the lotuses. Rice grains shall be half of that. Barley grains; etc. shall be still half of it. A Droṇa measure of that shall be put in the chief pot. Rice grains shall be half of it.

38-43. An Āḍhaka of gingelly seeds is put in the middle. Half that quantity of barley grains is also put. He shall then sprinkle the lotus with water repeating the Praṇava. He shall fix the Praṇava in all of them duly and in order. After concluding this and sprinkling the thousand excellent Padas, he shall make a thousand Kalaśas (water pots) of gold, silver or copper. They shall be splendid having the characteristics mentioned. They shall be duly sprinkled with the Arghya water repeating the Praṇava. Each of the Kalaśas shall be twelve aṅgulas wide at the belly and shall curve downwards. Its umbilicus shall be half of it in width. The neck shall be two aṅgulas in height and its width shall be four aṅgulas. The lip shall be two aṅgulas in height. The Nirgama, the spout through which the water comes out, shall be two aṅgulas (in length). In the Śivakumbha (the vessel pertaining to Śiva) all these measurements are doubled.

44-50. A space to the extent of a barley grain shall be tied well with a thread. The vessel shall be closed, sprinkled with water and placed on Kuśa grass duly. As before, he shall fill it with scented water repeating the Praṇava. He shall instal the Vardhanī[225] vessel along with Śivakumbha in accordance with the injunctions in the middle of the central lotus along with Kūrca (bundle of Kuśa grass) and Akṣata (raw rice grains). Each of the thousand waterpots shall be severally wrapped with a pair of cloth and covered with a golden lotus studded with jewels of diverse colours. Śiva shall be installed in the Śivakumbha by means of Gāyatrī and the Praṇava—"We know the Purusa. We meditate on Mahādeva. Hence, may Rudra urge and guide us". Always Rudra's presence is invoked by means of this Mantra. He shall instal goddess in Vardhanī by means of Devīgāyatrī and worship with the mantra "We know the mother of the Gaṇas. We meditate on Mahātapa (the great scorcher). Hence, may Gaurī urge and guide us."

51. Vāmā and others are glorified in the first Āvaraṇa. The first Āvaraṇa has been mentioned. Now listen to the second Āvaraṇa.

52. O sages of good holy rites, here there are sixteen Śaktis beginning with and ending with the east. He shall instal and worship Subhadrā in the middle of Aindravyūha in the group in the east.

225. vardhanīm khaḍgākārām, a sword Cf. vardhanīm khaḍgarūpiṇīm—*Agnipurāṇa*--cited in *ST*.

53-54. In the group in the South-east he shall worship Bhadrā. He shall worship Kanakāṇḍajā (one born of golden egg) in the southern group, Ambikā in the south-western group as well as the group in the middle. In the western side he shall worship Śrīdevī; in the north-western quarter he shall worship Vāgīśā. He shall worship Gomukhī in the north as well as in the central vessel.

55. He shall worship Bhadrakarṇā in the middle of Rudravyūha (group belonging to Rudra in the north). In the middle of the east and south-east quarters he shall worship the excellent Aṇimā (the attribute of minuteness).

56. He shall fix Laghimā (lightness) in the lotus in the middle of south and south-east quarters. He shall worship Mahimā (greatness) in the middle of south and south-west.

57. He shall worship Prāpti (the power that procures every thing) in the middle of the west and south-west quarters. He shall fix Prākāmya (Irresistible Will) in the lotus in the middle of the west and north-west quarters..

58. He shall instal Īśitva (superiority) in the middle of the north and north-west quarters and worship. He shall instal Vaśitva (subduing of passions) in the middle of the north and north-east quarters and worship.

59. He shall worship Kāmāvasāyitva in the middle of the east and north-east quarters. Thus, the second Āvaraṇa has been mentioned. Now listen to the third Āvaraṇa.

60-61. There are twentyfour Śaktis in the chief lotuses. As before he shall worship them in the middle of the group in accordance with the injunctions. He shall worship Dīkṣā, Dīkṣāyikā, Caṇḍā, Caṇḍāṁśunāyikā, Sumatī, Sumatyāyī, Gopā and Gopāyikā.

62-69. Then he shall duly instal Nandā, Nandāyī, Pitāmaha, Pitāmahāyī beginning with the east and worship. After worshipping the excellent third Āvaraṇa thus in accordance with the injunctions he shall go over to Saubhadra group in the first Āvaraṇa. He shall duly instal the eight Śaktis beginning with the east and in order. Listen to the Śaktis beginning with the east. After worshipping the sixteen Śaktis he shall show the gesture of lotus (Padma mudrā). These are the eight Śaktis in the first Āvaraṇa—Bindukā, Bindugarbhā, Nādinī, Nādagarbhajā, Śaktikā, Śaktigarbhā, Parā and Parāparā.

The sixteen Śaktis mentioned in the second Āvaraṇa are:—Caṇḍā, Caṇḍamukhī, Caṇḍavegā, Manojavā, Caṇḍākṣī, Caṇḍanirghoṣā, Bhṛkuṭī, Caṇḍanāyikā, Manotsedhā, Manodhyakṣā, Mānasī, Mānanāyikā, Manoharī, Manohlādī, Manaḥprīti and Māheśvarī. The Saubhadra group has thus been mentioned. Now listen to the Bhadra group.

70-73. The eight Śaktis in the first Āvaraṇa are—Aindrī Hautāśanī, Yāmyā, Nairṛtī, Vāruṇī, Vāyavyā, Kauberī and Aiśānī. The first Āvaraṇa has been mentioned. Now listen to the second Āvaraṇa. The sixteen Śaktis in the second Āvaraṇa are —Hariṇi, Suvarṇā, Kāñcanī, Hāṭakī, Rukmiṇī, Satyabhāmā, Subhagā, Jambunāyikā, Vāgbhavā, Vākpathā, Vāṇī, Bhīmā, Citrarathā, Sudhī, Vedamātā and Hiraṇyākṣī.

Thus the group called Bhadra has been mentioned. Now listen to the group called Kanaka.

74. The Śaktis in the first Āvaraṇa are—Vajra, Śakti, Daṇḍa (staff), Khaḍga (sword), Pāśa (noose), Dhvaja (flag), Gadā (mace), aud Triśūla (trident).

75-76. The sixteen Śaktis (in the second Āvaraṇa) are—Yuddhā, Prabuddhā, Caṇḍā, Muṇḍā, Kapālinī, Mṛtyu, Hantrī, Virūpākṣī, Kapardī, Kamalāsanā, Daṁṣṭriṇī, Raṅgiṇī, Lambākṣī, Kaṅkabhūṣaṇī, Sambhāvā and Bhāvanī.

77-78. The Kanaka group has been mentioned. Now listen to the group called Ambikā. The eight Śaktis in the first Āvaraṇa are—Khecarī, Atmanāsā, Bhavānī, Vahnirūpiṇī, Vahninī, Vahninābhā, Mahimā and Amṛtalālasā.

79-80 The sixteen Śaktis in the second Āvaraṇa are—Kṣamā, Śikharādevī, Ṛturatnā, Śilā, Chāyā, Bhūtapatī, Dhanyā, Indramātā, Vaiṣṇavī, Tṛṣṇā, Rāgavatī, Mohā, Kāmakopā, Mahotkaṭā, Indrā and Badhirādevī.

81-84. Thus, the Ambikā group has been mentioned. O sage of good holy rites, now listen to Śrī group. The Śaktis in the first Āvaraṇa are—Sparśā, Sparśavatī, Sandhā, Prāṇā, Apānā, Samānakā, Udānā and Vyānā. The sixteen Śaktis in the second Āvaraṇa, approved by all are—Tamohatā, Prabhā, Moghā, Tejanī, Dahanī, Bhīmāsyā, Jālanī, Coṣā (or Uṣā),

Śoṣaṇī, Rudranāyikā, Vīrabhadrā, Gaṇādhyakṣā, Candrahāsā, Gahvarā, Gaṇamātā and Ambikā.

85-86. Thus, the excellent Śrī group has been mentioned. O sage of good holy rites, listen to the group Vāgīśa. These are the eight Śaktis glorified in the first Āvaraṇa—Dhārā. Vāridharā, Vahnikī, Nāśaki, Martyātītā, Mahāmāyā, Vajriṇī, and Kāmadhenukā.

87-89. The sixteen Śaktis in the second Āvaraṇa approved by all are—Payoṣṇī, Vāruṇī, Śāntā, Jayantī, Varapradā, Plāvanī, Jalamātā, Payomātā, Mahāmbikā, Raktā, Karālī, Caṇḍālī, Mahocchuṣmā, Payasvinī, Māyāvidyeśvarī and the dark Kālikā. The group of Vāgīśvara has been mentioned. Now the group of Gomukha is being mentioned.

90-93. Eight Śaktis are mentioned in the firts Āvaraṇa—Śaṅkhinī, Halinī, Laṅkāvarṇā, Kalkinī, Yakṣiṇī, Mālinī, Vamanī and Rasātmanī. There are sixteen Śaktis in the second Āvaraṇa viz. Caṇḍā, Ghaṇṭā, Mahānādā, Sumukhī, Durmukhī, Balā, Revatī, Prathamā, Ghorā, Sainyā, Līnā, Mahābalā, Jayā, Vijayā, Aparā and Aparājitā. Thus, the group of Gomukhī has been mentioned. Now listen to the group of Bhadrakarṇī.

94-97. The following eight Śaktis are mentioned in the first Āvaraṇa viz. Mahājayā, Virūpākṣī, Śuklābhā, Ākāśamātṛkā, Saṁhārī, Jātahārī, Daṁṣṭrālī and Śuṣkarevatī. There are sixteen Śaktis (in the second Āvaraṇa) viz. Pipīlikā, Puṇyahārī, Aśanī, Sarvahāriṇī, Bhadrahā, Viśvahārī, Himā, Yogeśvarī, Chidrā, Bhānumatī, Chidrā Saiṁhikī, Surabhi, Samā, Sarvabhavyā and Vegākhyā.

Thus, the eight major groups have been mentioned. Listen to eight minor groups.

98-99. The Śaktis in the first Āvaraṇa enveloping the Aṇimā group are—Aindrā, Citrabhānu, Vāruṇī, Daṇḍi, Prāṇarūpī, Haṁsa, Svātmaśakti and Pitāmaha. Thus, the first Āvaraṇa has been mentioned. Now listen to the second Āvaraṇa.

100-101. The following sixteen are in the second Āvaraṇa:—Keśava, lord Rudra, Candramā, Bhāskara, Mahātmā, Ātmā, Antarātmā, Maheśvara, Paramātmā, Aṇujīva, Piṅgala, Puruṣa, Paśu, Bhoktā, Bhūtapati and Bhīma.

102-103. Thus, the Aṇimā group has been mentioned. I shall mention to you the group called Laghimā. The first Āvaraṇa consists of—Śrīkaṇṭha, Anta (? Ananta), Sūkṣma, Trimūrti, Śaśaka, Amareśa, Sthitīśa and the eighth Dārata. Thus, the first Āvaraṇa has been mentioned. Now listen to the second Āvaraṇa.

104-106. There are sixteen Rudras in the second Āvaraṇa viz. Sthāṇu, Hara, Daṇḍeśa, Bhauktīśa, the chief of Devas, Sadyojāta Anugraheśa, Krūrasena, Sureśvara, Krodhīśā, Caṇḍa, Prachaṇḍa, Śiva, Ekarudra, Kūrma, Ekanetra, and Caturmukha.

Thus, the Laghimā group has been mentioned. O sage of good holy rites, now listen to Mahimā group.

107-108. The following sixteen constitute the group viz. Ajeśa, Kṣemarudra, Somāṁśa, Lāṅgalī, Daṇḍāru, Ardhanārī, Ekānta, Anta, Pālī, Bhujaṅganāmā, Pinākī, Khaḍgi, Kāma, Īśa, Śveta and Bhṛgu.

109-110. Thus, the Mahimā group has been mentioned. Now listen to Prāpti group. These constitute the first Āvaraṇa viz. Samvarta, Lakulīśa, Vāḍava, Hasti, Caṇḍayakṣa, Gaṇapati, Mahātmā and Bhṛguja the eighth. Thus, the first Āvaraṇa has been mentioned. Now listen to the second Āvaraṇa.

111-112. The following sixteen constitute the second Āvaraṇa viz. Trivikrama, Mahājihva, Ṛkṣa, Śrībhadra, Mahādeva, Dadhīca, Kumāra, Parāvara, Mahādaṁṣṭra, Karāla, Sūcaka, Suvardhana, Mahādhvāṅkṣa, Mahānanda, Daṇḍī and Gopālaka.

113-114. Thus, the Prāpti group has been mentioned. O sage of good holy rites, now listen to the group of Prākāmya. The following eight constitute the first Āvaraṇa:—Puṣpadanta, Mahānāga, Vipulānandakāraka, Śukla, Viśāla, Kamala, Bilva and Aruṇa. The first Āvaraṇa has been mentioned. Now listen to the second Āvaraṇa.

115-117. The following constitute the second Āvaraṇa—Ratipriya, Sureśāna, Citrāṅga, Sudurjaya, Vināyaka, Kṣetrapāla, Mohāmoha, Jaṅgala, Vatsaputra, Mahāputra, Grāmadeśādhipa,, Sarvāvasthādhipa, Deva, Meghanāda, Pracaṇḍaka, and Kāladūta. Thus, the group of Prākāmya has been mentioned. I shall mention the group of Aiśvarya.

118-121. The following eight Śaktis constitute the first Āvaraṇa viz.—Maṅgalā, Carcikā, Yogeśā, Haradāyikā, Bhāsurā, Asuramātā, Sundarī and Mātṛkā the eighth. The Śaktis of the first Āvaraṇa have been mentioned. Now listen to those who constitute the second Āvaraṇa—Gaṇādhipa, Mantrajña, Varadeva, Ṣaḍānana, Vidagdha, Vicitra, Amogha, Mogha, Aśvīrudra, Someśa, Uttama, Udumbara, Nārasiṁha, Vijaya, Indraguha the lord, and Apāmpati.

122-123. Thus, the Vyūha of Aiśvarya has been mentioned. Now listen to the group of Vaśitva. The following are in the first Āvaraṇa viz.—Gagana, Bhavana, Vijaya, Ajaya, Mahājaya, Aṅgāra, Vyaṅgāra and Mahāyaśas. Thus, the group of the first Āvaraṇa has been mentioned. Now listen to the group in the second Āvaraṇa.

124-127. They are—Sundara, Pracaṇḍeśa, Mahāvarṇa, Mahāsura, Mahāromā, Mahāgarbha, Prathama, Kanaka, Kharaja, Garuḍa, Meghanāda, Garjaka, Gaja, Chedakabāhu, Triśikha and Māri. The group of Vaśitva has been mentioned. Now listen to the group of Kāmāvasāyika.

The following constitute the first Āvaraṇa—Vināda, Vikaṭa, Vasanta, Maya, Vidyut, Mahābala, Kamala and Damana. The first Āvaraṇa has been mentioned. Now listen to the second Āvaraṇa.

128-130. They are Dharma, Atibala, Sarpa, Mahākāya, Mahāhanu, Sabala, Bhasmāṅgī, Durjaya, Duratikrama, Vetāla, Raurava, Durdhara, Bhoga, Vajrakālāgnirudra, Sadyonāda, and Mahāguha.

Thus, the second Āvaraṇa has been mentioned, so also the group of Kāmāvasāyika. Thus, the sixteen groups have been mentioned. Now listen to the second Āvaraṇa.

131. In the Dakṣa group of the second Āvaraṇa there are eight Śaktis in the first Āvaraṇa and sixteen in the external Āvaraṇa.

132-135. The Śaktis in the first are Manoharā, Mahānādā Citrā, Citrarathā, Rohiṇī, Citrāṅgī, Citrarekhā and Vicitrikā. The Śaktis in the first Āvaraṇa have been mentioned. Now listen to the second Āvaraṇa—Citrā, Vicitrarūpā, Śubhadā, Kāmadā, Śubhā, Krūrā, Devī Piṅgalā, Khaḍgikā, Lambikā,

Satī, Daṁṣṭrālī, Rākṣasī, Dhvaṁsī, Lolupā, Lohitā and Mukhī.

The sixteen Śaktis in the second Āvaraṇa have been succintly mentioned. Thus, the group of Dakṣa has been mentioned. Now listen to the Dākṣa group.

136-139. The following constitute the first Āvaraṇa:—Sarvāsatī, Viśvarūpā, Lampaṭā, Āmiṣapriyā, Dīrghadaṁṣṭrā, Vajrā, Lamboṣṭhī, Prāṇahāriṇī. Thus, the first Āvaraṇa has been mentioned. Now listen to the second Āvaraṇa. Gajakarṇā, Aśvakarṇā, Mahākālī, Subhīṣaṇā, Vātavegaravā, Aghorā, Ghanāghanaravā, Varaghoṣā, Mahāvarṇā, Sughaṇṭā, Ghaṇṭikā, Ghaṇṭā, Īśvarī, Mahāghorā, Ghorā and Atighorikā. Thus, the sixteen Śaktis in the second Āvaraṇa have been mentioned.

140-141. Thus, the Dākṣa group has been mentioned. Now listen to the Caṇḍa group.

These constitute the first Āvaraṇa:—Atighaṇṭā, Atighorā, Karālā, Karabhā, Vibhūti, Bhogadā, Kānti and the eighth one Śaṅkhinī. Thus, the Śaktis in the first Āvaraṇa have been mentioned. Now listen to those in the second Āvaraṇa.

142-147. They are:—Patriṇī, Gāndhārī, Yogamātā, Supīvarā, Raktamālā, Raktāṁśukā, Vīrā, Saṁhārī, Māṁsahāriṇī, Phalahārī, Jīvahārī, Svecchāhārī, Tuṇḍikā, Revatī, Raṅgiṇī, and Saṅgā. Thus, there are sixteen in the second Āvaraṇa. Thus, the Caṇḍa group has been mentioned. Now listen to the group of Caṇḍā.

The first Āvaraṇa consists of Caṇḍī, Caṇḍamukhī, Caṇḍā, Caṇḍavegā, Mahāravā, Bhrukuṭī, Caṇḍabhū, and the eighth one Caṇḍarūpā. Thus, the first Āvaraṇa has been mentioned. Now listen to the second Āvaraṇa:—Candraghrāṇā, Balā, Balajihvā, Baleśvarī, Balavegā, Mahākāyā, Mahākopā, Vidyutā, Kaṅkālī, Kalaśī, Vidyutā, Caṇḍaghoṣikā, Mahāghoṣā, Mahārāvā, Caṇḍabhā and Anaṅga Caṇḍikā. The group of Caṇḍā has been mentioned. Now listen to Hara group.

148-149. In the first Āvaraṇa the following Śaktis are mentioned Caṇḍākṣī, Kāmadā Devī, Sūkarā, Kukkuṭānanā, Gāndhārī, Dundubhī, Durgā and Saumitrā the eighth one. Thus, the first Āvaraṇa has been mentioned. Now listen to the second Āvaraṇa.

150-155. The sixteen Śaktis of the second Āvaraṇa are :—Mṛtodbhavā, Mahālakṣmī, Varṇadā, Jīvarakṣinī, Hariṇī, Kṣīṇajīvā, Daṇḍavaktrā. Caturbhujā, Vyomacārī, Vyomarūpā, Vyomavyāpī, Śubhodayā, Gṛhacārī, Sucāri, Viṣāhārī and Viṣārtihā. Thus, the group, pertaining to Hara has been mentioned. Now listen to the group of Harā.

The following constitute the first Āvaraṇa, viz. Jambhā, Acyutā, Kaṅkārī, Devikā, Durdharā, Āvahā, Caṇḍikā and Capalā.

The following constitute the second Āvaraṇa :—Caṇḍikā, Cāmarī, Bhaṇḍikā, Śubhānanā, Piṇḍikā, Muṇḍinī, Muṇḍā, Śākinī, Śāṅgarī, Kartarī, Bhartarī, Bhāginī, Yajñadāyinī, Yama-Daṁṣṭrā, Mahādaṁṣṭrā and Karālā. Thus, the group of Harā has been mentioned. Now listen to the Śauṇḍa group.

156-159. The first Āvaraṇa consists of the following Śaktis :—Vikarālī, Karālī, Kālajaṅghā, Yaśasvinī, Vegā, Vegavatī, Yajñā and the eighth Vedāṅgā.

Thus, the first Āvaraṇa has been mentioned. Now listen to the second Āvaraṇa :—

The following sixteen duly constitute the second Āvaraṇa :—Vajrā, Śaṅkhā, Atiśaṅkhā, Balā, Abalā, Añjanī, Mohanī, Māyā, Vikaṭāṅgī, Nalī, Gaṇḍakī, Daṇḍakī, Ghoṇā, Śoṇā, Satyavatī and Kallolā. Thus, the Śauṇḍa group has been mentioned. Now listen to the group of Śauṇḍā.

160-163. The following constitute the first Āvaraṇa:—Danturā, Raudrabhāgā, Amṛtā, Sakulāśubhā, Calajihvā, Āryanetrā, Rūpiṇī and Dārikā.

Thus, the first Āvaraṇa has been mentioned. Now listen to the second Āvaraṇa.

There are sixteen Śaktis in the second Āvaraṇa, viz. Khādakā, Rūpanāmā, Saṁhārī, Kṣamā, Antakā, Kaṇḍinī, Peṣiṇī, Mahātrāsā, Kṛtāntikā, Daṇḍinī, Kiṅkarī, Bimbā, Varṇinī, Amalāṅginī, Draviṇīs, and Drāviṇī.

Thus, the excellent and charming Śauṇḍāvyūha has been mentioned.

164-167. I shall mention the Śaktis pertaining to the very excellent group named Prathama. The Śaktis in the first Āvaraṇa are:—Plavanī, Plāvanī, Śobhā, Amandā, Mahotkaṭā, Mandā, Ākṣepā and Mahādevī. The following constitute the second Āvaraṇa. The goddess Kāmasandīpanī, Atirūpā, Manoharā, Mahāvaśā, Madagrāhā, Vihvalā, Madavihvalā, Aruṇā, Śoṣaṇā, Divyā, Revatī, Bhāṇḍanāyikā, Stambhinī, Ghoraraktākṣī, Smararūpā and Sughoṣaṇā.

O son of the self-born deity, thus, the group of Prathamā has been mentioned precisely.

168-169. I shall now mention the group of Prathamə. Listen to me. The following eight constitute the first Āvaraṇa:—Ghorā, Ghoratarā, Aghorā, Atighorā, Aghanāyikā, Dhāvanī, Koṣṭukā and Muṇḍā the eighth. Thus, the first Āvaraṇa has been mentioned. Now listen to the second Āvaraṇa.

170-171. They are sixteen, viz. Bhīmā, Bhīmatarā, great Śastā, Suvartulā, Stambhinī, Rodinī, Raudrā, Rudravatī, Acalācalā, Mahābalā, Mahā Śənti, Śālā, Śāntā, Śivāśivā, Bṛhatkakṣā and Mahānāsā.

172-174. The group of Prathamā has been mentioned. Now listen to the Manmathavyūha group. The following constitute the first Āvaraṇa :—Tālakarṇī, Bālā, Kalyāṇī, Kapilā, Śivā, Iṣṭi, Tuṣṭi and Pratijñā. The Śaktis in the second Āvaraṇa are :—Khyāti, Puṣṭikarī, Tuṣṭi, Jalā, Śruti, Dhṛti, Kāmadā, Śubhadā, Saumyā, Tejanī, Kāmatantrikā, Dharmā, Adharmavaśā, Śīlā, Pāpahā and Dharmavardhinī.

175-176. Thus, the Manmatha group has been mentioned. Now listen to the group of Manmathā.

The following constitute the first Āvaraṇa :—Dharmarakṣā, Vidhānā, Dharmā, Adharmavatī, Sumati, Durmati, Medhā and Vimalā the eighth. Thus, the first Āvaraṇa has been mentioned. Now listen to the second Āvaraṇa.

177-178. The following sixteen Śaktis constitute the second Āvaraṇa :—Śuddhi, Buddhi, Dyuti, Kānti, Vartulā, Mohavardhanī, Balā, Atibalā, Bhīmā, Prāṇavṛddhikari, Nirlajjā, Nirghṛṇā, Mandā, Sarvapāpakṣayaṅkarī, Kapilā and Atividhurā.

179-180. Thus, the group of Manmathā has been mentioned. Now I shall mention Bhīma group to you. It consists of Raktā, Viraktā, Udvegā, Aśokavardhinī, Kāmā, Tṛṣṇā, Kṣudhā and Mohā the eighth. Thus, the first Āvaraṇa has been mentioned to you. Now listen to the second Āvaraṇa.

181-182. They are Jayā, Nidrā, Abhayā, Ālasyā, Jalatṛṣṇodarī, Darā, Kṛṣṇā, Kṛṣṇāṅginī, Vṛddhā, Śuddocchiṣṭāśanī, Vṛṣā, Kāmanā, Śobhanī, Dagdhā, Duḥkhadā Sukhadā, and Balī. Thus, the Bhīma group has been mentioned to you. Now listen to the Bhīmāyī group.

183-186. Ānandā, Sunandā, Mahānandā, Śubhaṅkarī, Vītarāgā, Mahotsāhā, Jitarāgā and Manorathā. Thus, the first Āvaraṇa has been mentioned to you. Now listen to the second Āvaraṇa. The following constitute the second Āvaraṇa:—Manonmanī, Manakṣobhā, Madonmattā, Madākulā, Mandagarbhā, Mahābhāsā, Kāmā, Ānandā, Suvihvalā, Mahāvegā, Suvegā, Mahābhogā, Kṣayāvahā, Kramaṇī, Krāmaṇī and Vakrā. Thus, the very excellent Bhīmāyī has been mentioned to you.

187-188. O son of the self-born lord, I shall now mention the Śākuna group.

Yogāvegā, Suvegā, Ativegā, Suvāsinī, Goddess Manorayā, Āvegā, Jalāvartā the intelligent. Thus, the first Āvaraṇa has been mentioned. Now listen to the second Āvaraṇa.

189-190. They are:—Rodhanī, Kṣobhaṇī, Bālā, Viprā, Śeṣā, Suśoṣaṇī, Vidyutābhāsinī, Goddess Manovegā, Cāpalā, Vidyujjihvā, Mahājihvā, Bhṛkuṭikuṭilānanā, Phullajvālā, Mahājvālā, Sujvālā and Kṣayāntikā.

191-192. Thus, the Sākunavyūha has been mentioned to you. Now listen to the group of Śakunā:—Jvālinī, Bhasmāṅgī, Bhasmā, Antagā, Bhāvinī, Prajā, Vidyā and Khyāti the eighth. Thus, the first Āvaraṇa has been mentioned to you. Now listen to the second Āvaraṇa.

193-194. Ullekhā, Patākā, Bhogā, Bhogavatī, Khagā, Bhogā, Bhogavratā, Yogā, Bhogākhyā, Yogapāragā, Ṛddhi, Buddhi, Dhṛti, Kānti, Smṛti Śruti and Dharā. Thus, the Śākunā group that bestows desires has been mentioned.

195-198. O son of the self-born lord, now listen to the very excellent group named Sumati. They are: Pareṣṭā, Parādṛṣṭā, Amṛtā, Phalanāśinī, Hiraṇyākṣī, Suvarṇākṣī, Devīkapiñjalā and Kāmarekhā. Thus, the first Āvaraṇa has been mentioned to you. Now listen to the second Āvaraṇa:—Ratnadvīpā, Sudvīpā, Ratnadā, Ratnamālinī, Ratnaśobhā, Suśobhā, Mahādyuti, Śāmbarī, Bandhurā, Granthi, Pādakarṇā, Akarānanā, Hayagrīvā, Jihvā and Sarvabhāsā.

Thus, the group of Sumati (male) has been mentioned to you. Now listen to the group of Sumati (female).

199-202. Sarvāśī, Mahābhakṣā, Mahādaṁṣṭrā, Atirauravā, Visphuliṅgā, Viliṅgā, Kṛtāntā and Bhāskarānanā constitute the first Āvaraṇa. Thus, the first Āvaraṇa has been mentioned to you. Now listen to the second Āvaraṇa:—Rāgā, Raṅgavatī, Śreṣṭhā, Mahākrodhā, Rauravā, Krodhanī, Vasanī, Kalahā, Mahābalā, Kalantikā, Caturbhedā, Durgā, Durgamāninī, Nālī, Sunālī and Saumyā. Thus, the Sumati group has been mentioned to you.

203-204. Now I shall mention Gopa group here. O son of the self-born lord, listen to everything. Pāṭalī, Pāṭavī, Pāṭī, Viṭipiṭā, Kaṅkaṭā, Supaṭā, Praghaṭā and Gaṭodbhavā. Thus, the first Āvaraṇa has been mentioned clearly.

205-206. The Śaktis (in the second Āvaraṇa) are Nādākṣī, Nādarūpā, Sarvakārī, Gamā, Agamā, Anucārī, Sucārī, Caṇḍanāḍī, Suvāhinī, Suyogā, Viyogā, Haṁsākhyā, Vilāsinī, Sarvagā, Suvicārā, and Vañcanī.

207-208. Gopa group has been mentioned. Now listen to Gopāyī group.

Bhedinī, Chedinī, Sarvakārī, Kṣudhāśanī, Ucchuṣmā, Gāndhārī, Bhasmāśī and Vaḍavānalā—these constitute the first Āvaraṇa. Listen to the second Āvaraṇa.

209-210. The Śaktis are Andhā, Bāhvāsinī, Bālā, Dīpā, Kṣamā[226] Akṣā Tryakṣā, Hṛllekhā, Hṛdgatā,[227] Māyikā, Parā,[228] Āmayā, Sādinī Bhillī, Sahyā, Asahyā,[229] Sarasvati, Rudraśakti, Mahāśakti, Mahāmohā and Gonadī.

211-212. Thus, Gopāyī group has been mentioned. I shall now mention Nanda group to you: Nandinī, Nivṛtti, Pratiṣṭhā, Vidyā, Nāsā[230] Khagrasinī, Cāmūṇḍā and Priyadarśinī. Thus, the first Āvaraṇa has been mentioned to you. Now listen to the second Āvaraṇa.

213-214. The following Śaktis constitute the second Āvaraṇa:—Gṛhyā, Nārāyaṇī, Mohā, Goddess Prajā, Cakriṇī,

226. N.S. Edition reads dīkṣapāmā, obviously a misprint for dīpā kṣamā. *ST.* disjoins as dīpā akṣamā.
227. hṛdgatā māyikā. *ST.* disjoins as hṛdgatā amāyikā.
228. māyikā parā. *ST.* disjoins as māyikā aparā.
229. sahyāsahyā *ST.* takes sahyāsahyā as a single word.
230. Vidyānāsā. *ST.* takes it as a single word.

Kaṅkaṭā, Kālī, Śivā, Ādyā, Uṣā, Virā, Mā, Āyā, Vāgīśī, Vāhinī, Bhīṣaṇī, Śugamā, and Nirdiṣṭā.

215-216. Thus, Nanda group has been mentioned to you. Now listen to Nandā group. Vināyakī, Purṇimā, Raṅkārī, Kuṇḍalī, Icchā, Kapālinī, Dvīpinī and Jayantikā, these eight Śaktis are glorified in the first Āvaraṇa.

217-219. Thus, the first Āvaraṇa has been mentioned to you. Now listen to the second Āvaraṇa:—Pāvanī, Ambikā, Sarvātmā, Pūtanā, Chagalī, Goddess Modinī[231] herself, Lambodarī, Saṁhārī, Kālinī, Kusumā, Śukrā, Tārā, Jñānā, Kriyā, Gāyatrikā and Sāvitrī; these duly constitute the second Āvaraṇa.

220-221. Thus, Nandā group has been mentioned to you. Now listen to the group of Pitāmaha.

Nandinī, Phetkārī, Krodhā, Haṁsā, Ṣaḍaṅgulā, Ānandā, Vasudurgā, and Saṁhārā the eighth. Thus, the first Āvaraṇa has been mentioned to you. Now listen to the second Āvaraṇa.

222-224. Kulāntikā, Nalā, Pracaṇḍā, Mardinī, Sarvabhūtābhayā, Dayā, Vaḍavāmukhī, Lampaṭā, goddess[232] Pannagā, Kusumā, Vipulāntakā, Kedārā, Kūrmā, Duritā, Mandaodarī and Khaḍgacakrā. These duly constitute the second Āvaraṇa. Thus, the Paitāmaha group that bestows virtue, love, wealth and salvation has been mentioned to you.

225-228. Now I shall mention to you the group of Pitāmahā. Now listen to me. Vajrā, Nandanā, Śāvā, Rāvikā, Ripubhedinī, Rūpā, Caturthā, and Yogā constitute the first Āvaraṇa.

Bhūtanādā, Mahābālā, Kharparā, Bhasmā, Kāntā, Vṛṣṭi, Brahmarūpiṇī with two arms,[233] Saihyā, Vaikārikājātā, Karmamoṭī, Mahāmohā, Mahāmāyā, Gāndhārī, Puṣpamālinī,[234] Śabdāpī and Mahāghoṣā. These constitute the sixteen śaktis of the second Āvaraṇa in the final group.

229-233. These Śaktis[235] have two arms. They resemble the rising sun in refulgence; hold the lotus and the conch; are calm; wear red garlands, clothes and ornaments; are bedecked

231. sākṣāddevī. According to *ST.* it qualifies Lambodarī.
232. pannagā devī. According to *ST.* devi is an epithet of pannagā.
233. dvibhujā. It qualifies brahmarūpiṇī.
234. puṣpamālinī. It is an epithet of gāndhārī.
235. sarvāś ca. Verses 229 to 231 describe the common characteristics of all the goddesses.

in all ornaments and adorned by coronets etc. studded with pearls and divine exquisite jewels pleasing to the mind. The embellished goddesses white in colour should be severally meditated upon. Thus, a thousand[236] water pots made of copper or mud and with the characteristics as mentioned before are installed in the Rudra Kṣetra. After worshipping them with the thousand names uttered by Viṣṇu, Bhava, etc. the water pots shall be placed in front. The devotee shall then perform the ablution of the Bāṇa idol.[237] After this ablution the water shall be poured over the king.

234. These thousand water-pots are conducive to the achievement of all Siddhis. These are the forty[237a] major groups, each marked with its characteristic signs.

235-237. The vessels shall be made of gold. As before, they shall be filled with scented water and each shall have five jewels (precious stones) put within it, as also gold pieces. The vessels of the lord shall be filled with ghee, milk, curds, pañcagavya or brahmakūrca. The ablution[238] pertaining to the sacrifice is being ordained. O excellent one, listen. The Abhiṣeka of the king is performed by repeating the Rudrādhyāya mantras of Rudra.

238-239. Mantra—"Obeisance to you, obeisance to Aghoras who are terrible, nay more and more terrible. Obeisance to all, to all Śarvas. Obeisance to all Rudras." Repeating the above mantra the water shall be poured over the king. Homa shall also be performed with the mantra of Aghoras, that dispels all sins.

240-243. Homa shall be performed in the Kuṇḍa of the lord or on the bare ground with ghee, etc. beginning with the east (?). Sacrificial twigs, ghee, caru, fried grains or Śāli or Nīvāra rice grains shall be used for Homa. After pouring hundred and eight āhutis the king shall be rendered fragrant with the odorous smoke. Puṇyāha water shall be sprinkled

236. sahasra-kalaśam. The number 'one thousand' is obtained from the forty-eight principal and the nine hundred fiftytwo group goddesses as mentioned in the foregoing verses.

237. Bāṇa-vigraham—this refers to Bāṇa liṅga. It is so called because it was worshipped by the asura Bāṇa.

237a. Catvāriṁśad—this refers to the forty mahāvyūhas as described n the foregoing verses of this chapter.

238. N.S. reads 'madhyam' (i.e. the middle) on the authority of *ST*.

repeating the Svastirudra mantra. A holy golden thread shall be tied round the right hand and Bhasman shall be dusted over it with lotus stalk.

Mantra[239]—"We worship the three-eyed lord who has fragrance, who increases nourishment as the cucumber fruit from its root. May I be liberated from bondage, from death and attain immortality." Water shall be sprinkled over the king with this mantra. Homa shall then be performed.

244. The rite of ablution with all materials shall be performed with the materials of Homa in due order. Homa in the eastern Kuṇḍa shall be performed with Vedic mantras[240] together with all materials used in due order.

245-246. "We know Tatpuruṣa. We meditate on Mahādeva. May that Rudra, therefore, urge and guide us." The brahmin shall perform Homa in the eastern Kuṇḍa with this mantra ending with Svāhā. He shall perform Homa in the southern Kuṇḍa by repeating the Aghora mantra with a piece of black cloth.[241]

247. "Obeisance to Vāmadeva, obeisance to the eldest, obeisance to the most excellent one, obeisance to Rudra etc., by repeating this mantra the devotee shall perform Homa in the western Kuṇḍa.

248-250. Homa in the western Kuṇḍa is then performed by repeating the Sadya mantra with all materials in due order. "I resort to Sadyojāta. Obeisance to Sadyojāta. When attacked by worldly existence come to my succour. Obeisance unto the origin of the world. The intelligent devotee shall perform Homa by repeating this mantra ending with Svāhā. He shall perform Homa in the south-eastern Kuṇḍa by repeating the mantra pertaining to Rudra.[242] "In the sacrificial rite we shall extract the juice of Soma" etc.[243] By repeating this mantra Homa shall be performed in the south-western Kuṇḍa with all materials of worship.

239. tryambakam etc. *TS*. 1.8. 6.2; *SV*. 3. 60.

240. brahmabhiḥ—with the pañca-brahma mantras.

241. Kṛṣṇa-vāsasā. But *ST*. supplies 'ācāryeṇa' i.e. through ācārya who shall be clad in black robes.

242. raudreṇa—with the mantra of Rudra: yo rudro agnau yo apsu TS. 5.5. 9.3.

243. jātavedase sunavāma somam TA 10. 1. 16.

251. "Niminiśidiśaḥ (?) Śvāhā, O sword." With this divine mantra that brings about all Siddhis the rite of Rākṣasa-bhedana (piercing the demon) shall be performed.

252. "Svāhā unto Rudhirājyārdranairṛti (?) Obeisance, Svadhā, obeisance" with this mantra he shall perform Homa as he pases by means of all materials.

253. O excellent brahmins, in the southern Kuṇḍa,[244] Homa shall be performed by the Īśāna mantra with all kinds of materials. Then, he shall perform Homa in the north-eastern Kuṇḍa with the materials mentioned before.

254. "Obeisance to Īśāna, to Kadrudra, to the three-eyed Pracetas, to Śarva. Hence, may Rudra urge and guide us."

255-256. O excellent brahmins, the chief Homa[245] shall be performed as before with the usual materials repeating the Īśāna mantra. In the presence of the king he shall perform a thousand Homas with each one of the materials.

The king, a favourite devotee of Śiva, shall also perform Homa.

"Īśāna is the lord of all lores, he is the overlord of all living beings, he is the lord of Brahmā, he is the overlord of the Brahman. May Sadāśiva be auspicious unto me Om."

257-258. The rite of expiation shall be performed by repeating the Aghora mantra. The rest of the rite shall be performed in the usual manner. Then after rendering the king fragrant by means of the odorous smoke of Homa, water shall be poured on him accompanied with loud and splendid shouts of victory, Vedic chants, the sounds of conches, bheri drums etc. Or the excellent king shall be sprinkled with the Kūrca of Kuśa grass.

259-261. The king shall smear Rudrabhasman[246] all over his body repeating the Rudrādhyāya mantras.

The king shall have all the auspicious royal paraphernalia such as conch, cāmara (chowries), bherī (drum) etc., Śibikā (palanquin) and the royal banner Vaijayantī. These royal emblems are offered only to a Kṣatriya lord who has been

244. yamyām. But *ST.* takes it as the north-west quarter (vāyavī dik) presided over by Vāyu.

245. pradhānam mukhyam *ST.* the principal deity.

246. But according to ST. Rudra=Rudrākṣa—a rosary of rudrākṣa tree and bhasman (ashes).

crowned in his kingdom and not to other Kṣatriyas. The size of these shall be upto twelve Aṅgulas.

262. Twigs of Palāśa, Udumbara, Aśvattha or Vaṭa shall be fixed beginning with the east. The festoons shall be hung thereon. The Paṭṭikās shall be silken alone.

263-264. The king shall be encircled with garlands of Darbhas with the Aṣṭamaṅgalas (eight auspicious fragrant objects). There shall be eight flags in the eight quarters. They shall be enriched by Dvārakumbhas (water-pots at the entrances. Golden festoons shall embellish the king. The priests shall then bathe him. He shall be seated above all others. He shall be sprinkled with the water from the Śivakumbha.

265-266. "We know Maheśa. We meditate on the lord purified in speech. May Śiva hence urge and guide us".

The king shall be sprinkled with this mantra and the Gaurīgītā[247] with a broom. Again, he shall be sprinkled with Rudrādhyāya mantras or Aghora mantras.

267. Then, he shall be offered divine ornaments, crown, etc. exquisitely made and white silken garments.

268-270. With sixty-eight Palas of gold a lovely ornament shall be made and embellished with the nine precious stones. It shall be offered as charitable gift to the preceptor. Ten cows and a good field shall also be given along with garments. Hundred droṇas of gingelly seeds and hundred of rice grains, bed, vehicle, bedsheets, pillows etc. shall also be given. To the yogins thirty palas of gold shall also be offered.

271. With half of that he shall delight the remaining priests. With still half of that he shall propitiate devotees of Śiva. Then, the king shall perform the great worship of Śiva.

272. Thus, succinctly the excellent rite of Jayābhiṣeka has been mentioned to you. Indra whose Abhiṣeka had been performed thus, formerly, attained the status of the lord.

273. Brahmā attained the status of Brahmā, Viṣṇu of Viṣṇu and Ambikā of Ambikā as well as incomparable good fortune of married blessedness.

274. Sāvitrī, Lakṣmī and Kātyāyanī too attained the same. Formerly, Mṛtyu was conquered by Nandin by means of Rudrādhyāya.

247. **gaurīgītayā—by gaurī gāyatrī.**

275. Formerly, this Abhiṣeka was performed on the very powerful Asura Tāraka. Vidyunmālī and Hiraṇyākṣa were conquered by Viṣṇu.

276-277. Formerly the Daitya Hiraṇyakaśipu was killed by Nṛsiṁha. Tāraka and others were killed by Skanda. Formerly, the sons of Sunda and Upasunda worshipped by leading Daityas were conquered by the mother Kauśikī. Vasudeva and Sudeva were killed by Kṛtakṛtyā.

278. By this rite of ablution laid down by Brahmā, the sons of Diti were conquered.

279. It is by performing this ablution that divine Siddhis were achieved by the kings and brahmins. No doubt need be entertained in this respect.

280. Wonderful indeed is the greatness of this Abhiṣeka whereby death was conquered by those who became Siddhas due to Abhiṣeka.

281-284. There is no doubt about this that by ablution a king is liberated from sins even if the sins were accumulated in the course of a hundred crores of kalpas. A king who is laid down by the ailments of consumption, leprosy, etc. is liberated from them. He becomes victorious always. He is blessed with sons and grandsons. He is richly endowed with the love of the people like another Indra. Devoid of sins he rejoices along with his virtuous wife. Only a general idea of the benefit accruing from this splendid rite has been mentioned to you as I heard it from Manu, the son of the self-born Brahmā. It has been mentioned to you for the sake of helping kings.

CHAPTER TWENTYEIGHT

The mode of charitable gifts.

Sūta said:

1-6. Manu the son of the self-born lord performed ablution and bowed down to Śiva, the lord of Devas. He saw lord Rudra Nīlalohita by his divine vision. He eulogised Śiva the bestower of boons by repeating the Rudrādhyāya mantras.

With great pleasure the lord said for once—"At the close of your reign you will attain salvation by performing holy rites alone. After saying this he vanished there itself.

After bowing down to the bull-bannered lord, Manu the son of the self-born lord ascended the great Meru mountain like Śiva ascending the great bull.

There he saw the son of Brahmā, the golden-complexioned bestower of boons, Sanatkumāra who was endowed with all Yogic powers.

Manu, of great lustre joined his palms in reverence; he bowed down to the bestower of boons, of the form of Brahman, one favourable to the brahmins and he eulogised him.

Sage Sanatkumāra had the sense of horripilation on seeing Manu. He, the storehouse of kindness, then spoke kindly:

Sanatkumāra said:

7-11. "You have come here after seeing and obtaining the rite of ablution from Śiva the tranquil lord of all, from Nīlalohita. Whatever it be, if you are desirous of speaking, speak on"

On hearing his words Manu bowed down to him with palms joined in reverence and said:—"O saintly lord, it behoves you to tell us how one attains salvation by holy rites alone. O saintly lord, salvation is achieved by perfect knowledge. In some places it is attained by means of the combination of the two."

On hearing his words, the saintly lord Sanatkumāra, the storehouse of the wisdom of the Vedas and the foremost among the knowers of Śruti, said:—

"Salvation is obtained, O sage, by means of Holy rites and the combination of the two gradually. But it is attained instantaneously by means of perfect knowledge.

12-15. Formerly by not honouring[248] the lord Nandin duly, I had attained the state of a camel due to his curse. Thanks to the grace of Nandin, I worshipped lord Śiva and became the son of Brahmā. Thanks to the holy rites I attained the divine excellent goal. It was only by practising the holy rites pertaining to Śiva and by worshipping him in various ways and not otherwise.

248. See *Liṅga* II. Ch. 9. V-5, note 86.

Sixteen types of charitable gifts which the kings shall bestow upon were mentioned by Nandin for attaining virtue, love, wealth and salvation. Holy rites such as Tulādhirohaṇa (ascending the balance) and other holy charitable gifts were mentioned by the noble-souled Nandin. Now listen to them precisely.

16-19. During the auspicious occasions such as eclipses,[249] etc. a splendid raised Maṇḍapa (platform) or kūṭa (peak-like projecting mound) shall be erected in a holy spot. The extent of the Maṇḍapa etc. shall be twenty, eighteen or sixteen[250] Hastas. A vedi (altar) extending to nine Hastas, eight Hastas or seven Hastas shall be made in the middle. The Vedikā (smaller altar) of two or one and a half Hastas is very splendid.

The scale[251] shall be beautiful and shall have twelve (joining) supporting ropes. The devotee shall dig nine square sacrificial pits all round.

20-25. O son of Brahmā, the main Kuṇḍa shall be between the east and the north-east. The sacrificial pits may be square or triangular in shape. O leading brahmins, the sacrificial pits shall be made in the shape of the vagina of women. They shall be semicircular, triangular, circular or hexagonal. The triangle shall be in the form of a lotus. It may have eight angular points also. The bare ground also shall be used. The enclosure shall have four entrances and bedecked with four festoons. There shall be the eight elephants of the quarters. It shall be surrounded by garlands of Darbha grass. The eight auspicious articles shall be procured. There shall be a splendid

249. grahaṇādiṣu kāleṣu—at suitable times and places. These are etailed in *Matsya*, cited in ST.

अयने विषुवे पुण्ये व्यतीपाते दिनक्षये।
युगादिषूपरागेषु तथा मन्वन्तरादिषु ॥
यज्ञोत्सवविवाहेषु दुःस्वप्नाद्भुतदर्शने।
द्रव्यब्राह्मणलाभे वा श्रद्धा वा यत्र जायते ॥
तीर्थेष्वायतने गोष्ठे कूपारामे सरित्सु च।
गृहे वाऽऽयतने वापि तडागे रुचिरेऽपि वा।
महादानानि देयानि संसारभयभीरुणा।

250. kalāhastena—ṣoḍaśa-hastena *ST*.

251. bhramantikā—tulā *ST*. the weighing scale.

canopy above. The wood used for the pillars of the Tulā (weighing balance) shall particularly be Bilva, Aśvattha, Palāśa or Khadira. The wood for the pillar shall be one that is commonly used.

26-28. Or bamboo can be used alongwith other wood structure. The space (for erecting the Tulā) shall be eight Hastas long and two Hastas wide. If the main pillar is not well-chiselled it shall have three times girth (?). It shall be circular and free from cracks. The distance between the two pillars of the balance shall be six Hastas or four Hastas.

29. The upper portions shall be six Hastas apart. Its upper (horizontal staff) shall be a cubit in width, or in circumference (if round).

30. The hole in the upper shaft shall be in conformity with the length of the pillars. The suspended Tulā (balancing rod) shall be thirtysix (Aṅgulas)[252] in length.

31. The diameter shall be eight Aṅgulas and five yavas. The pivotal point (Nābhi) shall be thirtysix Aṅgulas in length (?) It shall be fine and circular.

32. A gold plate shall be fixed in the top, middle and bottom portions. In the middle of the plate shall be three fixing pins.

33. The three fixing pins shall be made of copper or brass. It shall not be made of iron.

34. The fixing pin shall be splendid and facing upwards (i. e. raised) in the middle. It shall be duly fixed to the tip of the Toraṇa (?) by means of threads.

35. The Toraṇa is made in the middle of the Tulā in the form of a tongue. In the middle of the upper shaft there shall be an excellent peg.

36. It shall be firmly fixed to the top of the canopy. O sage, a round ring with a hollow shall be tied to the peg.

37. Suspended pendant (Avalambana) shall be fixed to the hanging shaft (?) in the middle of the Tulā along with the canopy by means of circular rings.

38. It shall be fixed firmly to the middle of the tulā leav-

252. ṣaḍtriṁśanmātra—36 pieces of gold. Here mātra means gold. *ST.* quotes *Viśva* in support of this meaning.

ing nine aṅgulas (on either side). The width of the (binding) plate shall be five aṅgulas.

39. The two seats shall be made of hard blocks of any strong material and hung below the supporting strings each weighing a thousand palas and measuring five Prādeś as square (a Prādeśa=the span between the extended thumb and fore-finger).

40-42. Or they may weigh eight hundred or six hundred Palas. The width of the Kalaśa in the middle shall be four palms[253] and the mouth three and a half palms of the hand. The Pañcapātra vessel shall be fixed to it. It must have four openings[254] each opening an aṅgula in width. It must have pure and white suspended pendants.

43. Chains shall be fastened to every pendant all round. The loop supporting the chain shall be joined to the pendant.

44. After leaving four span-lengths from the ground the pans shall be suspended. Two jars of human size and splendid in appearance shall be taken.

45. They shall be filled with sand. Śiva idol two Hastas long shall be put in the hollow.

46. The learned priest shall fill it with sand completely. It shall be so made that it does not move easily.

47-48. May a great secret be heard. Over the Vedikā a mystic diagram shall be drawn with the auspicious materials eight in number bedecked with the auspicious tender sprouts and scattered with flowers and fruits. Incense and lights shall also be used. It shall be as refulgent as the surface of a mirror. The Maṇḍala shall be drawn in the middle of the altar.

49. The Maṇḍala shall be drawn at the outset with four entrances. It must be beautified fully with the pericarp and filaments.

50-51. It shall be of various colours. At least there shall be five colours. The picture of the thunderbolt shall be drawn in the east, the shining Śakti in the south-east; a staff in the south and a sword in the south-west. The noose shall be drawn in the west and the banner in the north-west.

253. **Catustālam—tāla is a particular measure. Cf. तालः करतला-ङ्गुष्ठमध्यमाभ्याञ्च कीर्तितः—cited in *ST*.**

254. **Catur-dvāra, i.e. (consisting of) four holes.**

52. The iron-club shall be drawn in the north and the trident in the north-east. To the left of the trident a discus shall be drawn and a lotus to its right.

53-56. After drawing thus the Homa rite shall be performed. The main Homa shall be performed by repeating the Gāyatrī mantra, Svāhā unto Śakra, to Vahni, to Yama, to the lord of the Rākṣasas, to Varuṇa, to Vāyu, to Kubera, to Īśvara, to Viṣṇu and Brahmā. Homa shall be duly performed with the Praṇava ending with Svāhā, through the fire generated in accordance with the tenets of one's own branch of the Vedas. Then the priest shall perform all the rites ending with Jayādi Homa Sviṣṭa Homa in accordance with the injunctions. In all these Homas and in the main Homa the sacrificial twig shall be that of Palāśa. Twentyone Homas shall be performed repeating the following mantra.

57-64. "This sacrificial twig[255] is your Ātman, O fire, be kindled thereby; be flourishing; make us prosper in progeny, cattle wealth, brahminical splendour, foodgrains, etc, and intellect, Svāhā. Svāhā unto Bhūr, Bhuvaḥ Svāhā, Svaḥ Svāhā. Bhūrbhuvaḥ Svaḥ." Homa of sacrificial twigs shall be interspersed with Caru and ghee in order. The milk pudding with white rice and cooked rice with green gram are the Carus intended.

He shall then perform a thousand, five hundred or one hundred and eight Homas repeating the following mantras.

"O fire, you sanctify our lives.[255a] In these you put energy and all desired things. Harass our enemies. Agni is the sanctifying sage.[255b] He is the priest. He is conducive to the welfare. He originates from the Pañcajanas. We praise him that is Mahāgaya(?) O Agni. purify us[255c] with good waters (?) giving unto us excellent virility; giving unto me wealth and nourishment. O Prajāpati,[255d] the constituents in the universe are not diverse from you. May we have that, desiring which we perform Homa unto you. May we be the lords of wealth."

255. ayanta idhmā—AG. 1. 10.12; HG. 1.2.11.
255a. agna āyūṁṣi—*RV*. ix. 66. 19; *TS*. 1.3.14.7.
255b. agnirṛṣiḥ pavamānaḥ—*RV*. ix. 66. 20; TĀ. 2.5.2.
255c. agne pavasva—*RV*. ix. 66. 21; *TS*. 1.3.14.8.
255d. prajāpate *TS*. 1.8.14.2,

The main Homa is performed by repeating Gāyatrī[256], using sacrificial twigs and offering Caru and ghee. Homas shall be performed to Śakra and others as well as to thunderbolt, etc. five hundred in number. Homa unto Brahmā shall be performed with the mantra beginning with "Brahma jajñānam" etc;[257] that to Viṣṇu by the mantra—"We know Nārāyaṇa. We meditate on Vāsudeva. Hence, may Viṣṇu urge and guide us."

This special thing about the splendid path of Homas has been mentioned.

Twenty Homas shall be performed severally with the Dūrvā grass mixed with milk.

We worship the three-eyed deity who increases nourishment and who is fragrant. Just as the cucumber fruit is separated from the root may we be separated from death, but never from nectar.[258]

This Dūrvā Homa is very splendid and Vāstu Homa is similar to that by all means. The expiatory Homa rite shall be performed with Aghora mantra by pouring ghee. Each of these Homas shall be performed hundred times. Brahmā stands to the left, Viṣṇu to the right. Śiva the preceptor of the universe is in the middle along with the goddess Umā. He is surrounded by Indra and others as well as his Gaṇas.

65. He shall worship also Āditya, Bhāskara, Bhānu, Ravi and lord Divākara along with Uṣā, Prabhā, Prajñā, Sandhyā and Sāvitrī respectively.

66-69. Worship shall be performed in fivefold ways unto the noble-souled Khakholka. After worshipping Viṣṭarā, Subhagā, Vardhanī, Pradakṣiṇā and goddess Āpyāyanī he shall worship Ravi many times in the lotus seat. Vimala is worshipped in the south, Sāra in the west, Ārādhya in the north and Sukha in the middle.

In the filaments in due order the following shall be worshipped—Dīptā, Sūkṣmā, Jayā, Bhadrā, Vibhūti, Vimalā, Amoghā and Vidyutā. Sarvatomukhī shall be worshipped in the middle.

256. gāyatryā – by reciting rudra-gāyatrī.

257. Brahma jajñānam *TS*. 4.2.8.2; *VS*. 13.3.

258. tryambakaṁ yajāmahe *RV*. vii. 59. 12; *TS*. 1. 8. 6. 2.

70-71. In due order the Moon, Mars, Mercury, Jupiter, Venus, Saturn, Rāhu and Ketu shall be worshipped and Homa performed unto them. Yogins shall be given special gifts. Yogins the sole masters of Śaiva philosophy shall be fed.

72-73. Yogins who are richly endowed with the divine Vedic study shall be duly honoured. After performing these rites in detail even while the Homas are being performed, the king shall be made to mount the scale in the balance that is to the east, repeating the Rudrādhyāya mantras. The king shall be made to sit there for twentyfour minutes.

74. The sacrificer shall repeat the mantra called Rudra Gāyatrī. For the period of a Ghaṭikā or half of it or still half of it, he shall be seated.

75-76. The intelligent devotee shall sit with concentration. He shall hold the Darbha in the hand and face the west.[259] The king is richly adorned with all ornaments. He holds the sword and the iron club Kheṭaka. The Puṇyāha rite shall be performed by brahmins who are masters of the Vedas and the ancillaries repeating the word "Svasti" in the beginning and in the end.

77-78. There shall be auspicious shouts of victory and chanting of the Vedic mantras, splendid vocal music as well as instrumental accompanied by dances. All these shall add beauty and splendour to the ceremony. He shall place the gold to the northern side till the scales of the balance become equal.

79. If the amount exceeds hundred gold coins it is very excellent. If it is half of that it is Madhyama (neither good nor bad). If it is still half of that (i.e. 25 coins) it is inferior. Thus they are divided into three types.

80-81. All the following articles that had been worn at the beginning of the holy rite viz.—two cloths, the turban, the earring, the splendid necklace round the neck, the ring that adorns the finger, and the ornament round the wrist, shall be given to the devotee who regularly performs the Pāśupata rite and who smears Bhasman all over his limbs.

82-83. All the ornaments mentioned before, along with the turban and cloths shall be given to those who perform the rites. The learned man shall give a cloth to cover all these

259. Vāruṇam. According to *ST*. it means 'the sun'.

along with a monetary gift of hundred gold coins or half of that or still half of it. To all the yogins he shall give gold coins severally.

84. He shall give all the divine materials used for the sacrifice, to the chief preceptor. To the other ascetics he shall give a gold coin each.

85-89. The gold pieces on the balance shall be dedicated to Śiva. The palace, Maṇḍapa, rampart, ornaments, gold flower, drum, sword and the case for the sword shall be formally dedicated to Śiva. Whatever remains, the intelligent devotee shall give unto the preceptor and particularly to those who have smeared their bodies with Bhasman. All the prisoners in the jail shall be released. He shall perform the ablution of the lord with a thousand Kalaśas. The lord shall also be duly bathed with ghee or milk, or curds or by all commingled. The ablution may be performed with Brahmakūrca (cow's urine) or Pañcagavya.

90-96. The cow's urine shall be mixed by repeating Gāyatrī with the cowdung by means of Praṇava, the milk by repeating the mantra "Āpyāyasva" and the curds by repeating the mantra "Dadhikrāvṇaḥ" etc. The ghee shall be added repeating the mantra "Tejosi" etc. The Abhiṣeka (with Pañcagavya) shall be performed with Īśāna mantra. Repeating the mantra "Devasya Tvā" etc. the ablution of the lord of Devas shall be performed with the water in the pot along with Kuśa grass. The lord shall be bathed with the Rudrādhyāya mantras. Thousand Kalaśas shall be used and thousand names of the lord uttered as repeated formerly by Viṣṇu, Taṇḍin or Dakṣa the chief of sages. This great worship of Mahādeva shall be performed with deep devotion. To the worshipper of Śiva and to one's own preceptor monetary gift shall always be given. The covering for the bodies, i.e., clothes of silk or blanket shall also be given along with the monetary gifts. Poor, blind, wretched, old, lean and sick people as well as children shall be duly fed and given Dakṣiṇās.[260]

260. For detail, see *Matsya*—tulāpuruṣadānavidhi.

CHAPTER TWENTYNINE

The mode of the charitable gift of Hiraṇyagarbha

Sanatkumāra said:

1. The first holy rite Tulā has been mentioned to you in a general form. I shall mention Hiraṇyagarbha, the second in the series. This rite is the bestower of all Siddhis.

2-3. The bottom vessel shall be made with half a thousand gold pieces. The upper vessel shall be made with half that number. The mouth shall be just wide enough for its entry.[261] Thus, the golden vessel shall be made embellished with all ornaments. In the lower vessel the devotee shall remember the goddess Māyā having the three Guṇas.

4. He shall remember the goddess of twentyfour[262] principles with the forms of Brahmā, Viṣṇu and Agni. In the upper vessel he shall remember about the lord of Umā, the twenty-sixth[263] principle beyond the Guṇas.

5. He shall meditate on the Ātman as the Puruṣa, the twenty-fifth[264] principle, the deity born at the outset, in the middle of the spot mentioned before on the upper surface of the Altar.

6. Śāli rice shall be put into the pot and the pot shall be wrapped in fresh cloth. After applying the powdered residue of black gram *dal* on it, it shall be worshipped with five articles of worship[265].

7. The devotee shall worship it with the five mantras Īśāna etc. duly. The worship of Śiva and Homa shall be performed as before in due order.

8-10. The devotee shall repeat Gāyatrī and sit facing the east. After performing all these rites the excellent brahmin

261. saṁveśamātrakam—with a narrow opening, of the form of modern 'surāhī'.

262. Caturviṁśatikāṁ devīm—i.e. Prakṛti constituted of twentyfour tattvas.

263. ṣaḍviṁśakam—the twentysixth principle, i.e. the transcendent puruṣa Īśvara.

264. pañcaviṁśakam—the twentyfifth category, namely, the individual soul, the enjoyer of Prakṛti. Cf. *Liṅga* 1. 28. 7; II. 17, 26-27.

265. pañca-dravyeṇa—pañcopacāraiḥ *ST*. with the five articles of propitiation.

shall perform rites beginning with Garbhādhāna using the sixteenfold articles of worship.[266] The sprinkling shall be made in the right hand side nostril with the tender sprouts of the Dūrvā grass along with the fruits of the Udumbara tree. Water shall be sprinkled twenty-one times by means of the Kuśa grass. In the rite of Sīmanta also water shall be sprinkled in the north-eastern direction.

11-13. With thirty gold coins a splendid image of a girl shall be made and the rite of marriage be performed. After embellishing the idol and performing Homa, the same shall be dedicated to Śiva.

In the course of the rite of Annaprāśana the learned devotee shall feed himself with milk pudding, etc. Thus the rites beginning with impregnation (Garbhādhāna) shall end with the rite of Viśvajita. All these rites shall be performed with the help of brahmins who are masters of Vedas. The rites shall be performed by repeating the Śaktibīja mantra.

The remaining rites shall be performed like the Tulāhema rite (mentioned before.)

CHAPTER THIRTY

The mode of gifting the mountain of gingelly seeds

Sanatkumāra said:

1-3. Now I shall narrate the excellent rite of Tilaparvata dāna (gift of a mountain of gingelly seeds). This rite shall be performed in the same spot as is mentioned before and at the same auspicious occasion. It shall be performed on a beautiful level plot of ground. O sage, after duly worshipping the staff fixed on the bare ground without an altar it shall be sprinkled with water. The staff shall have the length of ten palms of

266. ṣoḍaśa-mārgeṇa—in the manner as enjoined in the treatises dealing with the sixteen saṁskāras.

hands. After sprinkling the staff with water the excellent brahmin devotee shall put gingelly seeds over it. He shall water that spot with Pañcagavya.

4-5. The learned devotee shall draw the mystic diagram as before all round. New cloth shall be spread over the ground and beautfiul flowers shall be scattered. Bhāras of gingelly seeds shall be piled up there. If the pile of gingelly seeds is higher than the staff by a Daṇḍa, it shall be glorified as the excellent one.

6. O leading sages, if it is four aṅgulas shorter in height than before it is the middle one. If it is of the same height as the staff it is of mean order. No mound shall be made shorter in height than the staff.

7. It shall be wrapped with new cloth all round and duly worshipped. After fixing Sadya and others he shall worship them in accordance with the injunctions.

8. The deities mentioned before shall be duly installed in all the eight quarters. Each of the deities shall be duly made with three golden pieces.

9. The monetary gift shall be duly offered as in the case of the rite of Tulā Bhāra. O excellent sages, the Homa too shall be just as it has been mentioned before.

10-13. The worship of Śiva shall be performed by means of thousand Kalaśas. One shall have the vision of Umāpati, the lord of Devas seated in the middle of the mound of the gingelly seeds. The devotee shall worship the lord of the chiefs of Devas surrounded by the guardians of the quarters, seated in the middle of the mound of gingelly seeds. In fact, the lord shall be in the form of the mountain mound of gingelly seeds. After performing the rite of worship in accordance with the injunctions, the lord shall be ritualistically discharged. The devotee shall give away the mountain of gingelly seeds as a present unto a brahmin well-versed in the Śrutis but poor. Thus, the rite of gift of a mountain of gingelly seeds has been mentioned to you. It is the greatest of all rites of charitable gifts.

CHAPTER THIRTYONE

The mode of gifting the subtle mountain

Sanatkumāra said:

1. Henceforth, a rite called Sūkṣmaparvata (subtle mountain) is being laid down. The materials are few but the benefit is great. It can be performed at any time when the materials have been gathered. It is genuinely a holy rite.

2. The ground is scrubbed and cleaned with cowdung. Cloths are spread over it. The intelligent devotee shall deposit three Bhāras of excellent gingelly seeds in the middle of the cloths.

3. He shall make an eight-petalled lotus with pericarp and filaments. It shall be made with ten gold coins.

4. The lotus shall be fixed in the middle of the gingelly seeds. The idol shall be placed in the middle of the lotus. After duly propitiating the lord he shall worship Vāma and others.

5-6. The form of Śakti shall be made of gold with three gold pieces. The Nyāsa rite shall be performed. Vighneśas shall be installed all round.[267] The Vighneśas shall be made with the quantity of gold mentioned before. They shall be duly worshipped with scents and fragrant flowers and other materials in accordance with the injunctions.

CHAPTER THIRTYTWO

The gift of golden earth

Sanatkumāra said :

1-2. I shall succinctly mention the charitable gift of golden earth. The rites of japa, homa, worship, charitable gift and ablution, etc., shall be performed as before through sages in the place and on occasions mentioned earlier either in the Kuṇḍa or in the Maṇḍala.

267. kramāt—pūrvādi-krameṇa—in the order of the quarters beginning with the east.

3-4. The figure of the earth shall be made with a thousand golden coins. It shall be divine in form with a single hand, beautiful and splendid. It shall be surrounded by mountains and shall contain the seven islands, oceans, etc., as well as all the holy centres with the mountain Meru in the middle.

5-7 Or the island[268] with the nine Khaṇḍas shall be depicted in the middle. As before all rites shall be performed in the mystic diagram in the middle of the altar. One-seventh of the thousand gold coins shall be given to a devotee of Śiva as a gift in accordance with the Śāstraic injunctions.

He shall worship lord Śiva with the thousand water pots and other articles. This excellent charitable gift is called Suvarṇa Medinī Dāna.

CHAPTER THIRTYTHREE

The mode of gifting the kalpa tree

Sanatkumāra said:

1-2. Henceforth, I shall mention the excellent rite of kalpa tree. The kalpa tree shall be made in replica with a hundred gold coins. It shall have all the branches. Strings of pearls shall be suspended from the branches. The tender sprouts shall be depicted by means of illustrious emerald stones.

3. The new shoots of the tree shall be depicted by the devotee by using coral. He shall beautify the branches all round by means of rubies depicting the fruits.

4. The root shall be depicted by using the blue gem; the stem by using diamonds; the tip of the tree by Vaidūrya (Lapis Lazuli) and topaz.

5. O sage of good holy rites, the bulbos root shall be depicted by the Gomedaka gem. The platform round the tree shall be depicted by the solar or the lunar stone or by crystals.

6. The width of the tree including the eight branches, and the height of the tree shall be one cubit.

268. dvīpam—Jambūdvīpa with its nine divisions.

7-9. The devotee shall place the Liṅga at its root. It shall be surrounded by the guardians of the quarters. The tree shall be placed on the Maṇḍala in the middle of the altar mentioned before. The devotee shall then assiduously worship lord Īśāna and the guardians of the quarters. As before, Japa, Homa and other rites shall be performed as in the rite Tulādhāna. O king, the devotee shall dedicate the tree to the lord or offer it to yogins or to persons who smear their bodies with Bhasman. The king will become an emperor.

CHAPTER THIRTYFOUR

The mode of gifting Viśveśvara

Sanatkumāra said:

1-5. I shall mention the rite called Gaṇeśeśa in the Maṇḍapa mentioned before. After worshipping the lord of the chiefs of Devas surrounded by the guardians of the quarters, the devotee shall make the idols of Viśveśvaras as enjoined by the scriptures, with ten gold coins. They shall be bedecked in all the ornaments. He shall worship them in accordance with the injunctions. As before, he shall perform Homas, in the eight Kuṇḍas in the eight quarters, according to the way of five coverings and the traditional style. He shall worship seven brahmins and a virgin girl in the north. All the mantras shall be repeated[269] and the gifts shall be offered along with their respective mantras in order. By giving a gift thus one is undoubtedly liberated from all sins.

269. sarvamantrāṇi—sarvadevatā-prasādanāni pratimārūpāṇi *ST.* mantras for the propitiation of all-gods in the form of idols.

CHAPTER THIRTYFIVE

The mode of gifting the golden cow

Sanatkumāra said:

1. Henceforth, I shall mention to you the procedure of the gift of a golden cow. It dispels all sins and destroys evil planets and famine.

2-3. It suppresses all evil portents and calamities. It despels all ailments.

The form of the cow shall be made in gold using a thousand, five hundred, two hundred and fifty or hundred gold coins. It shall be endowed with all attributes.

4. The form of the cow shall have beautiful hoofs and endowed with all divine characteristics. At the tip of the hoof a diamond shall be fixed. Ruby stone shall be placed on the horn.

5. O excellent sages, a divine pearl shall be fixed in between the eye-brows. The four udders shall be made by means of Vaidūrya (Lapis lazuli). The splendid tail shall be made by means of blue gem.[270]

6. In the place of the teeth a splendid topaz shall be fixed. After making the mother cow the devotee shall make a splendid calf.

7-8. The calf shall be made by means of ten golden coins. It shall be beautified by means of all gems. After drawing the mystic diagram in the middle of the altar mentioned before, the devotee who knows all principles shall place the cow in its middle along with the calf. With a pair of clothes he shall wrap the cow along with its calf.

9-11. He shall worship the cow and the calf by repeating the Gāyatrī mantra. He shall perform the Homa duly in accordance with the injunctions relating to the single fire. Using sacrificial twigs or ghee in accordance with the injunctions he shall perform the remaining rites too as before. After bathing the Liṅga with ghee, etc. the worship of Śiva shall be performed. After touching the splendid cow with Gāyatrī mantra it shall be dedicated to Śiva. O highly intelligent one, thirty gold coins shall be given away in gift.

270. nīlataḥ—nīla-ratnena *ST*. with the blue-coloured gem.

CHAPTER THIRTYSIX

The mode of gifting Lakṣmī

Sanatkumāra said:

1-3. I shall recount the rite of Lakṣmī Dāna which is a great holy rite. It causes the increase of prosperity. The rites should be performed in the mystic diagram over the altar in the Maṇḍapa mentioned before. The replica of Śrīdevī shall be made with unparalled beauty and endowed with all characteristics. It shall be made of gold by means of a thousand, five hundred, two hundred and fifty or one hundred and eight gold coins. The devotee shall then place Lakṣmī embellished with all ornaments in the Maṇḍala.

4-5. He shall worship Viṣṇu on the bare ground to the right hand side of Lakṣmī. After worshipping Sureśvarī by means of Śrīsūkta in accordance with the injunctions, he shall worship Viṣṇu, the preceptor of the universe by means of Viṣṇu Gāyatrī. After duly propitiating the goddess he shall perform the Homa as before.

6-9. After performing the Homas with the sacrificial twigs the devotee shall perform Homa with ghee. Each of these Homas shall be separately performed hundred and eight times through excellent brahmins. The sacrificer shall be called to spot[271] in the eastern quarter and the goddess shall be pointed out to him. He shall then prostrate on the ground like a staff. After bowing to Viṣṇu, he shall, as before, worship Śiva stationed there. A twentieth of the cost of the idol is considered to be the due Dakṣiṇā. Half of that should be given to others in the manner they deserve. Then the devotee, particularly the yogin, shall perform the Homa of Śiva.

271. tasyāḥ—Lakṣmyāḥ *ST.* of Lakṣmi.

CHAPTER THIRTYSEVEN

The mode of gifting the golden cow along with gingelly seeds

Sanatkumāra said :

1. Henceforth, I shall recount the mode of performing the rite of Tiladhenu Dāna. The devotee shall perform the worship of Śiva in the west of the Maṇḍapa mentioned before.

2. In front of it, in the middle of the ground he shall draw the diagram of a splendid lotus. The excellent gold lotus shall be wrapped in cloth and placed in its middle.

3-6. He shall cause the gingelly flower to be made and put the gold lotus therein. It shall be made with thirty, fifteen, or seven and a half, or five, or two and a half, or one and a quarter gold coins. After worshipping the deity[272] by means of scents, fragrant flowers and the like in accordance with the injunctions he shall cause eleven brahmins to sit in the northern quarter of the lotus. They shall be duly worshipped with scents and fragrant flowers in accordance with the injunctions. He shall then give the brahmins clothes to wear and upper cloth to cover themselves. A turban as well as a pair of ear-rings to embellish themselves should also be given to each.

7-9. The devotee shall give a gold ring to the brahmins duly. He shall then spread eleven pieces of cloth in front of them. Gingelly seeds and other articles shall be placed on those cloths separately. A bell-metal vessel of hundred Palas shall be split into eleven parts and given to the brahmins along with a sugarcane tree stump. The devotee shall cause the horns of the cow to be made in gold with two gold coins.

10. The hoofs shall be made of silver costing two gold coins. After giving all these severally the devotee shall place them amongst the gingelly seeds.

11-12. He shall repeat the eleven Rudra mantras and offer these to Rudras.

In the eastern side of the lotus he shall seat twelve brahmins and worship them. In the same manner as before he shall perform all the rites, repeat the twelve Āditya mantras and offer the materials to them.

272. **taṁ—hema-padma-vigraham** *ST*. **that idol of golden lotus.**

13. As before, he shall seat sixteen brahmins on the southern side of the lotus. The idol shall be dedicated as before by means of Vighneśa mantras.

14-16. All these rites shall be performed in due order by the sacrificer. It is enough if he makes over the gifts unto the Rudras or the Ādityas. The idols etc. shall be given in accordance with the extent of one's wealth. The king shall perform the rites of offering Pādya etc. as well. Dakṣiṇā shall be offered in the form of an ornament costing five gold coins.

CHAPTER THIRTYEIGHT

The mode of offering thousand cows as gift.

Sanatkumāra said:

1-2. O sage of good holy rites, I shall mention the rite of gifting a thousand cows.

The devotee shall collect together a thousand splendid cows endowed with good qualities along with their calves. He shall assiduously worship eight[273] among them in accordance with the scriptural texts. Each of the horns of these shall be covered with as much gold as there is in a gold coin.

3-5. The hoofs shall be covered with silver. The neck shall be tied round with a gold coin suspended from it. A splendid diamond shall adorn the ears. These shall be dedicated to Śiva and gifts shall be offered severally to the brahmins; each being given ten gold coins, or five, two and a half or one and a quarter gold coins or one niṣka in accordance with one's wealth. Or gold coins alone shall be offered. A pair of good clothes shall be offered to the brahmins.

6-9. The cows should be propitiated and given as gifts. They must be beautiful. After giving the gift duly the devotee shall worship lord Śiva. Thereafter, he shall repeat the excellent hymn of cows precisely. Cows are continuously in front of me.

273. aṣṭau—the number eight refers to the cows that are to be worshipped assiduously.

Cows are behind me. Cows are always in my heart. I stay in the midst of cows. The devotee repeats this hymn, circumambulates the cows and offers them to deserving brahmins.

The devotee who does like this is honoured in the heavenly world for as many years as there are hairs on the cows offered.

CHAPTER THIRTYNINE

The procedure for the gift of golden horse

Sanatkumāra said:

1. I shall mention the rite of the gift of golden horse. It is conducive to victory. It is more excellent than the horse sacrifice. O sage of good holy rites, I shall mention it. Listen.

2-9. With the gold of a thousand and eight gold coins or of a hundred and eight gold coins the devotee shall make the image of a horse endowed with all the characteristics and having all ornaments. It shall have the five[274] auspicious marks. It shall be of divine shape and form. It shall be endowed with all characteristics and shall have all the limbs and all the weapons. It shall be like the excellent vehicle of Indra. After placing the horse endowed with all attributes in the middle of the Maṇḍapa the devotee shall consider it to be on a par with Uccaiśśravas and worship it with devotion. To the east of it a brahmin who has mastered the Vedas shall be made to sit. He shall be worshipped as if he is Indra. He shall be given five gold coins. That horse shall be given to a devotee of Śiva. After making the gift of the golden horse the devotee shall worship the preceptor also in accordance with the extent of his wealth or he shall be given five gold coins. The devotee shall delight the wretched, the blind, the miserly, the helpless children, old men, lean and sick ones by giving them food. In particular, he shall feed the brahmins.

The man who performs this holy rite of giving away the gold horse enjoys the pleasure of Indra for a long time. He attains great prosperity.

274. **pañca-kalyāṇa-sampannam—pāde mukheṣu śvetavarnam** *ST.* **the nails of whose hoofs are white.**

CHAPTER FORTY

The mode of gifting a virgin

Sanatkumāra said:

1-7. I shall mention the rite of offering a virgin. It is the most excellent of all charitable gifts. The devotee talks to the parents and buys a virgin endowed with all characteristics and devoid of all defects. He gives much wealth to the parents and takes possession of her. She is bathed and robed in a fresh and splendid cloth. She is bedecked in all ornaments. She is then worshipped with scents and fragrant garlands. She is then given in marriage to a brahmin well-versed in the Śrutis or to an ascetic, a religious student who has learned the Vedas. The devotee shall observe the omens properly. He shall consider the lineage, the star of birth etc. of the virgin and the religious student; he shall consider the mental inclination of both and worship them assiduously. He shall give men slaves and women slaves, riches, ornaments, fields, money, grains and garments. He is honoured in the world of Rudra as many thousand years as there are hairs in the bodies of the progeny of that girl.

CHAPTER FORTYONE

The gift of the golden bull.

Sanatkumāra said:

1-2. I shall succinctly mention the rite of gifting the golden Bull. The intelligent devotee shall make the form of a bull with a thousand or five hundred or two hundred gold coins or even with hundred and eight gold coins. He shall make the bull in the form of Dharma.

3-4. The Puṇḍra (sectarial mark) shall be made on the forehead with crystals in the shape of the crescent moon. The hoof shall be made of silver; the neck of ruby and the hump of Gomedaka gem. The circular rope for the bells shall be tied round the neck. It shall be made wonderfully exquisite by means of gems.

5-6. There the bull-emblem shall have tinkling bells and bangles. The devotee then instals the leading bull on the Maṇḍala above the altar on the occasion and in the spot mentioned before. The bull shall face the West. At the outset, the devotee shall affectionately worship the bull-bannered Īśvara seated on the bull.

7-10. The devotee shall worship the leading bull by means of the Vṛṣa Gāyatrī and bow down to it with great concentration—"We know the bull with the sharp-edged horns. We meditate on one with the virtue constituting the feet. Hence, may the bull urge and guide us". For increasing virtue, the devotee shall worship the bull with this mantra. According to the extent of one's affluence one shall perform Homa by means of ghee, cooked rice and other things. The bull shall be worshipped and given to the brahmins, or to Śiva. Dakṣiṇā should be in accordance with one's capacity. He who devoutly performs the excellent charitable gift of bull shall become a follower of Śiva and rejoice along with him.

CHAPTER FORTYTWO

The mode of gifting an elephant

Sanatkumāra said:

1-6. I shall mention the rite of gifting an elephant in due order. It shall be worshipped as before and given to a brahmin or dedicated to Śiva. The devotee shall make an image of an elephant endowed with all good characteristics, out of gold or silver with a thousand, five hundred or two hundred and fifty gold coins. It shall be embellished with all characteristics. It shall be dedicated to the lord at the time and on the spot mentioned before. Or it shall be offered to Śiva,[275] Parameṣṭhin

275. Read Śivābhimukhamāsīno for Śivābhimukhamāsīnā i.e. by the worshipper who faces Śiva.

on the eighth day. After worshipping Śiva as before, it should be given to a poor brahmin who is well-versed in Śrutis and who maintains the sacred fire. It shall be given keeping Śiva in view. He who performs this holy rite of gift with devotion to Śiva shall stay in heaven for a long time and then become a king and lord of elephants.

CHAPTER FORTYTHREE

The mode of gifting the eight guardians of the quarters

Sanatkumāra said:

1-2. The rite of the gift of eight Lokapālas is divine and very rare to be achieved. It is a secret rite bringing about all riches and destructive of all enemies. It guards one's own land. It causes increase in progeny, in divine elephants and horses. It is holy and conducive to the welfare of cows and brahmins.

3-6. The devotee shall worship Śiva in the middle of the Maṇḍala above the altar at the time and spot mentioned before, in due order. In the quarters and the interstices the bare ground shall be covered with sand. Fresh[276] cloth shall be spread and eight brahmins made to sit facing Śiva. They shall be masters of the Vedas and the ancillaries; they shall have conquered the senses, be born of noble families and endowed with all good characteristics. The devotee shall worship them with divine scents, fragrant flowers and good incense. They shall be duly honoured by means of clothes and ornaments repeating the mantras of the Lokapālas.

7-11. At the outset he shall perform Homa in the fire beginning with the east, repeating the mantras of the Lokapālas. Homa shall be performed gradually by means of sacrificial twigs and ghee. The preceptor, a favourite devotee of Śiva, shall duly perform Homa and then call the sacrificer. He shall adorn the brahmins with ornaments and give them wealth, severally repeating the respective mantras. A fee of ten gold

276. anāhateṣu--naveṣu. i.e. dressed in new robes.

coins is decent. The seat shall be made with ten gold coins for each one of them separately. The rite of ablution of Śiva shall be duly performed there. Monetary gifts shall be given in accordance with one's capacity. The learned man who performs this rite of the guardians of the quarters with devotion shall remain in the worlds of the guardians of the worlds for a long time and shall become an emperor.

CHAPTER FORTYFOUR

The mode of gifting Viṣṇu

Sanatkumāra said:

1-4. Hereafter, I shall mention another rite which is the greatest of all excellent gifts. At the time and spot mentioned before, in the Maṇḍapa, in the middle of the Kuṇḍa or on the bare ground in the presence of Śiva, the devotee shall out of affection worship Viṣṇu and the lotus-born deity by means of the following mantras along with the Praṇava duly uttered.

"We know Nārāyaṇa. We meditate on Vāsudeva. Hence, may Viṣṇu urge and guide us."

"Svāhā unto Brahmā the old brahmin, to the creator of the universe, to Śiva, to Hari. Svadhā, Vauṣaṭ and Vaṣaṭ."

5-9. After worshipping in accordance with the injunctions he shall perform Homa. All materials shall be offered for Homa by two priests in accordance with the injunctions. There shall be two Ṛtviks who have mastered the Vedas through a preceptor. With them in view, the devotee shall give monetary gifts to the brahmins. One hundred and eight gold coins to each of them separately is decent. Garments, ornaments and other adornments shall accompany the gift. Though the preceptor is one he represents the glorious Brahmā, Viṣṇu and Maheśvara. They shall be given the gift, separately. The brahmins shall be fed. Worship of Śiva shall be performed beginning with ablution, etc. in due order.

CHAPTER FORTYFIVE

The mode of performing Jīvacchrāddha rite.

The sages said:

1. Thus, the sixteen auspicious rites of charitable gifts have been mentioned by you. Now it behoves you to narrate the procedure of the Śrāddha rite for the living ones.

Sūta said:

2-3. I shall succinctly mention the mode of Jīvacchrāddha that is approved of by everyone. Formerly, it was mentioned by Brahmā, the lord of Devas to Manu, to Vasiṣṭha, to the well-disciplined Bhṛgu and Bhārgava. It is great and conducive to the achievement of all Siddhis. Listen ye with great fervour.

4. O sages of good holy rites, I shall mention the manner and order of the Śrāddhas, the order of those who deserve Śrāddhas and the peculiarities of the Jīvacchrāddha.

5-7. The Jīvacchrāddha shall be performed on a mountain, on the banks of a river, in a forest or in one's abode as also when death is imminent.[277] When it is performed he is liberated even as he is alive; whether he does or does not perform the functions (ordained for him), whether he possesses perfect knowledge or not, whether he is well-versed in the Vedic passages or not, whether he is a Brahmin or a Kṣatriya or a Vaiśya or whether he follows the path of the Yoga. There is no doubt about this.

8-13. The ground shall be carefully scrutinized by its smell, colour, taste etc. All the weeds and stumps shall be assiduously taken out. The middle of the ground, a cubit in extent, shall be covered with sand. If a Kuṇḍa is dug it shall be long and splendid or the bare ground shall extend to an arrow's length. The ground shall be scrubbed, cleaned and smeared with cowdung and fire shall be placed there in accordance with the injunctions in the scripture. Water shall be sprinkled all round. The rites pertaining to the fire shall be performed and concluded along the traditional lines as men-

277. mṛtakāle—when death is imminent, but according to ST. it means Vārdhakye—in old age.

tioned in one's own branch of the Vedas by repeating the following mantras. After worshipping on the bare ground he shall perform Homas by means of sacrificial twigs, etc. Homas shall at the outset be performed with the twigs; then with Caru and ghee sparkling splendidly in a separate vessel. Homas shall be performed by oneself invoking[278] the Tattvas and Bhūtas all round.

14-33. Om Bhūḥ, obeisance to Brahmā. Om Bhūḥ, Svāhā unto Brahmā. Om Bhuvaḥ, obeisance to Viṣṇu. Om Bhuvaḥ, Svāhā unto Visṇu. Om Svaḥ, obeisance to Rudra. Om Svaḥ, Svāhā unto Rudra. Om Mahaḥ, obeisance to Īśvara. Om Mahaḥ, Svāhā unto Īśvara. Om Janaḥ, obeisance to Prakṛti. Om Janaḥ, Svāhā unto Prakṛti. Om Tapaḥ, obeisance unto Mudgala. Om Tapaḥ, Svāhā unto Mudgala. Om Ṛtam, obeisance unto Puruṣa, Om Ṛtam, Svāhā unto Puruṣa. Om Satyam, obeisance unto Śiva. Om Satyam, Svāhā unto Śiva. Om Śarva protect my earth, smell in the nose, obeisance unto lord Śarva, Bhūḥ, obeisance Om Śarva, protect my earth, smell in the nose; Bhūḥ, Svāhā unto Śarva. Om Śarva, protect my earth, smell with nose. Bhūh, obeisance to the wife of lord Śarva. Om Śarva, protect my earth, smell in the nose; Bhūḥ, Śvāhā unto the wife of Śarva.

34-37. Om Bhava, protect my waters, taste in the tongue; Bhuvaḥ, obeisance to lord Bhava.

Om Bhava protect my waters, taste in the tongue. Bhuvaḥ, Svāhā unto lord Bhava.

Om Bhava, protect my waters, taste in the tongue. Bhuvaḥ, obeisance unto the wife of lord Bhava.

Om Bhava, protect my waters, taste in the tongue. Bhuvaḥ, Svāhā unto the wife of Bhava.

38-41. Om Rudra, protect my fire, colour in the eye; Svaḥ, Om obeisance to Rudra.

Om Rudra, protect my fire, colour in the eye. Svaḥ Svāhā, unto lord Rudra.

Om Rudra, protect my fire, colour in the eye. Svaḥ Om, obeisance unto the wife of Lord Rudra.

278. tattvabhūtāni manasā uddhṛtya—lit. extracting the twentyfour tattvas along with the mind. But ST. explains 'uddhṛtya' as 'vicārya',—'thinking upon', i.e. distinguishing one tattva from the other.

Om Rudra, protect my fire, colour in the eye. Svaḥ Svāhā, unto the wife of lord Rudra.

42-45. Om Ugra, protect my wind, touch in the skin; Mahaḥ, obeisance unto lord Ugra.

Om Ugra, protect my wind, touch in the skin; Mahaḥ Svāhā, unto lord Ugra.

Om Ugra, protect my wind, touch in the skin. Mahaḥ Om, obeisance to the wife of lord Ugra.

Om Ugra, protect my wind, touch in the skin. Mahaḥ Svāhā unto the wife of lord Ugra.

46-49. Om Bhīma, protect my cavity, sound in the ears; Janaḥ Om, obeisance unto lord Bhīma.

Om Bhīma, protect my cavity, sound in the ears; Janaḥ Svāhā, unto lord Bhīma.

Om Bhīma, protect my cavity, sound in the ears; Janaḥ, Om, obeisance unto the wife of lord Bhīma.

Om Bhīma, protect my cavity, sound in the ears; Janaḥ Svāhā unto the wife of lord Bhīma.

50-53. Om Īśa, protect my Rajas (Guṇa), thirst for wealth; Japaḥ Om, obeisance to lord Īśa.

Om Īśa, protect my Rajas (Guṇa) thirst for wealth; Tapaḥ Svāhā unto lord Īśa.

Om Īśa, protect my Rajas (Guṇa) thirst for wealth; Tapaḥ Om, obeisance unto the wife of lord Īśa.

Om Īśa protect my Rajas (Guṇa), thirst for wealth; Tapaḥ Svāhā unto the wife of Īśa.

54-57. Om Mahādeva, protect my truth, faith in virtue; Ṛtam, obeisance to Mahādeva.

Om Mahādeva, protect my truth, faith in virtue; Ṛtam Svāhā unto Mahādeva.

Om Mahādeva, protect my truth, faith in virtue; Ṛtam obeisance unto the wife of Mahādeva.

Om Mahādeva, protect my truth, faith in virtue; Ṛtam Svāhā unto the wife of Mahādeva.

58-63 Om Paśupati, protect my noose, the state of the enjoyer and the enjoyment; Satyam, obeisance to lord Paśupati.

Om Paśupati, protect my noose, the state of the enjoyer and the enjoyment; Satyam Svāhā unto lord Paśupati.

Om Paśupati, protect my noose, the state of the enjoyer and the enjoyment; Satyam, obeisance unto the wife of lord Paśupati.

Om Paśupati, protect my noose the state of being the enjoyer and the enjoyment; Satyam Svāhā unto the wife of lord Paśupati.

Om obeisance to Śiva. Om Satyam, Svāhā unto Śiva[279].

64-66. Thus, Homa of Śiva shall be performed; that of Viriñci, etc. as before. Om at the outset unto Viriñci[280] and others, according to the paths of creation, O sages of good holy rites.

He shall, thereafter, worship the wife of Paśupati and Paśupati in order. After worshipping the lord, Homas shall be performed as before serially by using mantras. The article of Homa at the outset shall be ghee, then Caru and it shall conclude with sacrificial twigs. The sacrificer shall have concentration and mental purity.

67-68. Om Śarva, split my earth, split the smell into the nose, dispel the dense fat—Bhuḥ Svāhā, Bhuvaḥ Svāhā, Svaḥ Svāhā. Bhūr Bhuvaḥ Svaḥ Svāhā. Thus, the devotee shall perform Homa separately a thousand, and five hundred, or a hundred and eight times with ghee alone.

A separate Homa shall be performed a hundred and eight times with ghee alone repeating the Virajā mantras[281].

He shall perform Homa with ghee alone repeating the following mantra beginning with "Prāṇa" (as follows)—"Om, I am placed within Prāṇa, I perform Homas of Amṛta (nectar).

O Śiva, enter me. Svāhā unto the burner unto Prāṇa. Svāhā unto the overlord of Prāṇa, unto Rudra, unto the slayer of Vṛṣa (?).

Om Bhūḥ Svāhā; Om Bhuvaḥ Svāhā; Om Svaḥ Svāhā; Om Bhūr Bhuvaḥ Svaḥ Svāhā."

79. Thus, Homa shall be performed in this order as is mentioned in the treatises on Śrāddha. On the seventh day he shall feed leading Yogins and those who deserve to partake of the Śrāddha

279. Śivāya, but ST. adds 'mokṣāya', i.e. for the achievement of salvation.

280. Viriñcādyam—beginning with Viriñci (Brahmā).

281. Virajā—by reciting Virajā mantras.

80-81. To the brahmin devotees of Śiva,[282] garments, ornaments, shawls, vehicles, beddings, bell-metal, copper and other vessels, pots made of gold and silver, cows, gingelly seeds, fields, other assets as well as male and female slaves shall be given. Dakṣiṇā also shall be given.

82. Balls of rice shall be given as before in eight[283] ways separately. He shall feed a thousand brahmins and give them Dakṣiṇās too.

83. Or the devotee shall feed a single person engaged in the practice of Yoga. He shall strictly adhere to the Bhasman and shall have strict control over his senses. The Mahācaru shall be dedicated unto Rudra for three days.

84. Only particular things (about Jīvacśrāddha) have been mentioned here as other things are similar to all other Śrāddhas. If the devotee dies the Śrāddha may or may not be performed, since he becomes a liberated soul.

85. He can perform or eschew the obligatory and the optional rites. Even if any kinsman of his dies there is neither pollution nor purification of the same.

86-89. His post-natal pollution can no doubt be cleansed by mere bath. If afterwards he himself begets a son or a son is born to his wife, he shall perform all the holy rites for him. That son shall become a knower of Brahman. If a daughter is born to him, O sages of good holy rites, she will become one like Ekaparṇā or Aparṇā. Persons born in her family are liberated from hell. There is no doubt about this. By means of this holy rite his ancestors on his father's as well as mother's side are liberated.

90-94. When this brahmin passes away he shall either be buried after digging the ground or he shall be cremated. By performing all the duties of a son there cannot be any defect. He is not to attain any further salvation by means of later holy rites. Everything has been mentioned by Brahmā to the sages of sanctified souls. Again this was mentioned to Sanatkumāra by that intelligent lord.[284] It was mentioned to Kṛṣṇa Dvaipā-

282. śarvādīnām i.e. the Brahmins representing Śiva and other deities.

283. aṣṭaprakārataḥ—in the eightfold manner, i.e. in the order of the eight-formed (aṣṭamūrti) Śiva.

284. tena—i.e. by Brahmā.

yana by the son of Brahmā. It was due to the grace of the intelligent saintly lord Vedavyāsa that everything was known by me. It was at his behest that everything was performed by me.

Thus, the secret doctrine has been mentioned to you. It yields the achievement of Brahman. O sages of good holy rites this should be imparted to a devotee having control over his senses and never to one who is not a devotee.

CHAPTER FORTYSIX

Installation of the Liṅga

The sages said:

1. O Sūta of great intelligence, O Romaharṣaṇa, the mode of performing Śrāddha of living persons has been recounted by you for the sake of our liberation despite the fact that we are foolish.

2-6. O sage of good holy rites, how is the installation of Rudra, Āditya and Vasus, of Indra and others; how is the installation of Śiva the deity represented by the Liṅga; how are the following deities installed:—Viṣṇu, Indra, Brahmā, Agni, Yama, Nirṛti, Varuṇa, Vāyu, Soma, Yakṣa, Kubera, Īśāna, Earth, Śrī, Durgā, Śivā the excellent daughter of the Himavān, Skanda, Gaṇarāja and Nandin in particular ? It behoves you to describe in detail the characteristics of the installation of other Devas and Gaṇas.

7. O sage of good holy rites, you are conversant with the reality of all objects. You are another physical form of Kṛṣṇa Dvaipāyana.

8-9. "Sumantu, Jaimini and Paila are great sages. Romaharṣaṇa is capable of devoutly serving his preceptor." Thus is the great story sung about Vyāsa on the banks of the Bhāgīrathī. You are the chief disciple of that lustrous person, equal to or non-different from him.

10. You are equal to Vaiśampāyana among the disciples of Vyāsa on the earth. Hence, it behoves you now to mention everything to us.

11-13. After saying thus, the sages stood there for a while. At that time a mysterious thing happened in front of him (Sūta) and the sages. Goddess Sarasvatī herself uttered these words from the sky:—

"May the questions of the sages stop. The whole world is identical with the Liṅga. Everything is founded on the Liṅga. Hence, one shall eschew everything, instal the Liṅga and worship it.

14. One shall pierce the cosmic egg instantaneously by performing the rite of installing the Liṅga which acts like a large sword fixed to the path of the good. The devotee shall then unhesitatingly go out.

15-21. All these are firmly founded on the Liṅga:—Upendra, Brahmā, Indra, Yama, Varuṇa, Kubera, Īśvara and others. They have installed Maheśvara Śiva, whose physical form is the Liṅga. O brahmins, they have become the chief among their kinsmen by installing Śiva thus.

Brahmā, Hara, Viṣṇu, Ramā, Dharā, Lakṣmī, Dhṛti, smṛti, Prajñā, Dharā, Durgā, Śacī, Rudras, Vasus, Skanda, Viśākha, Śākha, Naigameśa, guardians of the quarters, planets, the Gaṇas, Nandin, Gaṇapati, Pitṛs, sages, those lustrous ones beginning with Kubera,[285] Ādityas, Vasus, Sāṁkhyas, the excellent physicians Aśvins, Viśvedevas, Sādhyas, Paśus, birds and animals—nay everything beginning with Brahmā and ending with an immobile thing is founded on the Liṅga. Hence, one shall eschew everything and instal the unchanging Liṅga. If one worships it, it is as good as worshipping everything installed assiduously.

285. Kuberādyāḥ—yakṣas with their leader Kubera.

CHAPTER FORTYSEVEN

Installation of Liṅga

Sūta said:

1-4. On hearing these words in the Heaven, the great sages joined their palms in reverence. Deciding to instal the Liṅga they bowed down mentally to the unchanging lord identical with tha Liṅga. Indra the lord of all Devas, the unborn lord Viṣṇu, the lord of everything, the excellent sages including Guru—the preceptor of Devas, the groups of Devas, Asuras and excellent men—all these imagined themselves to be identical with the Liṅga. On hearing these words in the Heaven the sages of the six great spiritual families,[286] endowed with concentration eschewed everything and attempted to instal the lord. The sages of holy rites then asked the sinless Sūta about the installation of the Liṅga. Their voices were choked with delight.

Sūta said:

5. I shall mention succinctly duly and precisely the installation of the lord in the form of Liṅga for obtaining virtue, love, wealth and salvation.

6-10. The Liṅga shall be made with great assiduity in accordance with the injunctions. A Liṅga shall be made of rock. It shall be identical with Brahmā, Viṣṇu, and Śiva. It may be made of gold studded with jewels, or of silver or copper. It shall have its pedestal and the exit for water.[287]. The top portion shall be sufficiently wide. The devotee shall clean Liṅga along with the pedestal and then devoutly instal it. The pedestal of the Liṅga is goddess Umā and the Liṅga is Maheśvara himself. By worshipping these two the lord and the goddess are worshipped. By their installation, the lord of Devas is installed along with the goddess. Hence, the most excellent among the installers shall instal the Liṅga along with the pedestal.

11. Lord Brahmā resides at the root; lord Viṣṇu in the middle. The unborn Rudra, Paśupati, the lord of all, the most

286. ṣaṭkulīyāḥ—belonging to six different families.

287. sasūtram—pañcasūtrādiyuktam ST. embellished by five sacred threads.

excellent one resides at the top. Since this lord of the Gaṇas is worthy of being worshipped by all Devas the devotee shall instal and worship a very weighty Liṅga.

12. Those who always worship Maheśa the most excellent lord among Devas, in his physical form of Liṅga, those who worship him by the pious articles of worship viz:—scents, garlands, incense, lights, ablutions, Homas, oblations, prayers, chanting of mantras and offerings of presents become free from the fear of birth and death. They become worthy of being saluted and worshipped by Siddhas, Devas and Gandharvas. They are bowed to even by the most excellent Gaṇas.

13. Hence, one shall instal the great Liṅga with devotion and fervent offerings of services. He shall worship the Liṅga for the achievement of all objects.

14-18. After worshipping it he shall install the Liṅga in the middle of the holy centre[288] in the seat of Śivā. The Liṅga shall then be wrapped in cloth, Darbha grass, etc.Eight pots with the guardians of the quarters as their deities shall be placed in a circle with Darbha grass bundle inserted into each of them. Akṣata grains shall be put into the pots and they shall be tied with threads of various colours. Svastika and other auspicious signs shall be drawn over them. The thunderbolt and other weapons shall be represented therein; they are then to be covered with cloth, and installed round the Liṅga by repeating the Īśāna mantra. The canopy above shall be fumigated with incense and lamps. Cloths are spread with the pictures of the emblems of the guardians of the quarters and their vehicles such as elephant buffalo etc. The devotee shall tie all round the place garlands of Darbha grass, with all their characteristic marks and woven into various beautiful forms.

19. The devotee shall then keep it within water along with incense and lights for five days, three days, or only for a single night.

20-26. The devotee shall spend this period studying the Vedas, performing dances and singing auspicious songs or playing on Vīṇā and other instruments to the accompaniment

288. tīrthamadhye—kṣetramadhye ST. in the midst of the soil, i.e. in the vaginal passage. ST. quotes Viśva in support of this meaning.

of tingling of small bells. The sacrificer shall have mental concentration and be free from excitement. After taking it out he shall meditate on the Svastika. The Liṅga shall then be placed in the Maṇḍapa endowed with characteristics. There shall be nine pits all round endowed with their characteristic marks. The eight auspicious articles called Aṣṭamaṅgalas shall be spread there. There shall be the eight emblems of the guardians of the quarters. The pits shall have the auspicious signs mentioned before. They shall be placed in the directions beginning with the east. The chief pit shall be made in the north-east oblong in shape. Or five pits made into one and a bare spot of ground shall constitute one unit. They shall be endowed with the paraphernalia and requisites of the sacrifice and ornaments, used in the worship of Śiva (?). In the middle of the altar there shall be a great bed bedecked in gold. A five-wicked lamp shall be kept nearby. The bed shall be covered with a white cloth. After arranging these he shall place the idol of the lord thereon.

27. He shall place the Liṅga with its head towards the east. He shall place it duly repeating Īśāna mantra. After performing the rite of Ratnanyāsa (fixation of jewels) he shall place the Kalaśa (water-pot) above.

28-29. The Liṅga shall be wrapped all round by two cloths and the Darbha grass. After doing the Ratna nyāsa the nine Śaktīs, Vāmā[289] etc. shall be fixed. The nine precious stones accompanied by gold, Pañcagavya and all kinds of grains shall be placed on the rock.

30. One shall instal the Brahmaliṅga by repeating Śivagāyatrī. One shall instal the unchanging Śiva by repeating the Praṇava alone.

31. He shall fix the Brahmā portion[290] of the lord with the mantra beginning with "Brahma jajñānam."[291] He shall fix the Viṣṇu portion[292] with Viṣṇu Gāyatrī.[293]

289. Vāmādyā nava-śaktayaḥ—vide *Liṅga*. II. 27.26.

290. brahma-bhāgam—Vedikādhobhāgam ST. the lower part of the pedestal.

291. Brahma jajñānam—TS. 4. 2. 8. 2.

292. Vaiṣṇavam bhāgam - madhyabhāgam ST. the middle part.

293. Viṣṇu-gāyatriyā—the correct form would be Viṣṇu-gāyatryā. This form is enforced by the exigency of metre.

32-33. He shall fix Śarva in the pedestal consisting of the three Tattvas by means of Praṇava with the mantras "Namaḥ Śivāya," "Namohaṁsa Śivāya" or by reciting the Rudrādhyāya after scrubbing Śarva (i. e. the Liṅga). He shall instal the Kalaśas all round by means of Vedic mantras.[294]

34-37. He shall place them in the middle of the altar along the lines mentioned before. He shall fix Śiva in the middle and the goddess Śivā in the southern pot. He shall place Skanda in the pot intended for him or he shall instal Brahmā in the pot pertaining to Skanda and Viṣṇu in the pot pertaining to Īśa. It shall be wonderfully decorated or he shall fix the body of Brahmā" in the pot pertaining to Śiva. The Brahmans are briefly—Śiva, Maheśvara, Rudra, Viṣṇu and Pitāmaha. These, Hṛdaya etc. and the mother goddess shall be fixed in the middle of the altar in accordance with the injunctions mentioned before.

38. He shall fill the Vardhanī[295] vessel with scented water and instal goddess therein. He shall place gold, silver and jewels in the pot pertaining to Śiva.

39-40. O sages of good holy rites, the Vidyeśvaras[296] shall be fixed in the Vardhanī assiduously by reciting the Gāyatrī and ancillary mantras. He shall fix Ananta, Īśa and other Devas in the pots pertaining to the quarters and filled with Brahmakūrca (cow's urine). The mantra begins with Praṇava and ends with Namaḥ. He shall cover with a fresh cloth each of the eight pots.

41. He shall put gold, jewels etc. in the pots of Viśveśvaras. Homas should be performed in the order of the faces (of Śiva)[297] with Gāyatrī and ancillary mantras.

42-43. The rites ending with "Jaya" and "Sviṣṭa" shall be performed as before. Water shall be sprinkled all round

294. brahmabhiḥ—pañca-brahma-mantraiḥ ST. by reciting the pañcabrahma mantras.

295. vardhanyām—khaḍgākārāyām ST. Vardhanī is an instrument of cutting in the form of sword.

296. Vidyeśvarān—probably viśveśvarān. Cf. v. 41 below, where ST. reads Viśveśvarāṇām for vidyeśvarāṇām and explains as aṣṭadikpālānām. But is not vighneśvarāṇām more suitable? The guardians of the quarters are stationed to ward off evil from their respective directions.

297. vakra-krameṇa—in the order of faces beginning with Īśāna.

from Śivakumbha, Vardhanī, those belonging to Viṣṇu and Brahmā, the Brahmā portion particularly the vessel belonging to Pitāmaha. He shall sprinkle Parameśvara with water from the pots of Vidyeśvaras.

44-45. As before he shall fix all the mantras with concentration and worship after performing the rite of ablution. The Dakṣiṇā shall be a thousand Paṇas[298] at the most. Half of that or one-fourth of it shall be given to others if possible.

46-50. Garments, fields, ornaments, cows and cash shall be given to the chief.[299] A great festival shall be celebrated. Homa, Yāga and Bali shall be offered in due order for the duration of nine, seven or three days or even for one day. Homa shall be done as mentioned before daily after worshipping Śaṅkara. Homas on behalf of Devas, Bhāskara etc. shall be done as before. They shall be daily worshipped within and without[300] as also in the fire. He who instals the Liṅga in this manner becomes identical with Parameśvara himself. By doing this Devas, Rudras, sages and the Apsarases shall be installed and worshipped by him. In fact, the three worlds of the mobile and immobile beings are being worshipped by him.

CHAPTER FORTYEIGHT

The different varieties of Gāyatrī

Sūta said :

1-2. I shall mention the installation of all Devas in detail. The Yāgakuṇḍas of Devas shall be fixed with their respective mantra and Devas installed and worshipped after the celebration of festivities in accordance with the injunctions. The worship of the sun shall be performed with five or twelve sacred fires.

298. Uttamaṁ sahasra-palam—one thousand palas of gold. pala is a particular measure, approximately equivalent to twenty māṣas.

299. pradhāne—i.e. the head-priest who represents lord Śiva himself.

300. ābhyantare tathā bāhye—in the internal (i.e. mental) as well as the external (physical) fire.

3-4. O sages of good holy rites, the Kuṇḍas shall be circular in the form of a lotus; the Kuṇḍa of Ambā shall be triangular. Only one Vardhanī is ordained for all together. In all the rites relating to the Śaktis the Kuṇḍa shall be triangular in shape. The Gāyatrī of Śiva shall be used assiduously for all other deities since all of them are born out of the parts of Rudra. I shall mention them briefly to you.

The different Gāyatrīs.

5-26. "We know Tatpuruṣa. We meditate on Vāgviśuddha (one purified by speech). Hence, may Śiva urge and guide us."

"We know Gaṇāmbikā. We meditate on Karmasiddhi (achievement of the benefit of the rite). Hence, may Gaurī urge and guide us."

"We know Tatpuruṣa. We meditate on Mahādeva. Hence, may Rudra urge and guide us."

"We know that Tatpuruṣa. We meditate on Vakratuṇḍa (lord Gaṇapati of curved snout). Hence, may Dantin (lord with elephantine face) urge and guide us."

"We know Mahāsena. We meditate on Vāgviśuddha. May thus, Skanda urge and guide us."

"We know Tīkṣṇaśṛṅga (one with sharp painted horns). We meditate on Vedapāda (one with the Vedas for feet). Hence, may Vṛṣa (virtue, bull) urge and guide us."

"We know Harivaktra (one with the face of a monkey). We meditate on Rudravaktra (one with a terrible face). Hence, may Nandin urge and guide us."

"We know Nārāyaṇa. We meditate on Vāsudeva. Hence, may Viṣṇu urge and guide us."

"We know Mahāmbikā (great mother). We meditate on Karmasiddhi (the achievement of the benefit of the holy rites). Hence, may Lakṣmī urge and guide us."

"We meditate upon and we know one who has been redeemed by Viṣṇu alone. Hence, may Rādhā urge and guide us."

'We know Vainateya (son of Vinatā). We meditate upon the golden-winged one. Hence, may Garuḍa urge and guide us."

"We know the lotus-born. We meditate on Vedavaktra (in whose mouth the Vedas reside). Hence, may the creator Brahmā urge and guide us."

"We know Śivāsyajā (one originating from the face of Śiva). We meditate on Devarūpā (one having divine form). Hence, may Vācā (speech) urge and guide us."

"We know the king of Devas. We meditate on Vajrahasta (one armed with the thunderbolt). Hence, may Indra urge and guide us."

"We know the eye of Rudra. We meditate on one armed with Śakti. Hence, may Agni urge and guide us."

"We know the son of Vivasvat. We meditate on one armed with a staff. Hence, may Yama urge and guide us."

"We know Niśācara (the Demon). We meditate on one armed with the sword. Hence, may Nirṛti urge and guide us.

"We know Śuddhahasta (one whose hands are pure). We meditate on one who is armed with the noose. Hence, may Varuṇa urge and guide us."

"We know the vital airs of all. We meditate on one armed with a stick. Hence, may Vāyu urge and guide us."

"We know the ruler of the Yakṣas.[301] We meditate on one armed with the iron club. Hence, may Yakṣa urge and guide us."

"We know the lord of all. We meditate on one armed with the trident. Hence, may Rudra urge and guide us."

"We know Kātyāyanī. We meditate on Kanyākumārī. Hence, may Durgā urge and guide us."

27. Thus, Gāyatrī shall be differentiated according to the deities; they shall be installed and worshipped. Their seat shall be Praṇava.

28-30. Or the devotee shall instal the incomparable Viṣṇu by reciting Puruṣasūkta. The devotee shall conceive of Viṣṇu, Mahāviṣṇu and Sadāviṣṇu in due order and instal them duly by reciting Deva Gāyatrī. Vāsudeva is the chief deity. Saṁkarṣaṇa, Pradyumna and Aniruddha are the different forms[302] of the lord. His forms are many due to the curse of Bhṛgu.

301. yakṣeśvarāya—to the lord of yakṣas, i.e. Kubera.

302. mūrtibhedāḥ—this refers to the group of four called Caturvyūhamūrti, comprising Vāmadeva, Saṅkarṣaṇa, Pradyumna and Aniruddha.

31-32. The forms are conducive to the welfare of worlds. They occur at every cycle of yugas[303] viz.—Matsya (fish), Kūrma (tortoise), Varāha (boar), Narasiṁha (man-lion), Vāmana (dwarf), Rāma (of solar race), Rāma (Paraśurāma), Kṛṣṇa, Buddha and Kalki. There are other forms[304] of lord Viṣṇu due to the curse of Bhṛgu.

33-35. The Gāyatrīs too of these forms shall be evolved, the deities shall be installed and worshipped. Perfect knowledge, yantras, mantras and the Upaniṣads (esoteric doctrines) are the secret of Viṣṇu, Nārāyaṇa the lord of Devas. Born of the five Brahmāṅgas[305] they are identical with the five Bhūtas. The mantra of Viṣṇu viz., "Namo Nārāyaṇāya" prefixed with the Praṇava is highly auspicious. It consists of eight syllables.

36. There are other mantras too, viz.—Oṁ Namo Vāsudevāya, Oṁ Namaḥ Saṅkarṣaṇāya, Oṁ Namaḥ Pradyumnāya, Oṁ Namaḥ Pradhānāya, Oṁ Namaḥ Aniruddhāya.

37-38. Similarly, he shall instal Parameśvara with a single mantra. The idols of lord Śiva, Parameṣṭhin shall also be installed and worshipped like the Liṅga, O excellent sages. The sacred auspicious threads along with the fixing of the jewels shall also be duly performed for Viṣṇu, as for the Liṅga.

39. Every rite shall be performed in the immovable liṅga. In the movable ones also, the rites shall be performed in accordance with the śāstraic injunctions. O sages of good holy rites, he shall cause eyes to open by means of the mantras of the eyes.

40. The circumambulation of the shrine, park and the city as well as the rite of keeping it in the water shall be performed as before.

41-42. The erection of the Maṇḍapa, the digging of the Kuṇḍas and keeping the deity lying down—these are the rites prescribed. The installation of the deity shall be performed after the Homa in the nine Kuṇḍas with nine sacred fires, or five Kuṇḍas or in the chief Kuṇḍa alone. Thus the splendid

303. sarvāvarteṣu—in all cycles of yugas.

304. It refers to the other incarnations of Viṣṇu, such as Kapila, Dattātreya, etc.

305. pañcabrahmāṅgajāni, such as Sadyojāta, Īśāna, Tatpuruṣa, etc.

rite of installation has been recounted as handed down traditionally.

43. The Jalādhivāsana rite is mentioned in regard to all rock-cut idols and picture-like[306] carvings. This is also recommended for Nandin the leading bull.

44-46. The installation of the parts of the palace is at the time of the installation of the palace in the same way as that of the parts of the body. The following shall be assiduously installed by reciting Gāyatrī duly—the Vṛṣa (bull, virtue), Agni, the mothers, Vighneśa, Kumāra, the goddess Durgā and Caṇḍī. The excellent eightfold covering of the lord shall be installed beginning with the east. The guardians of the quarters, Gaṇeśa and others shall be fixed in regard to him.

47-50. The following shall be worshipped in the north,[307] in due order—Umā, Caṇḍī, Nandin, Mahākāla, Mahāmuni, Vigneśvara, Mahābhṛṅgī and Skanda. He shall fix Indra and others in their respective places; Brahmā, Viṣṇu and the lord of the shrine in the north-east.[308] Ananta and others and Vidyeśas shall be installed in thrones in due order with Praṇava alone. The private parts[306] etc. shall be installed in the lotus. Thus, the, installation of the mobile Devas and goddesses has been mentioned to you in brief.

306. citrābhāsasya—according to ST. the lord of bulls (Nandin) shall be bathed in the idol of stone but not in the painted picture. This is the logical interpretation of the verse offered by ST., but the text is wanting in the negative particle 'na' to be construed with 'Citrābhasasya'.

307. saumyāditaḥ—uttaradigāditaḥ ST. beginning with the northern direction.

308. Īśa-gocare—Īśānadigbhāge ST. in the north-eastern direction.

309. guhyāṅgādini—dharmādini ST. Dharma, etc.

CHAPTER FORTYNINE

Installation of Aghoreśa

The sages said:

1. The greatness of Aghoreśa had been mentioned by you formerly. O saintly lord, it behoves you now to recount the installation and worship of the lord Aghora.

Sūta said :

2. O leading sages, the installation of Aghoreśa is in accordance with the general injunctions regarding the Liṅga, with the distinction that it shall be accompanied by the Aghora mantra and its ancillaries.[310]

3-4. The devotee shall perform the worship of the sacred fire. Homas shall be performed in the same manner[311] as the worship, one thousand, five hundred, or hundred and eight times. Homas shall be performed with gingelly seeds mixed with curds, honey and ghee. Homa performed with ghee, fried grain flour and honey dispels all miseries.

5. It is destructive of ailments. Homa with gingelly seeds bestows prosperity. A thousand Homas bring about great prosperity and a hundred Homas destroy ailments.

6-7. By means of japa performed in accordance with the injunctions, hundred and eight times and thrice a day, one shall undoubtedly be rid of all miseries. If he performs the japa, a thousand and eight times, Siddhis occur to him within six months. Even the kings and rulers of provinces achieve Siddhis. There is no doubt about this.

8-10. By means of a thousand times japas, fever is dispelled. If a devotee performs a thousand Homas thrice a day with milk and continues this for a month, he attains excellent good fortune within a mouth. If a devotee performs Homa with the mixture of honey, ghee and curds for a year, he achieves Siddhis. If Homa is performed by means of barley, milk and ghee or good rice, lord Aghora is delighted.

310. aṅgayuktena—along with the ancillaries, hṛdaya, etc.

311. yathāpūjā i.e. agnipūjā (fire-worship) shall be performed in the manner of Liṅga-pūjā (Śiva's worship in the form of Liṅga).

11. By performing Homa with curds, kings gain prosperity. By performing Homa with milk one attains tranquillity. By performing Homa with ghee for six months all ailments are destroyed.

12. By performing Homa with gingelly seeds consumption is dispelled within a year. By performing Homa with barley one attains longevity and with ghee one gains victory.

13. For despelling leprosy one shall perform ten thousand Homas everyday with rice-grains smeared with honey, regularly for six months.

14. Ghee, milk and honey constitute a trio of sweets. If one performs Homa with these three, one can dispel fistula of the pudendum.

15-17. By performing Homa with ghee alone all ailments are dispelled. Meditation, installation and due worship remove all ailments. This is the mode of installation of Aghora the great Ātman. Formerly this was mentioned by Nandin to the son of Brahmā[312] who was his disciple. O sages of good holy rites, by him it was mentioned to Vyāsa.

CHAPTER FIFTY

Mastering the mantra of Aghora

The sages said :

1-2. How to check and control the guilty has been mentioned by the trident-bearing lord of auspicious face. O sage of good holy rites, it behoves you to recount it. O Romaharṣaṇa, O highly blessed sage of good holy rites, there is nothing, Vedic or secular, that is not known to you. You know the rites laid down in Śrutis and Smṛtis perfectly well.

Sūta said:

3-5. O sages of good holy rites, the mode of checking and controlling had been formerly recounted to Hiraṇyākṣa by the

312. brahma-putrāya— to Sanat Kumāra, son of Brahmā.

illustrious Śukra, son of Bhṛgu and disciple of Aghora. Due to its grace Hiraṇyākṣa became the valorous leader of Daityas. He conquered the three worlds along with Devas, Asuras and men. He begot a son, Andhaka of charming exploits, who became the chief of the Gaṇas. He ruled over the world and was ultimately killed by lord Varāha (Boar).

6. Perpetual victory cannot be attained by one who commits atrocities on women, children or cows in particular. There is no prosperity in this world by following this path.

7-9. Goddess earth was brought down to nether regions by that Daitya. But the power was rendered ineffective by lord Aghora. At the end of a thousand years, he was killed by Varāha (Boar). Hence, in order to master Aghora mantra, one should not harass brahmins, women or cows. I am telling you the greatest of secrets, nay, the secret of secrets.

10-12. This rite should be performed by mighty kings against violent assailants and desperadoes. It should not be practised against brahmins or against the overlord of one's own realm. This excellent rite shall be performed when a very formidable and invincible enemy has arrived, or when one's entire army has been slain or when the battle has been waged on sinful lines. The rite shall be performed by one who is devoid of mercy through a merciless person. There is no doubt, that the moment it is performed the power of Nigraha is attained.

13-17. O excellent brahmins, the man shall repeat the Aghora mantra of terrible form, a hundred thousand times. To the extent of ten thousand times he shall perform Homa with gingelly seeds. He shall duly worship the lord with hundred thousand white flowers, on a Bāṇa liṅga or in the sacred fire. The mantra is mastered thereby, otherwise he does not become a seer nor has he any Siddhi etc. Only one who has mastered the mantra shall perform the following rite in the cemetery. Only a scholarly and intelligent brahmin who has mastered the mantra and who is sanctified by Śiva, shall perform the rite for his own or for the welfare of the king. The learned man shall fix eight tridents in the eight quarters beginning with the east and ending with the north-east.

18-19. On the top of the twentyfour edges of the tridents he shall make the three-tufted, trident-bearing form of Aghora.

He shall get the forms blended together. He shall perform the rites after meditating on the all-destructive deity. He shall conceive of his body as resembling a crore of blackfires.

20. The eight weapons in order are trident, skull, noose, staff, bow, arrow, Ḍamaruka, drum and the sword.

21. Nīlakaṇṭha has eight hands. He is the bestower of boons. He is nude. He rides on the five Tattvas[313] and holds the crescent moon on his forehead.

22. His face is terrible due to the curved fangs. His eyes are terrible. He is fierce. He makes all the quarters resonant with the sounds of Hum Phaṭ, etc.

23-26. The devotee shall meditate on Śiva Aghoreśa as follows :—He has three eyes. His coronet is tied well by means of the serpent noose. He is richly bedecked in all ornaments. The ashes from the cremation ground are smeared all over his face. He is surrounded by goblins, ghosts, spirits, Ḍākinī witches and Rākṣasas. He is wrapped in elephant's hide. He is adorned by serpents serving the purpose of ornaments as also by scorpions. He has a resonant voice like the sound of the blue cloud. He resembles the mountain of blue collyrium. The lion's hide serves the purpose of his upper garment. He is very very terrible. O sages of good holy rites, the devotee shall perform Prāṇāyāma with thirtysix mantras as mentioned before. He shall show the mahāmudrā and then begin all the holy rites.

27-33. The devotee who has mastered the mantras shall duly instal the deity in the funeral pyre or the spot of the dead. He shall duly make five Homakuṇḍas—one in the middle and one each in the east, south, west and north—in accordance with the injunctions in the sacred treatises. The preceptor shall sit in front of the middle Kuṇḍa and the aspirants in front of the Kuṇḍas in the quarters. He shall spread Darbha grass in an anti-clockwise manner and hold the trident. He himself shall be seated in the middle of the seat of black fire accompanied by his disciples similarly placed. He shall then meditate on the terrible deity Aghoreśa with the

313. **pañca-tattva-samārūḍhaḥ— according to ST. the expression means 'mounting on Nandin who embodies the five gross elements : earth, water, fire, wind and ether.'**

mantra of thirty-two syllables.[314] With the branch of Vibhītaka (Terminalia Belerica) cut into pieces of twelve aṅgulas he shall prepare replicas of his king's enemy and place them on the pedestal along with the coal. Then he shall furiously dig the Kuṇḍas and place the replicas of the king's enemy inside the Kuṇḍas with the face down and the feet turned upwards. He shall bring burning coals from the cremation ground and burn the branches along with paddy husks. The devotee maintaining strict celibacy shall place the fire silently.

34-35. He shall then kindle the fire in the navel with the Māyūrāstra. (peacock missile). He shall burn the bodice of red cloth, along with the seeds of cotton plant and husks of grains. He shall then perform Homa with the oil extracted by manually-operated machine. Other articles of Homa also shall be used along with the oils.

36-37. He shall begin Homa on the fourteenth day in the dark half of the month and perform a thousand and eight Homas till the Aṣṭamī day. He shall avoid touching the spot of burning coal and the circle round the spot. If this rite is performed, the enemies of the king will be faced with all calamities. They will die along with their kinsmen.

38-42. Repeating the mantra of Aghora the devotee shall gather the following in a human skull :—the nail, hair of men, coal, husk, bodice, a piece of bark garment, the dust particles from the sweepings, the fangs of a poisonous serpent, the teeth of a bull and of cows, the claws and the teeth of a tiger and deer, a cat, a mongoose and a boar. O sages of good holy rites, after gathering these fangs, etc. he shall repeat the excellent mantra of Aghora a hundred and eight times.

43. That skull with the nail,[315] etc. shall be wrapped in a cloth taken from a dead body. The entire thing shall be

314. The thirtytwo-syllabled mantra of Aghora: अघोरेभ्योऽथ घोरेभ्यो घोरघोरतरेभ्यः । सर्वेभ्यः सर्वशर्वेभ्यो नमस्तेऽस्तु रूद्ररूपेभ्यः ।। *Liṅga* II. 27. 238. but ST. explains, द्वात्रिंशाक्षरसंयुतम् as 'mantra of thirtythree syllables' with reference to *Liṅga*. I. 17. 85, dissolving the compound द्वात्रिंशाक्षरसंयुतम् as द्वात्रिंशच्च अक्षरञ्च द्वात्रिंशाक्षरे ताभ्यां संयुतम् ।"

315. nakham—not empty. According to ST. the skull shall not be empty (nakhaṁ nāsti khaṁ śūnyaṁ yasmin, paripūrṇam ityarthaḥ). But it omits to mention the article that shall fill up the skull.

buried in a field, or house or the cremation ground in the city or country of the enemy.

44-50. When the moon has entered the eighth sign of Zodiac, or when the sun is covered by Parivesa,[316] O sages of good holy rites this mantra shall be repeated. The enemy shall be deposed from his position and he shall perish. When the campaign of conquest starts, the picture of the enemy shall be drawn on the ground that has been scrubbed well to resemble the polished surface of a mirror. Above that ground there must be a splendid canopy with four festoons suspended and surrounded by clusters of Darbha grass. There must be chanting of the Vedic mantras indicating the affluence and flourishing state of the kingdom. The devotee then kicks the head of the enemy with his right leg. When this is performed the enemy of the king will be destroyed. If an evil-minded person performs this rite of Abhicāra against the king of his own country he will surely kill himself and his family. Hence, one shall always protect the king who protects his kingdom by means of mantras, medicines and holy rites. This secret that has been told to you shall not be given to anyone and everyone.

CHAPTER FIFTYONE

The Vidyā of Vajreśvarī

The sages said :

1. The excellent and terrible rite of Nigraha pertaining to Aghora has been recounted to us. O excellent one, it behoves you now to recount the Vajravāhanikā Vidyā.

Sūta said :

2-5. The Vajravāhanikā Vidyā is terrifying unto all enemies. One shall sprinkle the adamant with this mantra and try to achieve the objects of kings.[317] The Vajra shall be

316. pariveṣa—eclipse.

317. sādhayet—samarpayet ST. shall give it to.

made in accordance with the śāstraic injunctions and then sprinkled. This mantra shall be engraved in gold in that piece of adamant. Then the learned devotee shall repeat each syllable a hundred thousand times with great concentration. He who has this Vajra shall perform ten thousand Homas in the Vajrakuṇḍa with ghee etc. That adamantine piece shall always be guarded well and given to the king. If the king marches against the enemies taking this Vajra along with him he shall conquer them in the battle.

6. Formerly this Vidyā[318] of Goddess Vajreśvarī was assiduously obtained by Brahmā for rendering help to Indra.

7-8. O sages of good holy rites, formerly Tvaṣṭṛ, Prajāpati's son, was killed by Indra. He became inimical to Indra and performed a sacrifice wherein Soma juice was extracted. Indra of huge arms who had suppressed Viśvarūpa desired for the share in the Havis in that sacrifice.

9. "O Indra you have killed my son. I will not give you a share. You do not deserve that since you killed my son Viśvarūpa."

10-14. After saying this, he spread his power of delusion over the entire hermitage with his Māyā. But the suppressor of Viśvarūpa pierced through the Māyā and seized the Soma juice by force and drank it along with his attendants. Then the infuriated Prajāpati look the remaining part of Soma and consigned it to the fire saying—"O enemy of Indra, flourish. Svāhā". Then a demon named Vṛtra appeared there. He resembled a black fire. He was called Vṛtra because he abided by his vows. Indra fled from there. He abandoned Heaven instantaneously. Being terrified he fled along with his attendants. Then the delighted lord Brahmā the creator of the Universe, said to him:—

15-20. "O supressor of enemies, hurl this thunderbolt and kill him". Then the lord of Devas of mighty arms got ready along with Devas and killed him without any strain. He became free from ailments. Hence, Vajreśvarī Vidyā is a terror unto all enemies. The demons called Mandehas are conquered every

318. Vidyā prayatnataḥ—Brahmā received knowledge from lord Īśana. Cf. Īśānaḥ sarva-vidyānām—cited in ST.

day by means of this Vidyā. I shall mention that Vidyā which releases one from all sins.

"Om Bhūrbhuvaḥ Svaḥ. We meditate upon that excellent refulgence of the sun that urges and guides our intellect. Om Phaṭ, Jahi (kill) Hum phaṭ Chindhi (split) Bhindhi (pierce) Jahi, Hana Hana (kill) Śvāhā". This is the Vidyā named Vajreśvarī. It is a terror unto all enemies. O leading sages, even Śiva annihilates the Universe by means of this Vidyā.

CHAPTER FIFTYTWO

Rites for enslaving, fascinating etc.

The sages said :

1-5. The Vajreśvarī Vidyā of Brahmā which rendered help to Indra has been heard by us. We have also heard about the affairs of the kings realized through this Vidyā. O Romaharṣaṇa, now recount the mode of application of this Vidyā for different purposes.

Sūta said:

The various applications of Sāvitrī mantra are for enslaving, attracting, causing hatred, exorcising, paralysing, deluding, beating, extirpating, splitting, killing hindering, stunning the army and similar activities.

Mantra : "May the Goddess, the bestower of the boon come down to the earth on the top of the mountain. O Goddess, permitted on behalf of the brahmins go comfortably". O brahmins, it is only after taking leave of the earth by this mantra, one should know that she is to go and not otherwise.

6-7. After performing all the preliminary external rites and the rites of enslaving etc. he shall ritualistically dismiss the deity. Then he shall kindle another sacred fire duly. He shall invoke the goddess once again, perform Japa and worship too. He shall duly perform Homa too over again in the fire.

8. Then he shall accomplish the holy rites with the same mantra. He who seeks ability to enslave others shall perform thirty thousand Homas by means of Jātī flowers.

9-13. O brahmins, in the rite of attracting, Homa shall be performed with ghee and Karavīra flower. In the rite of causing hatred, Homa shall be performed with Lāṅgalaka flower. The rite of exorcising shall be performed with oil; the rite of paralysing shall be by means of honey; the rite of deluding with gingelly seeds, that of beating with the blood of a donkey or elephant or camel. The rite of paralysing shall be performed with mustard seeds. The rite of tearing up shall be performed with Kuśa grass. O sages of good holy rites, the rite of killing and exorcising with Rohī[319] seeds, the rite of binding with Ahipatra[320] and that of making the army stunned with Kunati[321] (trumpet flower). Then he shall perform the worship of Parameśvarī with ghee, for the achievement of all Siddhis. Purification is obtained by Homa with milk pudding.

14-16. The destruction of ailments is caused by gingelly seeds; wealth can be gained through lotus; splendour with Madhūka flower, Homas in each case being thirty thousand in number, repeating the Sāvitrī mantra. All the rites beginning with Jaya and ending with Sviṣṭa shall be performed as before.

Thus the application of mantras which is very vast has been succinctly mentioned to you. Or one can repeat mantra alone after worshipping in accordance with the injunctions. Even then he shall attain all Siddhis. No doubt need be entertained in this respect.

CHAPTER FIFTYTHREE

The rite of conquering Death

The sages said :

1-5. O Sūta, it behoves you to recount now the rite of conquering death relating to the Brahmins, Kṣatriyas and Vaiśyas. O sage of great intellect, you are omniscient.

319-321. Rohi, Ahipatra and Kunati. Some particular plants are intended.

Sūta said :—

O excellent brahmins, I shall mention the rite of conquering death. Of what avail is much talk? Repeating the Rudrādhyāya mantras the devotee performs a hundred thousand Homas with ghee, in due order. For Homas the following materials can be used: Gingelly seeds with ghee, lotus, Dūrvā grass mixed with ghee and cow's milk, honey, Caru along with ghee or mere milk. Thus the remedy against Death or the god of Death has been recounted.

CHAPTER FIFTYFOUR

Worship with Triyambaka mantra

Sūta said :

1. With the Triyambka[322] mantra one shall worship the three-eyed lord of Devas in a Bāṇaliṅga or in a self-born Liṅga.

2-6. Those who wish to prolong their lives and those who are conversant with the Vedas shall worship Śiva with a thousand and eight white lotuses or a thousand red lotuses or a thousand blue lotuses. After the worship one shall give milk pudding, cooked rice soaked in ghee, cooked green gram and rice mixed with honey, fragrant sweets and other edibles. He shall perform Homa in the fire with the flowers mentioned before as well as with Caru in particular. He shall perform japa a hundred thousand times and perfectly conclude everything in due order. He shall then feed a thousand brahmins and offer them Dakṣiṇās. After giving a thousand cows he shall in the end give gold also.

7-8. Thus, everything including the secret doctrines has been succinctly mentioned to you. This had been formerly mentioned to Skanda of unmeasured splendour on the top of the mountain Meru by the trident-holding Śiva, the lord of Devas. This was then mentioned to the intelligent son of Brahmā by Skanda the lord of Devas.

322. triyambakena—with the tryambaka mantra. Cf. *Liṅga.* II. 28. 62.

9. This was then mentioned to Vyāsa by Sanatkumāra the well-wisher of the worlds. Thus, this has been handed down traditionally.

10. When Śuka passed away the highly-blessed great sage Vyāsa saw the three-eyed lord Rudra and dispelled his misery.

11-12. The sage listened to the story of the birth of Skanda. As he stayed there the glory of Triyambaka mantra was fully mentioned to him. Thanks to his grace I shall now mention everything to you.

13. One shall repeat the Triyambaka mantra after duly worshipping the lord. One is liberated from all sins accumulated in the course of seven births.

14. He shall gain victory in the battle and attain incomparable good fortune. He who seeks a realm shall acquire it by performing a hundred thousand Homas and shall be happy.

15. He who seeks a son shall undoubtedly attain a son with a hundred thousand Homas of this mantra. He who seeks wealth shall unhesitatingly repeat the japa a million times.

16. He will be fully and perfectly endowed with riches, food grains and all other auspicious materials. He will play with his sons and grandsons. When he passes away he will go to the heaven.

17. O sages of good holy rites, there is no mantra on a par with this one both in the world and in the Vedas. Hence, one shall continuously worship the three-eyed lord thereby.

18-23. The fruit thereof shall be eight times the benefit of Agniṣṭoma sacrifice.

The word Triyambaka is interpreted thus. He is the lord of the three worlds, three Guṇas, three Vedas, three Devas, and three castes—brahmins, kṣatriyas and vaiśyas. He is expressed by the three syllables "A", "U", "M".[323] He is the lord of the three fires, viz., the moon, sun and fire. Umā, Ambā and

323. akārokāramakāra—ST. dissolves त्रय: (अकारोकारमकारा:) अम्वा (अविशब्दे) यस्मात्—who is the source of origin of the three-syllabled a u m.

Mahādeva constitute the trio.[324] So he is Triyambaka the lord of the three.

(The word Sugandhi in the mantra is interpreted thus). The splendid fragrance of a tree in full bloom is wafted to a great distance. Similarly is the fragrance of the great lord. The lord is fragrance or the holder of fragrance unto all other Devas.[325] His fragrance is wafted in this world and in the firmament when the wind blows.[326] Hence, the attribute Sugandhi refers to the lord. Now the word "Puṣṭivardhanam" is interpreted.

24-26. Formerly, the semen of the lord Śiva was deposited in the womb of Viṣṇu. It was from this semen that the cosmic golden egg, the source of origin of Brahmā originated. The nourishment of his semen extends beyond the moon, sun, stars, earth, Bhuvaḥ, Svaḥ, Mahaḥ, Tapaḥ and Satya. The five elements, the cosmic ego, the cosmic intellect and Prakṛti are nourished by his semen virile. Hence, the lord is Puṣṭivardhana (the increaser of nourishment).

27-28. The word Yajāmahe (we worship) is interpreted. We worship that lord duly and devoutly by performing Homas with ghee, milk, honey, barley, wheat, black gram, Bilva fruits, lilies, Arka flowers, Śamī leaves, white mustard and Śālī rice grains in the Liṅga.

29-30. Now the latter half of the mantra is interpreted. By the grace of this Ṛta (systematic worship) let me be released from the bondage of actions and reactions as well as the fetters of death. Let me be released from the glitter of worldly existence. Just as the ripe cucumber fruits fall out from their stalks when the season arrives, so also the time for liberation has come by the grace of this mantra.

31-35. One shall worship Śiva's Liṅga after understanding the meaning and the rites of this mantra. That Yogin shall sever all bonds. He can control death. O sages of goodsholy rites, there is no other lord so merciful as Triyambaka. He is propitiated and delighted easily. So is the mantra. Hence, one shall forsake everything and worship the three-eyed lord of Umā by

324-326. ST. offers another set of three fanciful derivations of sugandhim (i) शोभनः गन्धोऽस्त्यस्येति सः (ii) सुष्ठु च तद्गं (गीतं) च दधाति इति सः (iii) सुशोभनां गां गिरं दधातीति सः ।

repeating this Triyambaka mantra. He shall worship with great concentration whatever may be his plight; he shall undoubtedly be liberated from all sins by the meditation on Śiva and he shall become Rudra himself. Although one incurs sins by killing and piercing living beings or by eating and enjoying unjustly he shall be liberated from all sins by remembering Śiva alone once.

CHAPTER FIFTYFIVE

The mode of propitiating Śiva

The sages said:

1-2. How shall the three-eyed lord, the bull-bannered lord of Devas be meditated upon for realizing all Siddhis, through the Yogic path ? O sage of good holy rites, everything has been heard by you formerly and in detail. It is equal to the knowledge of the Vedas. But it behoves you to recount everything succinctly once again.

Sūta said:

3-4. O sages of good holy rites, Nandin having the lustre of the sun was asked in a similar manner by the son of Brahmā on the mountain Meru formerly. He was surrounded by the group of sages. As Sanatkumāra, the son of Brahmā, bowed down to him he told him in confidence and with great concentration.

Nandikeśvara said:

5-8. Thus, lord Mahādeva, Nīlalohita was formerly asked by the goddess Ambā, the daughter of the mountain lord. On the peak of Kailāsa the lord was asked by the goddess while he sat in the same bed with her and while he was in the height of ecstasy.

Śrī Devī said:

How many types of Yoga have been mentioned? What are they like? How they function? How is divine knowledge that yields absolution and whereby the creatures are liberated?

The lord said:

The first is Mantrayoga, the second is Sparśa, the third one is Bhāva, the fourth is Abhāva and the fifth is Mahāyoga which is the most excellent of all.

Mantrayoga

9-11. The practice and repetition of the japas along with meditation is Mantrayoga. The blood vessels are to be kept-spotlessly pure by means of Recaka (exhaling). The Air (Prāṇa) is to be conquered cumulatively and severally.

Sparśayoga

There is firm and strong action due to the splendid activities of the retention of birth etc. The practice of Kumbhaka (retention of air), illuminated by the three Dhāraṇās, is called Sparśayoga. It cleanses the three viz. Viśva, Prājña and Taijasa.

Bhāvayoga

12-14. That state which is devoid of mantra and sparśa but resorts to Mahādeva is called *Bhāvayoga*. The lord is stationed dividedly within and without. The annihilatory aspect of the lord is manifest. It accords purity of the mind.

Abhāvayoga.

The parts of the universe consisting of the mobile and immobile beings become dissolved. Everything becomes void. The form too of the lord loses its semblance. This is called Abhāvayoga which causes extinction of the mind.

Mahāyoga

15-17. That meditation in which the pure form appears without colour, which is auspicious, independent, and unspecifiable, which has light and splendour always and is self-evident all round is called Mahāyoga. The Ātman alone pure and self-luminous[327] rises perpetually (in it). Self-luminosity, that

327. svayaṁ jyotiḥ—cf. yasya bhāsā sarvam idaṁ vibhāti—cited in ST.

is pure is known as Mahāyoga. It comes up from the entire mind.

All these Yogas bestow powers of Aṇimā (minuteness) etc. and perfect knowledge.

18-20. In these Yogas the latter are better than the former.

The state of Mahāyoga is devoid of contact with the ego. It is great and comparable to the vast firmament. It is devoid of all coverings. Although it is incomprehensible yet it is knowable by its own nature. It is great, submerged, self-evident, and self-knowable. It shines in its blissful body. Therefore, it is considered to be knowable.

21. It should be given to a tested disciple, a brahmin who maintains the sacred fires, who is virtuous and not ungrateful. It should be given in due order, gradually.

22-25. It should be given to one who is devoted to the preceptor and the deity. Otherwise it should not be given. If so, he will be born sick, short-lived and censurable. He who gives also becomes like this, O sinless lady. Hence, one should avoid giving without testing the disciple.

My devotee shall be free from all attachments, shall consider me as the greatest resort, be endowed with perfect knowledge, and become an expert in the rites laid down in the Śrutis and Smṛtis. He shall be devoted to the preceptor, meritorious, eminently qualified, and always devoted to Yoga. Thus, O gentle lady, the eternal Yogic path has been recounted. O lady of slender waist, it is the honey that exudes from the lotuses of the Vedic and Āgama lores.

26-28. After drinking the Yogic nectar the Yogin, the most excellent among the knowers of the Brahman, becomes liberated. Thus is the most excellent Pāśupata Yoga. It bestows all the prosperities and prowess of the Yogas and needs no other support. It is declared as such for the sake of salvation. By whom is it obtained ? O beloved one, it is obtained only by those who are engaged in worshipping Śiva and whose conduct is lovable.

After saying thus the bull-bannered lord bade farewell to the goddess. Posting Śaṇkukarṇa[328] at the gate he entered Sāmādhi (a state of yogic trance).

328. **Śaṁkukarṇa—a particular gaṇa.**

Śaīlādi said :

29-31. Hence, O leading Yogin, O son of the self-born lord, be engaged in the practice of Yoga. The supreme lord is certainly identical with Brahman. Hence, by all means, the wise person seeking salvation shall always perform ablution with Bhasman. He must be engaged in the Pāśupata Yoga. In due order, the Śakti pertaining to Viṣṇu shall be meditated upon. Thereafter,[329] the Parā Śakti of Maheśvara shall be meditated upon.

32-35. Thus, the stable practice of a leading yogin has been succinctly described to you.

Sūta said :

Thus, Pāśupata Yoga has been recounted by the intelligent Nandin, the son of Śilāda, who scrupulously adheres to Bhasman. Sanatkumāra the saintly lord mentioned it to Vyāsa of unmeasured splendour. I heard it from him. At their behest I mentioned it to the sages who perform the Satra. I am gratified. Obeisance to the brahmins and to the Yajñas. Obeisance to the tranquil one, to Śiva. Obeisance to sage Vyāsa.

36-43. This excellent *Liṅgapurāṇa* contains eleven thousand ślokas. The first section contains hundred and eight chapters. The second section contains fiftyfive[330] chapters. It yields virtue, love, wealth and salvation.

Then the sages of the Naimiṣa forest bowed down to lord Īśāna with great concentration and mental purity. Out of pleasure their body showed horripilation. After composing this branch of the Purāṇa, the eleventh one,[331] the self-born lord Brahmā spoke these words, "He who reads the *Liṅgapurāṇa* entirely, from the beginning to the end, he who narrates it to the brahmins, and he who listens to it, attains the highest goal. He attains that highest goal which is attained by penance, by

329. **Yathākrameṇa—beginning with Brāhmī.**

330. **ṣaṭcatvāriṁśad adhyāyam—but the extant text consists of fifty-six adhyāyas. ST. therefore, dissolves the compound ṣaṭ catvāriṁśat as ṣaṭ ca nava ca catvāriṁśacca (madhyamapadalopi karmadhāraya. But this exegesis is unauthentic. It is very probable that the second part originally consisted of fortysix adhyāyas.**

331. **ekādaśikām—In the serial order of the Purāṇas, the *Liṅgpurāṇa* is the eleventh.**

sacrifices, by charitable gifts and by the study of the Vedas. He attains the scriptural lore pertaining to the Vedas. The brahmin will attain the faculty of renunciation either by action or by knowledge or by the mixture of both. His devotion will become permanent. May that noble soul have faith in me and in lord Nārāyaṇa. Learning shall continue in his family and he shall not err in anything." This is the behest of Brahmā. Hence, all these are attained by his grace.

The sages said:

44-48. O Romaharṣaṇa, sage Sūta, we the sages have attained Siddhis. Nārada who is engaged in holy pilgrimages has also attained Siddhis. Our pleasure is vast. Let this pleasure be present everywhere, all round, by the benign grace of lord Śiva.

When the brahmins said this, the pious sages Nārada touched the body of Sūta with the tip of his splendid hands and said: "O Śūta, hail to thee. Welfare unto thee. May you have faith in the bull-bannered lord. May we too have the same. Obeisance to Lord Śiva."

INDEX

K

R

S

T